W9-CRF-329

RUSE

Related Titles from Potomac Books

Thinking Like a Terrorist:
Insights of a Former FBI Undercover Agent
by Mike German

Enter the Past Tense:
My Secret Life as a CIA Assassin
by Roland Haas

RUSE

Undercover with
FBI Counterintelligence

Robert Eringer

POTOMAC BOOKS, INC.
WASHINGTON, D.C.

To Dr. William J. Moloney,

my high school U.S. history teacher

Library of Congress Cataloging-in-Publication Data
Eringer, Robert.
  Ruse : undercover with FBI counterintelligence / Robert Eringer. — 1st ed.
    p. cm.
 Includes index.
  ISBN 978-1-59797-189-8 (alk. paper)
  1. Eringer, Robert. 2. United States. Federal Bureau of Investigation—Officials and employees—Biography. 3. Intelligence service—United States. I. Title.
  HV7911.E75A3 2008
  327.1273—dc22
                            2007041094

Printed in the United States of America on acid-free paper that meets the American National Standards Institute Z39-48 Standard.

Potomac Books, Inc.
22841 Quicksilver Drive
Dulles, Virginia 20166

First Edition

10 9 8 7 6 5 4 3 2 1

CONTENTS

PART III. BAMBOOZLING BEELZEBUB

ACKNOWLEDGMENTS

Huge heartfelt thanks go to my literary agent and good friend of many years Frank W. Martin for his insightfulness and excellent advice.

Thanks also go to Don Jacobs for his thoughtful support.

Kudos to Don McKeon, whose expertise as an editor greatly refined my musings. He wields a deft blue pencil—rare in book publishing these days.

Much gratitude to the late Walt Perry, who masterminded sting-undercover operations for the Internal Revenue Service in the 1970s and 1980s and whose exploits, never published, inspired me to practice the art of the ruse.

PART I

HOODWINKING HOWARD

1

DEATH IN MOSCOW

On July 12, 2002, an American traitor died in a mishap (it is said) at his home near Moscow. His name was Edward Lee Howard, and he liked to define himself as the only intelligence officer trained by both the Central Intelligence Agency (CIA) and the Soviets' Committee for State Security (KGB). Howard had resided in the United States until 1985—dubbed "Year of the Spy" after eleven spies were arrested in the United States—when, fearing he was about to be arrested for selling CIA secrets to the KGB, he defected to the Soviet Union. In addition to his concern that the FBI was gathering evidence to charge him with espionage, Howard was mindful that his five-year probation, after having pleaded guilty in March 1984 to three counts of aggravated assault with a deadly weapon, would have been revoked if arrested again.

Under the FBI's nose, Howard had executed a "jack-in-the-box" jump from the car his wife was driving. Howard had learned this tactic during CIA training at Camp Peary, Virginia: a dummy pops up in your place as you jump from the vehicle at a point in the road where your car temporarily disappears to anyone following behind. Howard then flew from Albuquerque to Tucson and, using his Trans World Airlines (TWA) Getaway credit card, flew to Copenhagen via New York, then traveled farther east to Helsinki, and ultimately ended up in Moscow. Howard had tried to settle in Budapest and Stockholm in the late 1980s and early 1990s, respectively, but both times he bolted back to Moscow when Hungary and Sweden came under intense pressure from the U.S. government to seize and extradite him.

The Russian authorities explained Howard's death to his ex-wife, Mary, and college-age son, Lee, both of whom live in the United States, this way: drunk, Howard had tripped on concrete stairs leading to the laundry room of his dacha (country home) and broke his neck. There was only one problem: no stairs led to Howard's laundry room, which was adjacent to his ground-floor kitchen.

The dacha, which Howard adored despite its back-drafting chimney and water pipes that froze every winter, sat about twenty miles west of Moscow, in the exclusive village of Zhukovka. Although Howard owned an apartment in the fashionable Arbat neighborhood of central Moscow, he rarely slept there, preferring as his full-time home the traditional summer residence with its garden, on perpetual loan to him by the state.

I learned of Howard's death one week after his supposed accident while waiting for him to respond to an e-mail of mine. An e-blast, headed "Sad News," was sent from his e-mail address—safehous@online.ru—to family friends: "This is Lee writing from my Dad's dacha to tell you all that he passed away on 7/12/02. . . . He has been cremated, and we will take his urn back to the U.S., where his mother in New Mexico will keep it. . . . He is in a better place now."

I immediately telephoned the FBI's Albuquerque Field Office to report this unexpected twist. The Howard investigation was run out of Albuquerque, where it had begun. Born in New Mexico, Howard was a resident of Santa Fe when he came under suspicion of espionage. Albuquerque's main concern was, had anyone seen the body? I quickly mustered an answer: no, not even Howard's ex-wife and son, who had rushed to Moscow upon notification of his death.

The Russians, meanwhile, handled the matter with traditional clumsiness. If they had nothing to hide, their actions conveyed otherwise.

Washington Post reporter Walter Pincus broke the story of Howard's death first, on July 21. "Howard's death would mark the end of one of the more memorable espionage stories of the Cold War," he wrote.

Just how memorable is the basis of this book.

After a week, and a smattering of media attention, the Russians changed their story about Howard's death. "There is talk of a car crash," said a former KGB official. "There's a lot of contradicting information." Forgoing an autopsy for Howard and opting for just a quick cremation lent further suspicion to the circumstances surrounding this American traitor's death.

I telephoned former KGB colonel Igor Prelin in Moscow. I had met Prelin, the general-director of the retired KGB officers association, through Howard years earlier. "What happened to Ed?" I asked.

"I know nothing!" Prelin responded, sounding like Sergeant Schultz in the old TV series *Hogan's Heroes*. "They're not telling me anything," he added.

Next I phoned Lena Orlova, Howard's longtime assistant and on-and-off intimate companion for more than ten years. It always seemed to me, watching Orlova and Howard together, that she had an emotional attachment to him beyond a physical relationship and beyond keeping tabs on him for Russian intelligence. Orlova professed to know little more about Howard's demise than Prelin had. Odder still, Orlova was not grief stricken and was seemingly unfazed by her lover's premature death.

"What a shock," I said.

"Life is full of surprises," Orlova replied with chilling nonchalance. She said she had last seen Howard a few weeks earlier at his dacha.

"Was he happy?" I asked.

"Was Ed ever happy?" said Orlova. "He was Ed."

Then I phoned George Blake, a British intelligence officer who admitted spying for the communists, escaped from Wormwood Scrubs Prison in England, and beelined to Moscow in 1966. Howard counted Blake among his few friends and looked up to him as a mentor; they shared birthday celebrations and holiday occasions. Yet Blake sounded neither concerned nor saddened by Howard's passing. "Ed never really adjusted to life here," he told me with the kind of matter-of-factness one normally uses in discussing the weather. "And he was drinking heavily again the last few months."

By early August, the Russians' story changed a third time. "He was walking at sunset at the territory of his dacha, and the terrain is very steep there," a former KGB officer, Viktor Andrianov, told the Russian daily newspaper *Pravda*. "It's likely Edward slipped and when he was falling hit his head very hard on a stone. He was found only in the morning, when everything was over."

A former CIA operations officer who had "called in a chit" from a special source in Moscow later recounted a fourth version to me: Howard had meant to take the stairs from his bedroom loft, but, being very drunk, he missed and flipped over the balcony's low rail. The problem I had with this story was the rail was not low, but high, and had been installed to prevent such an accident.

It was, at a minimum, an embarrassment to the Russians that the only CIA spy to evade capture and reach Moscow did not enjoy a long, happy life. As Howard once told me, "KGB chairman Vladimir Kryuchkov wants me to be a good example that he could use as positive propaganda. He wants to be able to say, 'Here's a man who came to our side and he's happy, healthy, and successful.'" If nothing else, Howard's untimely and freakish death at age fifty debunked such nonsense.

Howard may well have suffered a drunken accident, although he tried to confine his drinking to New Year's Eve and his birthday, October 27. It is also possible that some old Russian general coveted the government-owned dacha in which Howard lived, and all that stood between him and it was Howard. But most probably, Howard died at the hands of Russia's internal Federal Security Service (FSB). Howard had long outlived any usefulness to his hosts; furthermore, drunk or sober, toward the end of his life, he regularly bad-mouthed Russia and Russians to all who would listen. Even more significant, as Howard secretly laid plans in the autumn of 2001 to relocate to Phuket, Thailand, FSB investigators might have concluded that Howard was at least partly responsible for the unmasking of their prized FBI informant, Robert Philip Hanssen. Aleksandre "Sasha" Zhomov, chief of the FSB's America Department, was said to be obsessed with nailing those responsible.

As one cagey Polish operative told me in reference to Howard's death: "Stairs—real or contrived—are a hallmark of the Russian intelligence services, their silencing signature."

2

WRITER, EDITOR...

The bar inside Montgomery's Grille in downtown Bethesda, Maryland, was quiet the last day of September 1993. I grabbed a stool and ordered a dry martini. Wayne, the barkeep, a character straight out of the movie *Animal House*, said he was out of olives. I was already teed off at this saloon for becoming so popular since opening a few months earlier. And now no olives?

"OK, make it a Beefeater, rocks, lemon twist."

Joel Joseph of National Press Books was late for our five o'clock rendezvous. Truth be known, I didn't care if he'd forgotten. I was in the mood for a quiet cocktail, which I'd savor this warm afternoon and be gone.

But as I sipped my martini, Joseph appeared with his partner, Alan Sultan. The specialty of this duo's ten-year-old publishing house was political intrigue. They had recently published a book by James Earl Ray, the convicted killer of Martin Luther King Jr. Months earlier, I'd jocularly suggested to this publishing pair that they create an imprint called Ball and Chain Books as an outlet for celebrity prisoners around the world.

Joseph was in his mid-forties, with a graying mustache and a paunch exaggerated by tight blue jeans. A lawyer by training, Joseph was civil liberties minded and a devotee of the First Amendment. Years earlier, he had been part of a legal team that defended conspiracy theorist Lyndon LaRouche. Sultan was about fifteen years younger than Joseph and slim with a swarthy complexion, thick jet black hair, and a trimmed beard. He was the bean counter at National Press.

I had first met them in 1988 when they took an interest in a proposal I was circulating for a nonfiction book on the *National Enquirer*. Thereafter, they had been trying for several years to lure me into their mix as an investor. (How do you make a small fortune? Invest a large fortune into book publishing.) I'd explained to them my philosophy about the book biz: each book is a business unto itself. Bring me a single book that has serious money-spinning potential, and maybe I'll pitch in. So Joseph had telephoned me a few days earlier to say he had such a book and asked if I was still interested in investing or editing such a project.

"Maybe," I said. "What is it?"

"Arafat," Joseph had replied. "We have a writer from *Penthouse* magazine who knows his people."

I'd been through this kind of publishing quagmire once before, with Poland's Lech Walesa, whose disparate representatives had made three simultaneous "exclusive" deals. But I like good yarns. So there we sat in the Bethesda bar—me with my Beefeater and Joseph and Sultan sipping white wine.

"Did Joel tell you about our new book project?" asked Sultan.

"Yeah," I said. "Arafat."

"No," said Sultan. "Something a lot better came in yesterday." He cued his partner with a glance.

"Have you ever heard the name Edward Lee Howard?" asked Joseph.

"Sure," I replied. "He's the only CIA guy ever to defect to Moscow."

"He wants to write a book," said Joseph. "We have his proposal."

"How long is it?" I asked.

"Forty pages," said Joseph. "You interested?"

Yep, I was interested, but not for the same reason that Joseph and Sultan were. I wanted to nail the traitor and put his butt behind bars. A much worse fate had befallen Adolf Grigoryevitch Tolkachev, the Russian electronics engineer and invaluable CIA spy whom Howard had betrayed to the Russians. Tolkachev had been executed.

"Maybe," I said. "Tell me more."

"Howard says it wasn't his fault that he ran to the KGB," said Joseph. "The CIA put him in a corner, and he had no choice. He says he's the only guy who's ever been trained by both the CIA and the KGB in spy tradecraft. And get this: the KGB chief who took Howard under his wing—Kryuchkov?—is the same guy who led the putsch against Gorbachev in 1991. You've got to see the proposal."

The next morning, Friday, October 1, I telephoned the Former Spymaster. We had known each other three years, since we had worked together as independent contractors on several private-sector intelligence projects.

"You know the name Edward Lee Howard?" I asked.

"You kidding?"

"He wants to write a book."

"Really?" This bit intrigued the Former Spymaster.

"Not only that," I said, "I've been invited to participate. You see the potential here?"

National Press Books had its offices at Artery Plaza, a contemporary commercial building in Bethesda at 7200 Wisconsin Avenue and the corner of Bethesda Avenue, above Montgomery's Grille. That same morning I strolled into their suite of tube-lit, shoe-boxy rooms.

Joel Joseph thrust Edward Howard's book proposal at me. "Our photocopier is on the blink," he said. "Read it here."

I took a desk chair, sat down, and perused the proposal, entitled *Safe House.* A page about publicity suggested that all the big media outlets, such as *60 Minutes* and *Nightline,* at some point, wanted to interview Howard. But he was holding out until he had something to sell. This hook is partly what he was selling: while serving on the CIA's Neutral Countries Desk in Washington in 1983, he'd learned various things—which he had itemized—that, if and when they were revealed publicly, would likely harm U.S. relations with several European countries. But Howard's pièce de résistance, what he called "My Big Secret," was couched in this question: "Why is the CIA so hot to get me after all these years?" Howard's answer: "Because of the one project that has never been revealed to the public but will come out in this book—the Black Box." He revealed this operation's code name and its details, both of which remain classified.

The CIA had specifically trained Howard to undertake this secret mission in Moscow, but he had never made it to his target country. Howard was fired after failing a series of polygraph examinations regarding drug use and petty theft only weeks before his scheduled departure for the Soviet Union. Few disagree that the agency badly mishandled his dismissal. Thereafter,

9

Howard drank, stewed, and ultimately took this position: *they trained me to be a spy, so a spy I'm gonna be.*

A few days later I arrived at the Former Spymaster's house shortly before our expected guests from the Federal Bureau of Investigation (FBI). At ten o'clock sharp, the doorbell rang. Two agents from headquarters entered: Nicholas W., a section chief from foreign counterintelligence (FCI), and Allyson G., a supervisory special agent. They proffered calling cards and acted deferentially to the Former Spymaster, who opened the meeting.

"I met Eringer around the time I retired from the government," explained the Former Spymaster as he introduced me. "He moved into my neighborhood, and we became close friends."

I conveyed how National Press Books offered to let me handle Edward Lee Howard's book. Nick W. exchanged glances with Allyson G. and then spoke. "We already know people who have met Howard and reported to us bits and pieces of what he's said. I'm not sure how much more we're going to get by giving you questions to ask him."

"Wait a second," the Former Spymaster put up his hand. "This isn't about asking Howard questions. It's about trying to *capture* him."

"Oh." This news stumped Nick W. "We hadn't even thought of that."

The Former Spymaster and I exchanged glances. "A unique opportunity has presented itself," I said. "This situation is Howard-initiated. He is seeking a publisher. By an odd quirk of fate, National Press would put *me* in charge of Howard's book as his editor. Over time, I could gain Howard's trust. And I could lure him into a trap."

Nick W. warmed up to this idea. "Howard could certainly use a friend," he agreed. "But this isn't a bureau decision. This is the domain of the U.S. attorney out in New Mexico, because that's where the investigation is under way, in our Albuquerque Field Office. He's the one who has to prosecute this case. So he's the one who has to decide whether to use these kinds of tactics and how it's going to play out in court—a pretty complex thing."

"The U.S. Marshals have something called the 'Curved Frisbee Doctrine,'" I pointed out. "If we can lure Howard to an international corridor in an airport without violating his human rights, the courts won't object." I'd heard about this doctrine from Howard Safir, former chief of the U.S. Marshals Service, who'd coined the term himself after masterminding the international apprehension—known as an "extraordinary rendition"—of CIA renegade Edwin Wilson.

"It's nice of you to offer to do this," said Nick W., "to take trips, incur expenses. . . ."

"No," I said. "This operation would be on your nickel. I'm not planning to pursue this opportunity unless you folks sign on, cover my expenses, and hire me as a contract agent."

"What's your deadline on this?" asked Supervisory Special Agent Allyson G., who had been taking notes on a legal pad.

I shrugged. "I don't have one, but you can be sure this opportunity won't last forever."

"We'll pass it to the U.S. attorney in New Mexico," said Allyson G. "It'll be up to him."

After the Former Spymaster saw Nick W. and Allyson G. to their car, he returned with a look of astonishment on his face. "Typical 'feebies.' They only think in terms of collecting more incriminating information on Howard. As if they didn't have enough! I can't believe it didn't occur to them before they got here that we're talking about *catching* Howard." He shook his head. "That's government today. No imagination, no creativity." He paused. "It'll sound too complicated, too dangerous. Anyone with any clout in government is just a few years away from a pension. They'll never want to risk that."

In the meantime, Edward Howard phoned Joel Joseph from Moscow and pressed him for a commitment to his book proposal. Joseph asked for more time.

In turn, Alan Sultan called me. "I know how these things work," said Sultan. "If we're going to sign him, we've got to keep up the momentum. Otherwise another publisher will come along, and we'll lose him."

I relayed this update to Allyson G. "It's heating up," I said. "Can we get an answer?"

"They seem pretty interested," said the supervisory special agent. "Others have come forward in the past with plans to trap this guy, mostly from inside the bureau, but nothing as interesting as this. However, we still have to get the Justice Department on board."

It should have tipped me off there and then what it's like to work for a U.S. government agency: you spend your life getting smacked around like the silver ball inside a pinball machine. Hit this base, bang! Whacked over to another post, boing! Boomeranged someplace else, ba-da-bing! Until, after a good battering, you drop into a black hole.

Alan Sultan was guzzling a beer when I arrived at Montgomery's Grille about quarter after four on October 5. "Are you going to buy me a birthday drink or what?" I asked.

"Happy birthday," said Sultan. "Order anything you want." I opted for a glass of pinot grigio. "I'm convinced we should do this book," he continued. "But do you really believe Howard's story that he didn't help the Russians until after he was forced to flee?"

"Who cares?" I said. "The guy's a traitor whichever way you cut it."

"But I still wonder if he started off as a spy. What do you think?"

"I'm inclined to go with the evidence," I said. "Howard was identified by a Soviet defector named Vitaly Yurchenko, who also identified Ron Pelton, an NSA [National Security Agency] engineer who later admitted his guilt."

"But if we publish Howard's book, won't people say we're capitalizing on treason?"

"People can say whatever they want," I shrugged. "It's a publisher's job to publish interesting books. Howard's story is a piece of espionage history."

Sultan had another concern. "We have to assume Howard may run a background check on us. What will he find on *you*?"

"Well, I guess he might discover that I was William Colby's literary agent." Colby had been the CIA's director in the mid-1970s. I represented him as his literary agent and found a publisher for his book on Vietnam, *Lost Victory*.

"That's what I was thinking," said Sultan. "I don't think Howard would like that."

"I wouldn't worry about it," I said, trying to put his mind at ease. "And even if the Russians check *you* out—and that's iffy because they probably can't stomach Howard anymore—the most they'd do is send a flunky up to your office to make sure National Press really exists."

The next morning brought a call from Allyson G. "There's a guy in our office out West who wants to talk to you."

Ten minutes later my phone rang. "This is John H.," said a voice. "You know my name?"

We both chuckled. John H.'s name was all over Edward Howard's book proposal as the special agent tasked with tracking the fugitive traitor. John H. had even met Howard, in person, in Sweden and made a pitch for the turncoat to come home and face the music. This case, at the top of John H.'s docket, was his passion.

"I'd like to meet with you and discuss the legal ramifications of what we're talking about here," John H. said in his low-key, soft-spoken voice. "I have to tell you, I was negative on this when I first heard about it. But then I learned all the details, and I've come around. I'm in Albuquerque. I'd like to give you a ticket to fly out here. Would that work for you?"

"No, it would not work for me," I countered, suggesting, instead, that we meet in Washington. I wasn't about to go charging off anywhere, expending time and energy, until we set ground rules.

3

... PUBLISHER, SPY

FBI special agent John H. flew into Washington's National Airport on the rain-drenched Tuesday morning of October 12, rented a car, and asked directions to the Holiday Inn in Chevy Chase, Maryland. John H. had never been stationed in Washington, D.C., and had no desire for such a posting. When he visited the area, he did his business and got out of town as quickly as possible.

Initially, John H. couldn't get into the Holiday Inn only one mile from my home, because rooms allocated for special U.S. government (USG) rates were booked. So he'd made a contingency reservation at a Marriott in downtown Bethesda, Maryland. "I have to do it that way," John H. told me. "If I pay full rate, the difference comes out of my pocket. That's thirty or forty bucks." John H. called the Holiday Inn one last time, discovered a *cheaper* rate than the USG special, and booked a room.

I asked myself, "And I'm trying to turn this outfit into a paying client?"

That morning at nine o'clock on the dot, my phone rang. John H. confirmed his presence down the road. Punctuality, a principle of good intelligence work, could have been John H.'s middle name. Twenty minutes later, I knocked on his door, room 303. John H. wore slacks, black wing tips, a button-down shirt, and a tie featuring a Mickey Mouse pattern. He was my kind of guy. We shook hands and sat down at a small round table by the window, which overlooked the hotel's parking garage. If John H. had had a full head of hair, he'd have looked about thirty-five years old, or ten years younger than his actual age.

"The assistant U.S. attorney, Bob G., is flying in this afternoon," said John H. "He has to visit headquarters and meet with people about this situation, and then he wants to meet you. It's very important that you did not initiate this book project with Ed Howard. Otherwise, a judge might say we entrapped him."

I shook my head. "Howard initiated it. Not only that, National Press came to *me*."

"Good."

As we sat facing each other over legal pads, I ran John H. through the events that had brought us together that cool, wet October morning. "Let me tell you something about Ed," offered John H. when I'd finished. "I've studied him for a long time, eight years now. He's a good liar. Ed has lied his whole life, and it was lucky that the final polygraph beat him, because he'd been lying for years, and he's still lying. Did you ever get a copy of the book proposal?"

"Right here." I tapped my folio. I also had a copy of a fax Howard had sent to National Press, inviting us to visit him in Moscow, and I produced it for John H. It was signed "Mr. Roumanis," whom Howard said was the director of his consulting business, Westar, and it included telephone numbers for Howard's apartment, his dacha, and his assistant, Larissa.

John H., a Russian speaker, translated the invitation. "Do you know who this assistant is?" asked John H.

"He mentions Larissa in his proposal."

"Her name is actually not Larissa," said John H. "It's Lena Orlova. She's a Russian who was married to an American defector from the U.S. Navy named Glenn Michael Souther, who committed suicide. After Souther's suicide, the KGB moved Lena near Howard. They met, became lovers, and now she's his assistant." John H. glanced at the invitation and back to me. "And this guy, Roumanis—do you know who he is?" When I shook my head, he continued, "Roumanis *is* Howard. It's an alias. Let's move on. There's a difference between insider stuff and classified stuff. I'm going to give you an insider overview about where we are on this case."

I nodded.

"It's never been reported, not even by David Wise in his book about Ed, *The Spy Who Got Away*, but we were just about to issue a warrant for Howard's arrest when he escaped. It was his sheer good luck to have chosen that weekend to leave. The arrest warrant should have been ready the week before, but it got delayed by some grand jury hearing. So the warrant wasn't issued till Monday. By that time, unknown to us, Howard was gone.

"We feel we've got an airtight espionage case against Howard before he escaped, and there's an important delineation between pre- and post-September 1985. The way our case is written up, it's all about his espionage activities *before* September 1985. We're sure we can convict him on that. But we have never developed an espionage case for what he did *after* September 1985. That's where you become important. We may want to build a whole new case about his espionage post-September 1985 and try him on both. The crux of that would be his own admissions in his book proposal and whatever he tells you."

"Got it."

"We'd like to get updates on Howard's relationship with the Russian security services," John H. continued. "For instance, what's the fallout from the most recent events? [President Boris Yeltsin had just disbanded Russia's Parliament.] When is the right time to ask the Russians for Howard?" That, in a nutshell, was the FBI's strategy on Howard: at an opportune political juncture, perhaps with some incentive, to cajole the Russians into turning him over. "And this assistant I mentioned, Lena Orlova," said John H., "we'd like to know the details of their current relationship."

I scribbled a note.

"The idea," said John H., "is to draw Howard out, get him talking about these areas. Is that how you see it?"

"Not only that," I said, "the ultimate goal, I hope, is to capture him."

"Good. I'm glad you said that, because that's what *I* want this to be about." John H. paused. "How do you see doing that?"

"In his proposal, Howard says he's going to write about the KGB. I'd like to draw him out on that and say, 'Hey, maybe we should talk about the KGB in a place they can't hear us, like Zurich or maybe Poland.' If he'd meet me in Warsaw, maybe I'd be able to get him up to Gdansk, get him drunk, onto a boat, into international waters, and—bam!— we'd get him."

"I like the way you're thinking," said John H.

"It all comes down to how bold and daring you guys want to be," I said. "Just tell me where you want him. It'll be my job to get him there."

"I'm like you," said John H. "I'm ready to be real bold."

Our talk turned to Howard's book proposal. "I don't know if I should be telling you this," John H. paused and spread an open palm across his forehead, trying to work out separating "insider" from "classified" information. "I have to be careful here, but . . . Howard has *already* written a manuscript. I've seen it."

"How long ago?"

"Uh, I have to do this without getting into sources and methods," said John H. "That's the classified part. He wrote it about a year ago. It's poorly written. He's not a good writer. And it's different from what your notes say are in this proposal."

"How different?" I asked.

"For a start, there's nothing in the manuscript I saw about the Black Box [the secret mission for which the CIA had specially trained Howard]. The Black Box and other things in his proposal are classified information," said John H. "Just by telling someone this stuff, Howard is breaking the law. And his literary agent is breaking the law by being *told* this stuff."

"So I guess that means *I've* broken the law, just by reading it," I said.

"Uh-huh," John H. grinned. "You've got it."

"At the moment," I said, "National Press wants to publish Howard's book next spring, only eight months from now. I thought such an idea was ludicrous, not least because I hear Howard drinks a lot. But now you're telling me there's already a manuscript, the schedule becomes very feasible."

"Where did you hear Howard drinks a lot?" asked John H.

"Your colleague, Nick W. And didn't Howard call the U.S. attorney to try to cut a deal?"

"Where did you hear *that*?"

I chuckled. "Nick."

"Howard called *me*," said John H. "Once. He was drunk."

"What did he want?"

"He wanted to make a deal. I told him the bureau does enforcement. We're not allowed to make deals."

I broached a new subject, my expenses. I also told John H. that when I'd travel to Europe to meet Howard, I'd need a business-class seat and to stay in fine hotels.

John H. raised an eyebrow.

"I usually fly first class," I said. "Hell, when I went to Europe three weeks ago for a client I flew the Concorde both ways. But it isn't just that," I added. "If you want to sting your target, you've got to throw money around, show that you travel in style. Put yourself in his shoes. Who wants to do business with someone on a budget, who watches his pennies?"

"About how much is business class to Moscow?" asked John H.

I shrugged. "Maybe three or four grand."

He noted this detail. "How many trips do you think will be necessary?"

It wasn't as if I wanted a bunch of free trips to Moscow. I'd been before; it was definitely *not* my destination of choice. "As few as it takes to get him." I paused. "And now my fee."

John H. put down his pen and leaned back in his chair. "In Division Five, the Foreign Counterintelligence Division, we have a number of assets," he said. "Most of them help us for free as patriotic citizens."

"I respect that," I said, "but I do private-sector intelligence for a living. I view you as a potential client. I'd need a grand a day to work this."

John H. noted it in his folio and glanced at his watch. It was 11:25 a.m. "Shall we get a jump on lunch?"

PRINCE OF RUSE

On the drive up River Road through the horse farms and mansions of Potomac, Maryland, John H. spoke of his love for Albuquerque, where he had settled with his family twelve years earlier. About to celebrate his twenty-fifth year with the FBI, he had evaded the fast track—and administrative posts—preferring to ensconce his wife and two sons in one home after early stints in New York City and Seattle. The bureau offers this kind of non-ambitious career to those who want to hunker down and steer clear of supervisory roles at headquarters.

John H. told me he was born in Germany. His parents, of Russian extraction, spent the later part of World War II in a displaced persons camp. Given the choice of returning to the Soviet Union or emigrating to America, it was no contest. They settled in Michigan.

I parked the car in Potomac, and we nabbed a quiet table at an Italian restaurant called Renato's. During the next hour, John H. filled many pages with meticulous notes about my background.

"When I was fourteen, in 1969, and living in southern California, my family traveled to London for what was supposed to be a three-week summer vacation," I began. "We never returned, swapping sunny blue skies for dark clouds and rain. I think my father was suffering a mid-life crisis, long before that phrase became fashionable. Anyway, he wanted to grab a hold on life before it grabbed a hold on him.

"The project that caused our upheaval—transatlantic charter flights—disintegrated. So he developed a new idea—cheesecake. London didn't have any. And my mother had a killer recipe. The Hard Rock Café had just opened, and it became my parents' first customer. My mother baked five cheesecakes each day for the place. Pretty soon my parents were up to forty cakes a day for a handful of customers. My mother baked from six in the morning till eight at night, with an oven so small it had room only for two cakes at a time. My father delivered the cakes, my grandmother washed cake tins, and my brother and I earned our pocket money grinding cookies for the cake crust in an old milk-shake mixer. I'd eat cheesecake for breakfast and return from school every afternoon to rows and rows of cheesecakes cooling in the living room. Their operation was bursting out of our house, so my parents found a retail shop down the road and added chocolate cake and apple pie to their production schedule."

John H. smiled. He no doubt wondered what my family's cake business had to do with my ability to pull a ruse on Edward Howard. But he had to hear my whole story for it to make any sense.

"Soon, my parents needed even more space," I continued. "My dad wanted to buy the lease of a run-down restaurant next door, remove the wall dividing both premises, and create one large bakery. The landlord gave his oral approval, but after taking my parents' key money, he demanded a much higher rent to put the arrangement in writing. My dad refused on principle. So the wall didn't come down. My parents used the restaurant space for storage and finishing cakes. When the landlord saw this, he squawked: 'You can't run a baking operation in there. The lease stipulates it has to be a restaurant.' I was just out of high school, and I said to my parents, 'OK, I'll open a restaurant in the front part; that'll satisfy the lease.' We already had tables and chairs, an old microwave oven, and assorted kitchen appliances. With a little paint and some partitions, I had it up and running within a month. I called it 'Tricky Dick's Coffee House,' after our infamous president, who was on his last legs at the time. One of our menu specialties was Alger Hiss Pumpkin Pie."

John H. laughed. Hiss, a spy in the U.S. State Department, had given documents to Whittaker Chambers, who hid the incriminating film in his pumpkin patch. Richard "Tricky Dick" Nixon, then a young congressman on the House un-American Activities Committee, had successfully prosecuted him.

"It became an institution," I continued, "not because it was a front for a baking operation, but because it was an anarchist's sanctuary, full of eccentric characters.

"I left the place in my brother's hands sporadically and ventured off to college in the States—in Cape Cod and at the American University in Washington, D.C.—but I never stayed long enough to get a degree. I studied criminology and political science, though, and got to know a Georgetown University professor named Carroll Quigley, who took me under his wing and sent me out of his office with controversial books in brown bags.

"Meanwhile, Tricky Dick's was my practical education, with hiring and firing staff and dealing with the mentally insane, people with names like 'Bronco John' and 'Burned-out Paul.' Tim Hardin, the folksinger, was living in a squat around the corner and was a down-and-out, recovering heroin addict. He'd come in and sing 'If I Were a Carpenter' for his dinner. He'd make up new lyrics extemporaneously, and customers who had no idea he had written the song would try to correct him."

"So you dealt with all sorts of people?" asked John H.

"On-the-job psychology and sociology training. Later, on the basis of this life experience, I managed to weasel my way into a graduate program."

"Of course," said John H., much amused. "Where?" Undoubtedly he found my story mind-boggling and was thinking, "This will keep the security checkers busy."

"The University of Southern California had a master's program in international relations, which it ran out of the U.S. Navy's European headquarters in London. I took a couple of courses and some field trips to NATO [North Atlantic Treaty Organization] and the EEC [European Economic Community] in Brussels, the OECD [Organization for Economic Cooperation and Development] in Paris, and the U.S. Army's Russian Institute in Garmisch.

"Anyway, my family's cake business finally moved to a factory, so we folded Tricky Dick's when our lease ran out in 1978. I started writing for a folksy expatriate newspaper called *The American* that catered to Americans living in the UK."

"But how did you get into journalism without any training?" John H. scratched his head.

"Same way I got into the restaurant business—calculated serendipity. Have you ever heard of Bilderberg?" Like most other people, he had not. I continued, "While I was at American University I wrote a term paper on this group of so-called power brokers. When I got back to London, I rewrote it and submitted my piece to a magazine called *Verdict*. After they bought it and published it and I saw my scribing in print, even though the editors stole my byline, I wanted to become a journalist. My breakthrough came when I infiltrated the Ku Klux Klan [KKK]."

John H. put his pen down and shook his head, incredulous. "Tell me about that."

"In 1979 the KKK was trying to establish a branch—what it calls a Klavern—in the UK I penetrated the operation so well, the Grand Dragon from South Carolina appointed me its leader. I pitched the idea to the *Sunday People*, a high-circulation UK tabloid. We lured all the British Klan recruits to a London hotel, photographed them, and tape-recorded them saying horrible things about what they wanted to do in Britain, like tar-and-feather interracial couples. One guy and his two grown sons told us they kept illegal guns beneath their beds, ready for service."

John H. scribbled with gusto. "Go on."

"The Klan's Grand Dragon, Bob Scoggins, was impressed by my progress and decided I had to visit him in South Carolina and get 'naturalized'—his term for my initiation—to make it official. So two reporters from the *Sunday People* and I flew to Spartanburg, South Carolina, and checked into a Days Inn motel near the interstate. A welcoming committee collected us in a van full of guns and drove us to Scoggins's ranch house. Pickup trucks were parked everywhere. They guided us into his dark garage and pointed us up a creaky staircase. At the top, I knocked on a closed door. Scoggins opened it, decked out in a gold satin robe and hood. He beckoned us into his Klan den, with Klan posters hanging on the walls, illuminated by fluorescent black lights.

"First he took us for twenty bucks each—membership dues. Then he stood us near his altar—a table draped with an American flag, an unsheathed sword, and the Bible opened to Corinthians 12. Finally, he ushered in a bunch of robed Klansmen and women to form a semicircle behind us. And then began a thirty-minute ceremony during which the Grand Dragon tapped our shoulders with his sword and anointed us with 'holy' water. At the very end, Scoggins pointed to a snakeskin nailed to the wall and said, 'I got that rattlesnake before it got me, and that's what you've got to do with Klan traitors.' The lights went on, and we all had cookies and milk.

"And then they brought out a tape measure."

"A tape measure?"

"To size us up for our robes and hoods."

John H. grinned, shaking his head. "Tell me more."

"We spent a week there, attending meetings, handling illegal weapons, learning secret code words. On the last day of our visit, Grand Dragon Scoggins took us to a tri-state KKK cross-burning rally in North Carolina by way of a tour through the Blue Ridge Mountains. I drove our rental car, with Scoggins in the front passenger seat and the two reporters in the back.

"I used an alias with the Klan. My only ID was my genuine UK driver's license, which I'd packed with my clothes in the trunk. We took our little tour, during which Scoggins introduced us to the oldest Klansman in the country, who was about ninety-two and looked like the guy holding the pitchfork in Grant Wood's famous painting, *American Gothic*. At dusk we crossed the border into North Carolina and found the rally site.

"The state police had set up a roadblock, and we were behind a long line of cars on a single-lane dirt road headed into the rally. I could see up ahead a state trooper was asking to see drivers' IDs and car papers, and I was thinking, 'Shit, the KKK from three states is about to find out I'm not who I claim to be.' The reporters behind me, too, clicked to the notion that we were about to get caught out, and they were also looking for an exit ramp. But there was nowhere to drive, we were stuck in line, and there was nowhere to run.

"I inched closer. Finally, it was my turn. The trooper bent down and eyeballed me through the rolled-down window. 'License and registration,' he drawled. I plucked the car rental agreement from the glove compartment and handed it to him. He looked at it, grunted, and handed it back. 'License,' he said. 'It's in the trunk,' I said. 'Well, go get it, son,' he replied.

"I climbed out. The Grand Dragon got out, too, and met me at the back of the car. With the trooper on my left and Scoggins on my right, I opened the trunk. Both men watched as I rummaged through my dirty clothes. Just as I located my license, Scoggins turned to the trooper, offered his right hand, and drawled, "Hi, I'm Bob Scoggins, Grand Dragon for South Carolina." The trooper broke into a broad smile and said, 'Well, why didn't you say so? You boys go right on through.'"

"Wow! That's a good story."

"All true. Not one word of exaggeration. So I closed the trunk, and we rolled into the rally site. They had our robes and hoods waiting for us. They were red robes, because they made us *Kleagles*, which is Klan-speak for 'officer,' since they presumed we were going to command the KKK back in Britain. Instead, of course, the *Sunday People* ran a front-page, center spread exposé over two successive issues. The police raided the UK house where guns were said to be hidden beneath the beds, found them, and confiscated them. Our story and its consequences killed the KKK in Britain dead in its tracks.

"After that, I worked freelance for the *Sunday People's* investigative department. It was a great place to train in the early 1980s. Under a legendary investigative editor named Laurie Manifold, I developed my own stories and specialized in undercover penetrations. I infiltrated cults, Ponzi schemes, neo-Nazis, and a pro-violence anarchist group called Class War. I was the Prince of Ruse, exposing sleazeballs and scumbags. It was like being an actor, except I made up my lines as I went along. Main thing I learned, if *you* don't believe your own cover story, don't expect anyone else to believe you, either."

John H. sat, pen affixed to his timeline. "What was next?"

"In 1981 I was invited to Poland to write a book about the Solidarity movement, which had just exploded over there."

"How did *that* happen?" asked John H.

"I received a letter from a Polish journalist."

John H. eyed me with skepticism. "Out of the blue?"

"Yeah. Well, no, not entirely. I had expanded my article about Bilderberg into a short book, *The Global Manipulators,* which the publisher had advertised in *The Economist*. This journalist had read it, tracked me down, and interviewed me on his radio show about which persons Ronald Reagan, our newly elected president, would choose for his cabinet. I predicted almost all of them correctly, based on my investigation of Bohemian Grove and the power elite. A few months later his letter of invitation arrived, and soon afterward I traveled to Warsaw and Gdansk. My work resulted in a book, *Strike for Freedom!* which was published in 1982 by Dodd, Mead. After martial law was declared and Lech Walesa was imprisoned, I did more work in Poland for ABC News."

"When?"

"In 1984. They gave me a six-month contract to focus on the outlawed Solidarity underground."

"How did that come about?"

"My Polish contact was privy to a secret dialogue between Solidarity and the Polish government. ABC News was basking in glory over its documentary about secret negotiations behind the Iranians releasing the U.S. embassy hostages, so the bosses were gung ho on this sort of thing. I traveled to Poland a number of times, supplied video equipment to key activists in Solidarity, and coordinated what they produced. The secret dialogue came to nothing, but we were able to report on the effectiveness of the underground. For instance, Solidarity's technicians could cut into the TV nightly news broadcasts and announce, 'These newscasters are lying!' And when Jerzy Popieluszko, the priest, was kidnapped and murdered by members of the Polish secret police, we photographed the secret, uncensored transcript of their trial, and I smuggled it out of Poland."

John H. smiled and scribbled on. "How did you get in and out of Poland?"

"Business visas. I posed as a mushroom salesman. I even spent one full day traipsing around a city called Bydgozsz, tasting mushrooms and pretending to check out a chain of fast-food mushroom restaurants. One place fed me a four-course meal with everything made from mushrooms, including mushroom cake for dessert."

John H. raised an eyebrow.

"They take mushrooms very seriously in Poland," I said. "Anyway, New Year's Eve 1986, I moved back to the States and realized I had to do something different. In Britain, freelance journalism is a respectable occupation. In the States, 'freelance' is a euphemism for 'unemployed.' I wanted to stay in the information biz, so I became a literary agent."

"How did *that* happen?" John H. scratched his head again.

"Serendipty, as usual. Before leaving Britain I attended a conference on international terrorism at Ditchley Park and met Robert Kupperman, one of the early pioneers of terrorism studies. Later, we lunched in Washington. Kupperman told me he wanted to write a book. I knew a few people in book publishing, so I offered to help. I drafted his proposal for a book called *Final Warning* and sold it to Doubleday for six figures. It was published in 1989."

"So you're still a literary agent?"

"Not really. I wear that hat once in a while. If somebody comes to me with something good, I try to help them place it."

"So what hat do you wear most of the time?" asked John H.

"Hold on, we're getting there," I said. "In 1988 I moved to Monaco."

"*Where?*"

"Monte Carlo, on the French Riviera."

John H. put his open palm to forehead and scribbled some more.

"My parents had retired to Monaco, and I'd visited them a bunch of times through the eighties. I always thought it would be an interesting place to live for a while. In the summer of 1988 my parents called to say a small apartment near theirs had become available. I flew over to take a look and signed a lease on impulse. Monaco is like a glass bubble; it's a very busy city-state removed from reality."

"What accounts for that?"

"Thirty-thousand people, comprised of ninety-three nationalities, squeezed into a mile and a half square."

"What did you do in Monaco?"

"Mostly, I rationalized that I was there to discover literary talent. I met many interesting people. Out of that came a comic novel."

"You wrote a novel?"

"*Zubrick's Rock*. It's about a reclusive mega-millionaire who lives in Monaco but loses his residency status after getting involved in a scandal. He has nowhere else to go. So he takes a long walk, wanders into Monaco's wax museum, and discovers that the reigning Grimaldis took Monaco by force from the Spinola family seven hundred years ago. So this character, who's always wanted his own country, digs up a descendant of the Spinolas to legitimize a coup d'état. The only Spinola he can find on short notice, though, is a low-life dentist in Hoboken who's an alcoholic and a compulsive gambler."

John H. had stopped taking notes and studied me.

"After Monaco I moved to Washington," I said, "where I met the Former Spymaster and became a consultant."

"What kind of consultant?"

"Creative problem resolution."

John H. smiled. "Go on."

"My consulting is confidential. I engage in private-sector intelligence, by appointment, for billionaires and royalty."

"Can you tell me *something* about it?"

"I'll tell you about an assignment I had recently, because it relates to my ability to handle Howard by creating the right illusion. I was involved in a complicated international child custody case. I represented the mother's side. The father was given generous visitation rights, but he used the child as leverage to extract money from the mother, who came from one of Europe's wealthiest families. The child hated being forced to spend time with his nutcase father, who once tried to kidnap him. So the mother was on pins and needles every summer when the boy was forced to spend five weeks with dad, who was under no obligation to disclose where he went with the boy. For five weeks the mother didn't know where her son was or if the father would return him or try to kidnap him again. He'd been heard to mutter under his breath that one day he'd run off with his son to South America.

"So the mother hired me. I figured what I had to do was monitor this guy, especially when he had custody of his son. And, if possible, I needed to influence, even manipulate, his actions to render him harmless to my client and her son. To do this, I had to get to know the father and insert myself into his existence." I paused. "Shall I continue?"

"Of course."

"First thing I did was to hire a former CIA operative in Europe to collect as much information about the father as possible. Out of this, I learned what made him tick. This aspect was important, because I needed to refine the right story that would get him to invite me into his life. You only get one shot at this from out of the blue.

"I called him on the phone, made my pitch. One week later, we were having lunch together at a fancy restaurant in Paris. After an hour of fine food and wine, he was telling me all about his personal problems, including his ex-wife and their son. By the end of lunch, I was his new best friend. Come summer, not a day went by that I didn't know where the kid was and what he was doing." I paused. "I only like jobs with a high L.Q."

"L.Q.?"

"Laugh quotient, my main criteria. The job's got to be funny, or I won't do it."

John H. grinned. In his profession, he did not often see this kind of perspective. He settled the eighteen-buck tab, and we walked to my car.

"Sorry my background is so eclectic," I said.

"You kidding?" said John H. "You seem tailor-made for this job."

"So what's your gut," I said. "Am I heading East?"

"We've still got hurdles," said John H., "but I like what I hear. My gut instinct is that you'll be heading East. Your name is Robert," he added, attuned to some kind of metaphysical wavelength. "That's the code name Yurchenko used to identify Howard." He seemed tantalized by the poetry at play, as if these events had been directed by the stars.

John H. phoned me next morning from the J. Edgar Hoover Building, FBI Headquarters. "It's coming along," he said. "Can you get to the Holiday Inn at three? The U.S. attorney I mentioned wants to meet you."

"OK to wear blue jeans?"

"That's the most welcome thing you've said so far. I'll tell *everyone* to wear blue jeans."

John H. was not having an easy time down at headquarters. He had rediscovered that things were not as laid back in Washington as they were in New Mexico. Nobody but nobody wanted the buck to stop with him. This new project had to be pushed higher and higher up the ladder.

I returned to the Holiday Inn's room 303. John H. had been joined by Bob G., the slight, boyish U.S. attorney, and by Jim S., who was John H.'s boss and a supervisory special agent in Albuquerque. Jim S. had rugged features and a Wyatt Earp mustache.

"Dammit," said Jim S. in a resonant broadcaster's voice. "I didn't bring any blue jeans. When I come to D.C., I expect to suck up big time."

We all laughed. I sat at the small round table; Jim S., at a table next to the window. Bob G. sat on one bed while John H. sprawled on the other, folio in hand.

John H. looked me squarely in the eye. "Did you ever use the name Michael Dunsmore?"

The question took me by surprise. "Yes," I replied. "Michael Dunsmore was the alias I used to infiltrate a neo-Nazi organization called the Liberty Lobby. I exposed the group in a couple magazine articles." I chuckled, "The guys sued one magazine, owned by Jack Anderson, for libel. In a petition to the Supreme Court, they referred to me as 'the mysterious Robert Eringer' and questioned whether or not I really exist."

The poker-faced men nodded, preoccupied with their experience earlier at headquarters.

"Things are moving slower than we hoped," said John H. "It looks like a decision will take at least a week. Headquarters wants you to write a letter that explains your understanding of what this operation is all about."

I shrugged. "Easy."

"Good. They'd like to have it in three parts, starting with your relationship between the parties involved."

"The players," I said.

"Exactly. Part two is what you need."

"The deal," I said.

"Right. Three, they need an assurance of what you will do and not do if we proceed."

"Uh, I'm not clear on that," I said. "I'd do whatever we agree needs to be done."

Bob G. addressed this point. "We have to make sure you're not thinking of any kind of drastic action on your own that might embarrass the Justice Department."

"You mean like if I killed Howard?" I said, tongue in cheek.

The three men exchanged glances, lightening a tad to my level of levity.

"You could state that you would not break any laws," said Bob G.

"OK," I said, "but we're talking about operating outside the United States, and it'll get real gray real fast out there. Wouldn't it be better if I write that I won't break any *U.S.* laws?" When the trio agreed that approach would be better, I then asked, "Where will this memo go?"

"To the top of the Justice Department," said John H. "You can take the weekend to write this letter and—"

"The weekend?" I said. "I can write it in ten minutes."

They were astonished. This was not how bureaucracy operated.

Bob G. had a question for me: "What's your motivation for doing this?"

"Look," I said, "it has never been my burning desire to catch Ed Howard. Until two weeks ago, the only thing I knew about Howard was what I'd read in the press years ago. But the minute I heard about this book proposal, I immediately tweaked to its sting potential. I think I'm pretty good at sting-undercover operations. This situation poses an inviting challenge."

"Would you be willing to tape-record Howard?" asked John H.

"I don't like to rely on gadgets," I said. "I have a very good memory."

"Yeah, but if Howard incriminates himself on tape," said John H., "Bob could use that in court."

"OK."

"So you're not concerned about carrying a mini-cassette recorder into Russia?"

I shrugged. "Why? Millions of businessmen carry mini-cassette recorders for note taking while on the move."

"What if it's discovered?"

"You mean if it's in my jacket pocket and running? So what? It got switched on by accident."

Bob G. asked, "Isn't National Press worried about breaking the law by publishing classified information?"

"I don't think the guys have given it much thought," I said.

"No? It's a serious issue."

"Right now," I said, "National Press is focused on signing this book. It's just too early to deal with the legality of publishing classified information."

"What do you think they'll do?" asked John H.

"Joel Joseph is a lawyer who loves fighting constitutional issues, especially those involving freedom of speech," I said. "He might relish a challenge like this one and argue it all the way to the Supreme Court. And I'll tell you this: National Press would absolutely love the publicity. That's what sells books."

Bob G. and John H. looked at each other. Even if they chose *not* to proceed with a sting, they realized they still had a situation on their hands.

The Albuquerque contingent flew home the next afternoon, leaving headquarters to fret about the risks. It was headquarters' favorite pastime, I would soon learn.

5

THE CHEESE FAMILY

By mid-October, the guys at National Press Books wanted to get moving. I, conversely, was bent on slowing all movement until the FBI could get a grip. Joel Joseph and Alan Sultan called a meeting at their office.

"So what's happening?" asked Joseph. "Are you in or what?"

"Still thinking about it," I said.

"We want to publish this book next spring," said Sultan. "We need to know immediately if we're going ahead with you on this."

"Do you really think Howard will write a book in time for spring publication?" I asked.

"He's already written a hundred pages," snapped Joseph.

"Huh?" The manuscript John H. had referred to earlier had apparently surfaced. "Have you seen it?"

"Sure," said Joseph. "We've got it here in the office. It's good."

Time to change gears. "Another thing that concerns me," I said, "is the legality of publishing Howard's secrets."

"We'd never publish anything we know to be classified," said Joseph without hesitation. "That's a felony. The CIA will hate this book. We don't want to give those guys a reason to jump all over us."

"What will Howard say about that?" I asked.

"We won't even bring it up," replied Sultan. "Ultimately, we control the editorial content of the book."

"May I see Howard's material?"

"Sure," said Joseph.

Sultan left the room and returned with a sheaf of manuscript pages. I thumbed through it and discovered neat, polished prose that was nothing like John H.'s description. Sultan said, "We've got to know whether or not you're in by tomorrow. Take the material, read it, and let us know."

Back home, I called John H.'s direct line. "I'm under pressure to make a decision," I said. "The guys at National Press are convinced they can publish Howard in the spring because they received a hundred pages of his manuscript."

"Did you get a copy?"

"Of course."

"Will you mail it to me?"

"I've already posted it."

"I'll phone headquarters," said John H.

He phoned me back the next morning. "This is the situation: there's a Big Cheese who needs to make the final decision, but he's out all this week. So no decision till the Big Cheese returns on Monday. But," John H. added, "it's at the top of his pile. You've got a lot of people behind you at headquarters who want to do this."

I played for time with National Press.

John H. phoned me the following Tuesday. "There's been a non-decision," he said.

"A what?"

"The Big Cheese saw the memo this morning. It's going higher than the Big Cheese."

"Bigger Cheeses?"

"Our people are putting a lot of pressure on the people dealing with the super-superiors," he continued. "They promise a decision tomorrow."

The next day, I had no word from John H. till late in the afternoon.

"I still don't have an answer," he said. "It has to go to the Biggest Cheese."

"Jeez," I said, "I thought it had already reached that Cheese."

"No, things don't move that fast around here. We work in a unit, which works for a section, which works for a department. . . . We're lucky it's gone up the ladder as quickly as it has."

Lucky? I was beginning to think *bad* luck had gotten me into this *fromagerie*. *Quickly*? Bad guys might have less to worry about than they think.

"So when will it reach the Biggest Cheese?" I asked.

"Tomorrow."

Which is exactly what I'd been telling National Press for five days straight: tomorrow. I felt like the bologna between two pieces of stale rye.

"It had to get everybody's initials on it," said John H. "And that's done. This is a reputation maker. But now the Biggest Cheese has to decide. He's the one who will have to face the cameras if things go wrong."

The bottom line was the division chief, the assistant director for national security, the deputy director—none of them had the *cojones* to take the buck.

The guys at National Press, although going up a wall, issued me a deadline five days hence. After what I'd been going through on a daily basis, it felt like a vacation. John H. called. "The Biggest Cheese has a few questions."

"Will it have to go *beyond* him?" I asked.

"No. Now it's coming back down again, to get his questions answered."

"What kind of questions?"

"Like, should we really be doing this kind of thing," he said.

Should we really be doing this kind of thing? You mean, instead of conducting the equal opportunity meetings the Federal Bureau of Investigation did so well? (I had good sources on the inside.) If the FBI higher-ups had to ask whether we should really be doing this kind of thing, I'd have to ask myself, "Should *I* really be involved in this kind of thing?" After all, it wasn't *my* job to enforce the laws of the United States and to catch spies.

Later I related my conversation with John H. to the Former Spymaster.

"'Should we really be doing this kind of thing?'" he repeated, incredulous. "Sounds like the Clinton administration, all right." He added, "It's over."

Two days after National Press's deadline, John H. phoned. "Good news," he said. "It looks like we're in business. The confusion's been sorted out, and everybody agrees we should do this. There's just one more meeting tomorrow."

"Tomorrow? Let's say you get a go-ahead," I said, "at what level will this project be managed?"

"I'll be the guy who deals with you," said John H.

"So what happens," I said, "if we're into this and we have to move on something? Are we going to have to wait three weeks for the Big Cheese Family to approve something?"

"Well, at some stage it may involve the State Department."

"Ah," I thought, "the Headcheese."

John H. phoned late in the afternoon the next day. "The meeting that was supposed to take place today is going to take place tomorrow."

The delays weren't funny anymore; in fact, the L.Q. was way low on the yuk-o-meter.

The next day Joseph and Sultan phoned me, all huffy. I apologized and promised a decision soon. Then I phoned John H. "Any word?"

"It's very discouraging," he said.

"National Press just gave me a final deadline," I said. "Four o'clock today."

"That's fine by me," said a dispirited John H. "I'll call headquarters and tell them if they don't have a yea or nay by four o'clock they will no longer have to worry about making a yea."

At two o'clock, I'd heard nothing from John H. Three o'clock—still nothing. At one minute to four, my cell phone whistled. "I guess it's over," said John H. "The latest is, they have to show it to the number two man under Janet Reno. Probably—"

"Don't say it!"

"Tomorrow," said John H, adding, "I told them it didn't matter anymore."

The Biggest Cheese apparently didn't want the buck, either. The Former Spymaster had called it right. I faxed National Press a letter bowing out of the Ed Howard book. I was disappointed, but given how this project had been handled so far by a variety of cheeses, perhaps it was for the best.

Eight days later, I received an unexpected call from Alan Sultan. "Any news on your end?" he asked.

"Jeez," I said, "after my waffling the last few weeks, I didn't think you guys would even want to *talk* to me again."

"Nah, we're not like that," said Sultan. "We're doing the book anyway. If you want to participate, we're still interested. It's perfect for you. We've got a cover designed. You want to see it?"

Fate would not loosen its grip. A minute later, a slick book cover mock-up arrived by fax.

I phoned the Former Spymaster. "Dammit," I said, "I could get this guy."

"I know you could," he said. "I'll make a call." A few days earlier, the Former Spymaster had filled me in on what had transpired at the highest level. The FBI director was gung ho about my proposal, but the deputy attorney general had given it to seven lawyers to study.

The Former Spymaster phoned me back later that day. "I talked to a guy named Tom T. [the Current Spymaster], and Tom called the number two guy at the FBI to tell him the CIA is strongly in favor of this operation."

Two days later the Former Spymaster called me with an update. "I just got a call from a senior guy. He wanted to get to the bottom of this. So I filled him in and told him about the bureaucratic foot-dragging. He said, 'Jesus Christ, this is one of the most important things we could be doing!' He's charging over to the bureau this morning to raise a ruckus and try to get it back on track."

Soon after, I received another call, this one from John H. in Albuquerque. "If you're still interested, it looks like we're getting somewhere," he said, a tad puzzled. "I've been called to Washington. And I have the power to get you started."

And that's how it became my job, on behalf of FBI foreign counterintelligence, to create a sting that would snare America's most wanted spy.

Once John H. reached town, we agreed on an hourly fee for me. He issued me a code name, and we agreed on an alias for communication purposes. Only a handful of officials inside the bureau with a need to know would be aware of my true identity.

6

SPOOK WRITER

Time for business. National Press Books gave me the use of a desk and the Edward Howard file. I sifted through his publishing contract, perused a media correspondence file containing news organizations' requests for interviews with Howard, and reread his partial manuscript.

At noon, Sultan and I broke for lunch at Melio's in Washington's Spring Valley neighborhood. "Wouldn't it be great if Howard came back to the States?" mused Sultan. "Think of the publicity!"

"Working on it," I felt like saying.

Sultan was now consumed with selling the book. "I've got the sales director from our distributor coming to see us. He's giving me a hard time, saying something about Cold War books being tough to sell these days. But if we could get Howard to return. . . ."

Soon after, on December 16, I had my first encounter with Edward Lee Howard. I punched in his Moscow telephone number and left a message on his answering machine. An hour later he returned my call. We exchanged greetings, and Howard sounded serious and sober. When I asked how much material he'd already written, besides what National Press possessed, he told me, "About a hundred pages."

"How much more do you intend to write?"

"Another hundred pages," said Howard.

"Sounds light, Ed. Even three hundred pages would work out to only 220 book pages."

"Hmmmm, I guess I could write more," said Howard. "I wrote my story a couple of years ago. A lot has happened since then." He also said he had plans for a Christmas vacation in Siberia, which was his own code word for Switzerland. "I'll be back on the twenty-seventh. That's when I intend to start writing."

"National Press wants to publish this book in May or June, which means we need a finished manuscript by early March. Do you think you can do it?"

"The contract says March 15," said Howard. "I intend to comply with it."

"Don't worry about spelling or grammar," I said. "Just let it roll. Write it as if you're at a bar telling your story over a couple of beers."

Howard chuckled. He could relate to that; it probably made him thirsty.

A few weeks later Howard's computer disk arrived, labeled in Howard's hand "ELH Book WP5.0." I slipped the disk it into my laptop and read Howard's files, which came to about a hundred additional pages, as promised. It was rough, very rough, and not at all like the first batch. Howard needed more than an editor. He needed a ghostwriter.

Although they had a signed contract with Howard, the guys at National Press had thus far withheld his advance payment, not least because they had no cash flow. "Everybody was conning everybody else," I reflected.

It was already January when I shot Howard a fax: "Your material has big problems. I'm planning to be in Monaco on business in February. Can we meet?"

A Federal Express envelope from Howard arrived one week later. Inside, he'd enclosed a letter saying he would meet me in Zurich, Switzerland on April 2, at "1300 hours" at the reception desk of Hotel Kindli. Hereafter, he instructed, we should refer to it in all communications as "the kids' place."

This news greatly relieved Joseph and Sultan. A promise of a face-to-face meeting with Howard suggested progress, though they conceded his book would not be a spring title.

"And we're still hurting for financing," said Joseph. "If we don't get any, we may have to kill Howard's book. His literary agent is bugging us every day for the advance, and we don't have it."

I phoned Howard soon after CIA official Aldrich Ames was arrested on February 22 for conspiracy to commit espionage. "Big news, huh?"

"Yeah." Howard sounded shaken *and* stirred. "It brings back old memories."

"We still on for 'the kids' place'?"

"Yeah," said Howard. "When can you get there?"

"Four days after the date you suggested."

"That'll be fine."

Next I phoned John H. "You boys have been busy."

"We sure have," he said. "Now that it [the Ames arrest] is out the way, headquarters can focus on *our* project."

John H. was intrigued when I told him about Howard's shaken response to the Ames arrest. In his book proposal, Howard had claimed that he had visited the United States with a phony U.S. passport in 1986, a year after his defection to Moscow, and that he had met in a Washington, D.C., park with an authoritative American, as arranged by the KGB. The American had warned Howard against seeking out his wife, Mary, because she was cooperating with the FBI.

"Do you remember that guy in the park the author wrote about?" asked John H.

"I remember it well."

John H.'s implication: the man Howard met on that Washington park bench was Ames.

I telephoned Howard and discussed with him National Press's inability to pay his advance at that time, Howard's writing progress, and our imminent rendezvous. I also brought up the American spy he had met during his clandestine trip to the States in 1986. "Is it your belief that there's somebody else [another spy beyond Ames]?"

Ed replied, "Well, I think that you, um, go to the last part of my trip to America, uh. . . ."

"Yeah, I remember that. Is that the guy [Ames]?"

"No. The man I met in the States was different."

His answer tipped me, and the FBI, to an extremely important truth: *another* high-ranking man within the U.S. intelligence community was passing secrets to the Russians.

John H. arrived in Washington in November along with a thunderstorm of flashflood proportions. The hunt for the new mole was about to commence.

He greeted me at the door of the Holiday Inn's room 922 in Chevy Chase. A heavy, relentless rain lashed the window beside the small table where we got down to business. We went over a two-page "shopping list" John H. had compiled while vetting Edward Howard's manuscript. Some items pinpointed contradictions in what Howard had written compared to what he had told other people. John H. suggested I get Howard to trip up, further contradict himself, and thereby weaken his resistance to telling the truth by catching him in a web of lies. First, Howard had proposed to write about the classified Black Box, and John H. wondered what other secret operations Howard would reveal.

Howard had then written about traveling to Havana and giving Cuban intelligence officers insights into how the CIA thinks and behaves. The Cubans, wrote Howard, also knew of a lesbian within the CIA's ranks and wanted to compromise and blackmail her. John H. wanted to know what had become of their operation to entrap this officer.

Howard had also revealed his good relationship with former KGB chairman Vladimir Kryuchkov. "If Ed had nothing to offer the Russians, as he claims, how come he was able to get so buddy-buddy with Kryuchkov?" posed John H.

John H.'s next item concerned Howard's assertion that the KGB had shown him photographs of suspected CIA personnel and asked him to identify them. "This act itself would be considered espionage," said John H. "Will he confirm that he positively identified these officers?"

Item five dealt with a CIA operative Howard was believed to have compromised. Howard claimed the Russians had already identified this officer "a year before my arrival," but how did Howard *know* that?

John's next item covered Howard's view that he could never be convicted for espionage. "So why doesn't he return? The answer," said John H., "is because we *can* convict him. We have enough testimony. Ed knows this, and he knows *we* know. From your perspective, Ed's got to be more believable about why he chose to flee to Moscow if he hadn't done anything wrong."

Next he pointed out Howard's contradictions regarding Adolf Tolkachev, the Russian defense scientist arrested, tried, and executed for espionage after Howard compromised him. Item eight covered Howard's failed polygraph. "This is the pivotal point of his story," said John H. "He should be prepared to tell all."

"You'd make a good editor," I remarked. "I wonder what Howard would say if he knew you were shaping his book?"

Howard had also written about a CIA operation: "the idea of running a train car full of computers and spy devices right through the heart of the USSR was something that the boys at Langley could not resist doing." About this episode, John H. wanted me to ask Howard two questions: Is this for real? Do you know more details? "This really happened," said John H. "It's not so important now, but it was *very* important back then. It's another example, we think, of something Howard gave away."

Next, John H. wanted me to determine Howard's current drinking habits. "After too much drink," warned John H., "he gets weepy and admits he spied." Finally, Howard depicted himself as a faithfully married man, but this picture was far from the truth.

"Would addressing any of this be a problem for you to handle?" asked John H.

"Are you kidding? I'm his editor, which makes me a notch higher than a psychotherapist. It's my *job* to play devil's advocate."

"Good," said John H. "People at the top have confidence in your ability to pull this off." He produced an envelope stuffed with hundred-dollar bills, expense money for my trip. "You're on your own in Zurich. Usually, the CIA would watch the action, but we've told them to stay clear. No notice will be given to the Swiss government. You've got a clear playing field. The downside, of course, is that there'll be no backup. No one will be there for you."

Bad news arrived the next morning, by way of a fax from Howard: he would not be going to "the kids' place" after all in early April. The Russian government had instructed him to freeze all foreign travel until after Aldrich Ames's trial. Howard requested that I come see him in Moscow instead. This change of plans, of course, would require a whole new set of approvals from the Cheese Family.

John H. was disappointed. Finally, the FBI was all gung ho, and now he'd have to tell his people that our Swiss rendezvous was a no go.

Joseph and Sultan were none too pleased, either, when I visited their offices to commiserate with them. "And we finally paid part of his advance," said Sultan. "I bet the CIA would love to see this." Sultan showed me the wiring instructions, which identified Howard's numbered Swiss bank account: *234-877-60T, Union Bank of Switzerland, Zurich*. The Biggest Cheese apparently didn't want the buck, either.

I had John H. on the horn thirty minutes later. "Would you like the author's Swiss bank account details?"

"Are you kidding?"

I telephoned Howard, reaching him at his dacha. In the absence of a face-to-face meeting at this juncture, would he be prepared, I suggested, to engage in an editorial discussion over the phone?

"Yeah, I could do that."

"I have a list of things I'd like to discuss with you."

"Shoot."

"You mentioned a trip to Cuba where you gave insights into the CIA," I said. "It would be interesting to have those same insights in your book. A few pages about that would help your book."

"OK."

"Just tell your reader what you told the Cubans."

"Oh, OK."

"In another place, you refer to your relationship with Vladimir Kryuchkov. I think you need to personalize this to convince the reader just how close you are with the former KGB chairman."

"OK."

"At the moment you also come across like an angry man. I don't think that's how you want to convey yourself in this book. I think you need to lighten up, allow yourself some levity. Humor is the best way to make a point. Don't hold back, Ed. Let it rip."

"Yeah, I agree."

"Now, there's this business about how an American court could never convict you, yet you refuse to return. How do you reconcile that?"

"I have a probation problem, from a firearm conviction. And the other thing is, my life would be destroyed anyway. Plus I think some of my former CIA buddies would get me."

"'Get you'?"

"I would be hit by a truck."

"OK . . . detail those thoughts in writing. Reviewers are going to look for holes. We need to make sure they're all filled."

"OK."

"Good. Now, what you really need to address is the Ames case. Offer a good overview from your unique perspective."

"Right. OK, I'll do that."

"Do you think you were compromised by Yurchenko in order to conceal Ames?"

"What?"

"Did he give up information about you to divert attention from Ames?"

"OK, I understand. You know, I wrote the first part of this book a few years ago. I was doing it for Kryuchkov. He asked me to write this book. The book he wanted was *Glory to the Soviet State*. Fortunately, it never got published. Now I'm able to address these points and do my best job."

In April 1994, Howard's revision arrived. His new writing addressed my points and answered many of John H.'s questions. Howard also enclosed photocopies of his passports: one, Russian; the other, a KGB-fabricated U.S. passport under the alias Steve Roth that Howard had used when he secretly visited the United States in 1986. The package also included photographs of Howard's dacha, which detailed the security apparatus around him.

Joseph and Sultan invited me to a meeting at their offices and ambushed me about producing a finished Howard manuscript for autumn publication. I took the offensive. "You need a ghostwriter," I said. "Though I guess in this case, we say 'spook writer.'"

"Why a writer?"

"Because Howard's new material sucks. It needs to be completely rewritten." I explained that Howard's manuscript lacked cohesion. I pointed out that some of it was penned in 1988, part of it in 1990, and so on.

"We need a publishable manuscript no later than June 15," said Sultan. "Do you think we'll get it?"

"Honestly?" I said. "No. Howard thinks he's done his job. The only way to do this right is to hire a ghost to work with Howard and rewrite the whole thing. You don't believe me?" I plunked part of Howard's slapdash manuscript on the table. "Read it for yourself."

Later that afternoon, Joseph phoned me in a state of near panic. "We can't show this material to our sales reps! It's awful! Do you have other chapters that are any better?"

"Nope," I said. "Except for what his literary agent gave you, it's all like that. That's what I've been trying to tell you guys for three months: Howard can't write. We need a ghost."

Joseph responded by defining my role as Howard's editor, arguing that all the manuscript needed was heavy editing. I differed, pointing out that my accepting the editor's role had been based on Howard's proposal, which had included a section of clean, crisp, professional writing that was very unlike what Howard had delivered. "Howard and his literary agent misled you," I said. "You need to hire a ghost."

"We have no budget for a writer," said Sultan, who had joined the conference call. "You know what our cash flow is like. We just don't have the money."

I suggested that they confront Howard and his literary agent. They needed to point out that the manuscript was deficient, not what they promised, and thus unacceptable. They should threaten to reject it unless Howard and his agent found a ghostwriter at their own expense to rewrite the book.

"It's too late for that," countered Joseph.

"And we don't want a confrontation," said Sultan.

"In that case, there's only one solution." I paused. "The Dickster."

"The who?" they asked in unison.

"A book doctor I know. He works fast and—more important, for you guys—he works cheap."

"Could you talk to him?" asked Joseph.

One minute later, I caught Richard Côté at his home in South Carolina. We had met when he was looking for an agent. I outlined our project and its pitfalls. I did not mention that I was secretly working for the FBI.

"Can you do it?" I asked.

"Sure!" Côté had no reservations about working with Howard. He calculated the job at about ten grand's worth of work. I negotiated him down to two grand plus two net royalty points, a phenomenally low price for the job ahead.

I phoned National Press with the details. When I told them it was a great deal, they asserted they had no cash flow, nothing. They wondered if I could cough up the two grand.

"Yeah, right," I thought. "I'd already coughed up more than five hundred dollars in Fed Ex, phone, and fax expenses, not to mention my time. If I *weren't* working secretly for FBI foreign counterintelligence, I'd be a

world-class moron." I finally said, "Maybe I could pitch in five hundred bucks."
I didn't think the bureau would go for this, nor was it worth collecting the
twenty-two sets of initials for the necessary approvals, but this operation was
evolving fast and needed greasing.

Then Joseph and Sultan began questioning Côté's credentials. Well, he
had authored a handbook about how to score with women through personal
ads. That's why I called him "the Dickster."

"Look," I said, exasperated, "how many ghostwriters do you know who
would be ready to start immediately, who will travel to Moscow, conduct
extensive interviews, transcribe them, and rewrite a whole manuscript in six
weeks for two grand and pie-in-the-sky royalties?"

Next I phoned John H. "All hell has broken loose on my end."

"Really?" he said. "What now?"

"National Press has seen Howard's material, and these guys finally realize they don't have a book. They're going nuts."

I ran John H. through the new scenario: Richard Côté enters the picture, I give him the right questions to ask, he travels to Moscow in May and
works with Howard for ten days, and the book gets saved. I would travel to
Moscow in July and meet Howard for an editing session. Then I could get
him busy on my own book idea—our lure—and then we'd be off and running in a new direction, literally, to someplace where we could nail Howard.
John H. had no objections.

National Press signed an agreement with Richard Côté, and I wrote a
fax to Howard explaining Côté's involvement. On May 19, Côté arrived in
Bethesda. He and I met the National Press guys for a working editorial lun-
cheon at Montgomery's Grille. Côté was all business in a navy blazer, gray
flannel trousers, blue button-down shirt, a chili pepper–patterned tie, and
black penny loafers, with pennies tucked into their bands. Big and round, he
comes equipped with a twitchy neck and a set of rules that keep him regi-
mented and organized. While we ate, Côté took copious notes.

"Are there a bunch of defectors who hang together, maybe play poker
on Wednesday night?" I posed. "Find out. Howard has written that he's good
friends with George Blake, the British spy. Are there others? Also," I added,
"show a week in the life of Ed Howard. How does he live? We need this kind
of color to bring his manuscript alive."

"I'm a lawyer," said Joseph to Côté. "Ask Ed if he wants to make a deal to come back to the States."

I let Joseph posture. It couldn't hurt.

Côté noted our concerns and summed up his approach: "I'm going to tell Ed that this is his one shot to tell his story—he won't get another—and that he'd better make use of it and hold nothing back."

Two hours later, Alan Sultan dropped Côté at Washington Dulles International Airport for a six o'clock flight to Paris and a connection to Moscow.

7

NYET-NYUKS

Ten days later, Richard Côté came back through the looking glass, blasted and spacey from jet lag when he arrived at my house a little past five thirty. He had just flown four hours from Moscow to Paris and eight hours from Paris to Washington, and had all but lost his voice to laryngitis. He begged for a glass of milk and then another. We sat in my sunroom.

An awestruck Côté was in his glory. "I just had the most exhilarating ten days of my life!" he erupted.

Edward Howard had introduced Côté to George Blake, and they had lunched at a Moscow restaurant called Tren Mos Bistro. The British traitor, Blake, convicted of espionage and sentenced to a forty-two-year prison term, had escaped and fled to Russia two decades before Howard had. Blake had betrayed forty-two agents and given up many secret operations, including the CIA's tunnel under East Berlin. Now he wanted the Dickster's help to write his own book—a sequel to his earlier memoir, *No Other Choice*—so Côté wanted to get back to Russia as soon as humanly possible.

"Moscow has no logic," he rasped, "at least not our logic. It has a logic all its own. You're not in control in Moscow; Moscow is in control of you. Everywhere you go, the answer is no. I call Russians '*nyet-nyuks*.'"

"Slow down," I said. "Let's start from the beginning."

Côté rubbed his Adam's apple and begged off talking about his trip. "I asked Howard the entire laundry list of questions the FBI and CIA would dearly like to ask him, if only they could," he said. "I'll send you fifty pages of interview transcripts."

So rather than talk substance, we decided to talk color and gossip over pizza and white wine at nearby Melio's.

"Howard has a seventeen-hundred-square-foot apartment in the second-nicest neighborhood in Moscow," whispered Côté. "He was able to buy it, but he doesn't live there. He uses it to overnight in town and put up business associates [such as Côté]. His apartment is on the second floor," he continued. "This was better than a higher floor because the elevator was broken the whole time. It has two bedrooms; one has twin beds. The other is fitted as a home office with a computer and laser printer."

I asked Côté if he thought he'd been watched.

"Not for one minute."

"But what about Ed's security contingent?" Howard had written of a twenty-four-hour, sixteen-bodyguard arrangement.

The Dickster shook his head. "It doesn't exist. I asked him about it. He said, 'Sometimes I have a tail or two, if they're training somebody new.'"

"Did he drink any booze?"

"Not one drop."

"Did you go out to bars with him?"

"Yep." Côté nodded. "He drank soft drinks. Oh, you'll like this: Ed told me every head bartender in every bar in Moscow is a KGB agent. Anyway, Ed just doesn't drink. The Russian police can stop motorists for any reason. They don't need probable cause. And they come down heavy on drunk drivers. Ed says it's not worth chancing it. He wants to be a good Russian.

"What do you mean, 'a good Russian'?"

"Ed doesn't consider himself an American expatriate any more," said Côté. "He has Russian citizenship, and he considers himself a Russian. That's his self-image. He's in Russia for good, and he's going to live a Russian life. None of his friends are American."

"Who are his friends?"

"Ed has very few friends. Igor Batamirov, a KGB colonel I met, is probably his best friend. And George Blake. I loved Blake. He's like a big teddy bear. I wanted to put him in my suitcase and bring him back with me. And, yeah, he's a good friend to Ed."

"Girlfriends?"

"Yes," replied Côté, "he has a few. Ed has an interesting perspective on this. He says his wife knows that he's screwed around and that he has girlfriends, but as long as it's vague, it's cool. He doesn't want to get into specifics in his book because then it would be uncool. But, boy, his first three years in Moscow were wild. All he did was drink and screw every woman he could get his hands on. Igor vouched for this. But that's over. Ed's settled down. He's really a quiet country boy at heart."

"You think so?"

"Absolutely," said Côté. "He's sober and serious and very self-sufficient."

"What about a sense of humor?" I asked.

"Ed doesn't have a well-developed sense of humor," said Côté. "If you try to be funny, he misses it nine times out of ten." The Dickster reached into his sport coat and extracted a pack of color photographs. "Ed took me to places where tourists never travel. Our government," he whispered, "spent 250 million dollars on a manhole cover. Can you believe it? Here it is." Côté showed me a shot of Howard kneeling over a manhole cover. "That's it, the manhole cover, worth a quarter of a billion bucks!"

I flipped through the deck. There was Howard hunched over a laptop in his dacha and Howard picking through meat at an open-air stall. None of the photos showed him full face, but he was clean shaven—gone was the mousy moustache—and his hair was turning gray.

"Ed didn't want any full-face shots," explained Côté. "He doesn't want the FBI to have an up-to-date picture of him."

"What makes Ed think the FBI would see your photos?"

"You kidding? Ed was convinced they'd meet me at the gate at Dulles Airport and confiscate my tapes and photos."

"Really?"

"Yeah. He's really pissed at the FBI. Now, this is in confidence—it's not for the book, not for the guys at National Press, but just for you: Ed told me that his assistant, Larissa [Lena Orlova], came to the States to visit relatives. She was intercepted by the FBI and forced to give testimony before a grand jury. She was upset. Ed was livid. He's had it with the FBI. As for Joel Joseph's suggestion about making a deal and returning to the States? Ed says no deal making. He says no truce with the FBI, no compromises. His attitude about the FBI is, 'You won't leave me alone, so screw you. You want to play games? I'll reveal everything I know.'"

I perused Côté's other photos. He had one of himself with Ed's KGB friend, Col. Igor Batamirov, a senior officer whom the powers that be in Moscow had wheeled out for his first-ever interview with a Western writer.

Said Côté, when Howard first arrived in Moscow, it was Batamirov who met him at the airport. Another photo showed Côté with George Blake.

"George didn't really want a photo taken of him," said Côté. "Nobody knows what he looks like anymore. I assured him it won't be used in the book."

This much about Côté's visit was obvious: the Russians had put on a good show for the Dickster. They were very much behind Howard's book.

"Ames?" I asked.

"In the transcripts."

"Tell me *something*," I prodded, mindful that John H. would fly in the next day so I could brief him on Côté's trip.

"OK," Côté sipped water. "I put to Ed the Yurchenko theory—that Yurchenko was KGB stage-managed to take the heat off Ames at Ed's expense—but Ed doesn't buy that. He believes Yurchenko was genuine and knew that he, Howard, was on a KGB target list because they knew he was unhappy and ripe for an approach. So Yurchenko gave his debriefers hints about whom the KGB *might* target. The FBI ran with that, pinpointing Howard and assuming the worst because the FBI knew the KGB had been getting secrets from someone—and that someone was Ames. Ed says the FBI is gradually discovering that what the FBI thought the KGB had gotten from him had really come from Ames."

"Do you believe him?" I asked.

"Look, I had a minor clearance in the air force," said Côté. "And I was taught if something is stamped 'secret,' it's secret. It doesn't matter if the Russians already know about it. It's illegal to tell anyone, period. Clearly, Ed has done this. It's obvious to me he has given secrets to the Russians."

"Anything else?"

"Yeah, this is good," said Côté. "Ed told me that the Russians gave him a Toshiba laptop, a value of three or four thousand dollars, to write his book. And they promised him a new car when it's finished. Ed also said they wanted him to include CIA operations he knew nothing about—CIA operations in Latin America, CIA media propaganda operations."

The Dickster was spent. He'd been traveling all day. Just past eight o'clock he set off again, bound for his home in Charleston.

John H. phoned me just past six o'clock the next evening, Wednesday, June 1. "I'm here."

"And it's not even raining," I said.

"Of course not, because I brought an umbrella this time. I'm at the Holiday Inn Bethesda. Couldn't get into Chevy Chase."

"Let's have dinner at Houston's. It's walking distance from your hotel."

John H. and I greeted each other and grabbed a booth. "Let's start like this," I said. "If we didn't know each other, would you be aware that my ghostwriter just spent a week in Moscow with Ed Howard?"

John H. shook his head. "We'd have no way of knowing."

"The reason I ask is, Howard was convinced Côté would be met at Dulles by G-men. So I'm wondering if you *should* contact Côté lest Howard think something is amiss because the Dickster *wasn't* met. But you should contact Côté only if it would have been your natural inclination to do it."

"No, it wouldn't have been," said John H, "because we wouldn't have known about him."

"OK. I just wanted to be sure of our moves. Howard is *really* pissed off at you guys."

"Oh, no," said John H. in mock horror.

"Yeah, that thing you did to Lena Orlova? Howard says, 'No more mister nice guy.'"

"Oh, I see!" John H. chuckled.

"Howard says he's never coming back. No deals, no compromises. He thinks of himself as Russian."

Over prime rib, I ran through my notes. John H. was alternately intrigued and amused. The photographs riveted his attention: Howard and the manhole cover, Batamirov, and Blake. To a counterintelligence officer, they were a treasure trove.

"Here's what's happening," said John H. "Bob G. [assistant U.S. attorney] is flying in tonight. My boss, Jim S., is flying in tomorrow. The U.S. attorney for New Mexico is here, too."

"Jeez," I said, "sounds like a convention."

"It will be," he replied. "On Friday morning we have a meeting downtown with the four of us, plus about ten others, including the assistant FBI director for national security and the deputy attorney general."

I presented myself at John H.'s room, 1406, at nine thirty the next morning. Bob G. arrived a few minutes later in blue slacks and a short-sleeve madras shirt. I retold Côté's tale and had show-and-tell with his photographs, including some photos Howard had sent via FedEx to me a few weeks earlier. These photos also showed a manhole cover, labeled in Howard's own handwriting with the still-classified code name of the still-classified operation to which the manhole cover was associated.

John H. was gobsmacked. "This is evidence of espionage!" he said. "Even the code name is secret, but he's written it here, sent it to you, and even signed his initials."

Bob G. said he had loved the idea of inserting a ghostwriter into the process. Côté would make a great witness, he said, not least because he had been unaware of what was really going on. "That was pretty good," said Bob G. "You've put this writer in front of you as a shield."

"It's called a 'cutout,'" I said.

The three of us met Jim S. at O'Donnell's, a Bethesda seafood restaurant. Jim S. had learned his lesson and dressed casually.

"I have a question," I said, looking over my menu. "If I hadn't shown up with Howard's book proposal nine months ago, would you still not know about it?"

"We wouldn't know," said John H.

"You mean not one person has called the bureau in all these months?" I considered how by this time, *Safe House* by one Edward Lee Howard had been featured as a forthcoming title in a catalog produced by National Book Network, the distributors for National Press. The catalog had been sent to thousands of booksellers, libraries, and media organizations around the country.

John H. shook his head. "Not a one."

"People assume we know everything," said Bob G. "If only they knew the truth. We're too busy having meetings or fighting political battles."

John H. phoned me at three o'clock the next afternoon when the big powwow at FBI Headquarters had concluded. Bob G.'s pitch had been well received. The bottom line was the Cheese Family had given a green light to our proposal. I was going to meet Howard in Russia.

8

GOOD TO GO

My Air France flight on July 20 from Paris to Moscow was a slow three hours and fifteen minutes, a path that took us over Amsterdam, up to the Baltic Sea, and across Lithuania. Lunch in Le Club class was surprisingly inedible, which was fine by me as I had no appetite.

I was on my own, in both a literal and figurative sense, unprotected by diplomatic immunity. If the KGB caught me out as an *illegal* deep-cover spy, my friends at the FBI would deny any connection to me. The Russian definition of spying is purposely vague and stickier than flypaper on a humid day. Twenty years' imprisonment is the Russians' going rate for espionage.

I carried with me a pocketful of ideas to extend my relationship with Edward Howard beyond his business with National Press Books. Indeed, it had been determined on a legal level that a rendition of Howard should not involve National Press but should instead stem from a new project I would propose to him.

I sipped a quarter bottle of champagne and made a meal of *Time* and *Newsweek*. As we descended, my mood lightened. It was a sunny summer day in Moscow with clear skies. The fields and lakes looked appealing from on high.

As we landed and taxied to a terminal, I looked out my window to see Aeroflot aircraft everywhere, sleek and attractive on the outside. Like Russia itself, the truth lay beneath the surface: loose seats, missing life vests, disarray, and deteriorating infrastructure. Armed soldiers watched as we new arrivals negotiated drab corridors and descended a flight of stairs to baggage collection, which was a madhouse. I hadn't checked any luggage, so I aimed myself at Customs. I had two choices: Green (nothing to declare) or Red (something to declare). Green was closed, so I took my place in one of two long lines for Red.

"Do you speak English?" I asked the guy in front of me.

"I hope so. I'm from New York."

"Why is Green closed? I have nothing to declare."

"If you have more than fifty dollars," he said, "you have something to declare."

"Fifty dollars? Who has less than fifty dollars?"

"Exactly."

"But what if I did have less than fifty dollars?"

"You'd have even more trouble if Green was open. They'd detain you for having so little money. I saw that happen once."

The Dickster was right: Moscow defied logic. I was only ninth in line at Customs, but it took thirty minutes to reach an apparatchik resembling Mr. Potato Head's wife, who stamped and restamped my documents in quadruplicate.

I looked around for Edward Howard, but he found me first, coming up from behind me and whispering my name. I turned and shook his outstretched hand. Howard looked like a short, pudgy version of the actor Roy Scheider. He wore mismatched clothing: a red-and-white striped shirt, gray trousers, beige jacket, and black sneakers. He looked, well, Russian.

We made our way to Howard's powder blue 1987 Volvo station wagon with Russian tags T9415MK. The odometer registered more than fifty-two thousand miles, but his rusty vehicle had matured way beyond its physical age and mileage. Howard climbed behind the wheel and fastened his seat belt. "Mind if I smoke?"

"Not at all." I paused. "I'm staying at the Radisson. No offense or anything, it was nice of you to offer your apartment, but I prefer a hotel and the services that go with it when I travel."

"OK. The Radisson's good," said Howard. "I recently joined the health club so I'm there three times a week. It also houses the International Press Club, which I just got into."

"Really?"

"Yeah." Howard dragged on his Doral cigarette and started the car. "It's open to journalists, writers, and heads of business. So I thought, 'What the hell, I've got my own business as a consultant.' I went in, and they accepted me. It's kind of funny because the U.S. Embassy is on its board!"

"What kind of consultant are you?" I asked.

"I arrange introductions and things for people who want to do business in Russia."

Watching Howard's hands, I noted his school ring and a Rolex wristwatch with a stainless steel bracelet. His fingernails were bitten all to hell. As he swung into airport traffic, Howard mentioned that FBI director Louis Freeh had visited Moscow two weeks earlier. "I tried to get a photograph of him for my book. I stood watching outside Lyubyanka when he visited, but he didn't stop to talk to reporters. He rushed straight in. Later I found out why: his visit upset a lot of hard-liners. So he was asked to keep a low profile." Howard struggled against other motorists to merge onto a main road. "That's the mentality here," he commented, shaking his head: "beat out the next guy."

"Is that a Muscovite trait?" I asked.

"No, it's a Russian trait. I don't like these people. And they're even worse to do business with. Things are changing too fast here." Howard coughed, an incessant catarrh-like hack from smoking. "Used to be, everything was based on party privilege. Now everything is based on money. If you've got dollars, you can have anything you want." Howard seemed disgusted by this concept, not least because all he possessed had come through party privilege. "Not that I was ever in love with communism," he added. "It's just that people here aren't used to this. Look at all these cars." He motioned with both hands at the bumper-to-bumper traffic gridlocked around us. "There never used to be this many cars around. People had money, but they couldn't buy a car without the right contacts and getting on a list. It used to take fifteen years to buy a car. Now anyone with money can buy one. And what do you get? Traffic."

"Things are pretty ridiculous in the States, too," I said. "You've been away a long time, Ed. You're probably not familiar with all the political correctness going on. Real estate agents can't even use terms like *great view* any more because it may offend blind people."

Howard chuckled. And Côté said he didn't have a sense of humor.

"I've lived half my life overseas, Ed," I said. "You begin to see the United States through a different light. You ever think of going back?"

Howard grimaced. He rubbed his crooked boxer's nose. "I could beat the espionage charges. It's all the other stuff they could put me in jail for: interstate flight, taxes. . . . ."

"Taxes?"

"Yeah, uh-huh. I went to see a tax adviser about the amnesty they're offering for overseas Americans. I was told I could take advantage of that. It's the state tax in New Mexico that worries me."

I couldn't believe my ears. This fugitive, wanted for espionage, was worried that he hadn't paid his taxes. Plus he was under the erroneous impression that he should have been paying *state* tax all these years. I pointed out that as an overseas American, he had liability only for federal income tax, after an exemption for the first seventy-five thousand dollars of earned income.

"Really?" said Howard.

"Truly." I don't think he believed me.

Taxes aside, I asked whether there was any deal that could be made for his voluntary return. "Alan Sultan thinks it would be great publicity for your book," I said.

"If they'd just try me for espionage and drop all the other crap, I'd come back," said Howard.

"Who would you deal with?" I asked.

"The FBI, but the bureau doesn't deal. It's really up to the U.S. attorney in New Mexico."

"Have you had any offers to deal?"

"Yeah, I got a fax over a year ago saying they wanted to come to Moscow and talk to me."

"Out of the blue?"

"Well, I had phoned an FBI guy named [John H.]. I'd met him in Stockholm before the Swedes let me leave. I guess the fax was a result of that."

"What happened?"

"I faxed back and asked for an agenda."

"And?"

"They faxed me saying they wouldn't give me an agenda."

"Then?"

"Nothing," said Howard. "My KGB contacts said, 'Why bother?' So when the FBI didn't give me an agenda, I never faxed back."

"Forget the KGB," I said. "They have a vested interest in you staying here. If this guy wants to come to Moscow to talk, what have you got to lose?"

"It's just boondoggle," said Howard. "Those guys like taking trips. They'll come all this way not to deal."

"You've still got nothing to lose," I said.

"Yeah, yeah, I guess it's worth thinking about, but I don't think the Russians would be too happy."

"Screw the Russians, man. It's yourself you've got to worry about."

"I know, I know." Howard steered into the Radisson Slavyanskaya's forecourt. For a new luxury hotel, it was as ugly as sin. Howard circled twice and slipped into a space vacated by another vehicle. As we approached the hotel entrance on foot, Howard said, "The Russians think I'm crazy for including the Black Box in my book."

"Why?"

"Because they say the CIA is going to kill me for that."

"Why? It's old news, isn't it?"

"Yeah," said Howard, "but the CIA may be doing the same thing in other countries today, using current applications of the same technique."

Howard stood next to me at the check-in desk as a clerk accessed my reservation. "I'll put you a long way from noisy renovations," said the clerk.

"And I'd like a double bed," I said. "Not twins."

The clerk fingered his keyboard. "Can I have your passport?"

"When do I get it back?" I asked.

"Tomorrow."

"No good," I said. "I'm leaving early in the morning. Can't you just photocopy it?"

"No," said the clerk. "You need a receipt for Customs when you leave Russia."

Howard made faces. "What crap!" he erupted. "Foreigners stay in my apartment all the time and never show their passport."

The clerk shrugged. "I'll get it back to you tonight." He took my passport and issued me a key.

While Howard remained in the lobby, I ascended to the sixth floor and found my way to room 6056, which was adjacent to noisy renovations. I opened the door to find twin beds. Côté was right, no logic to Moscow. I then emptied my head, scribbling notes about Howard in handwriting so illegible *I* could barely make sense of it. Bad handwriting is less incriminating than encryption.

I returned downstairs, and we drove to Howard's office so he could check on incoming faxes. Howard told me his wife and son would arrive in Moscow five days hence and stay a month. They wanted to visit St. Petersburg, he said, so he intended to accompany them and play tour guide.

"How are you able to maintain your marriage like this?" I asked.

"It's tough," said Howard. "Mary and I see each other at Christmas and during the summer. I don't ask her questions and she doesn't ask me any. It's what you'd call 'mature' love."

"And when she's here, it's as if nothing has changed?"

"That's right." Howard added, "My in-laws are coming, too."

"Everything's cool with them?"

"It's OK now. At first they didn't want Mary to see me again. It took some time, but we got over the emotional difficulties. I've got their support. And that's the main reason I want to write this book: I just want my side of the story out there where my family can see it. Then I can move on."

"And your son?"

"We have a good relationship. We had a long talk when he was eleven, after he found a copy of the David Wise book. Lee knows that I'm not a spy, that I'm a political refugee."

I told Howard that National Press planned to submit his manuscript to the CIA for review. "They have to," I said, "to protect themselves from accusations of receiving and publishing classified material."

"I see." Howard was displeased by this news, not least because he anticipated, correctly, that the CIA would try to freeze all monies due him.

Traffic had slowed because a dozen large crates of bottled beer had fallen from a truck in front of us. Cars veered around the mess; some motorists jumped out of their vehicles to loot the few bottles that lay unbroken in the street. A half mile later, Howard parked, and we crossed the street to his office, housed within a yellow cinder-block structure. "I'm in a medical building," said Howard. "It's cheap."

We walked through an unlocked front door. A few yards on, at the first door on the left, Howard keyed a single lock, and we entered. The drab, two-room office was illuminated by dim wattage. It reeked of stale tobacco smoke, which had permeated the carpets and the furniture and stained the walls brown. Howard checked for faxes but had none.

57

"Who are your clients these days?" I asked.

"Some Germans, Swedes, and a Spaniard who paid for me to meet him in Vienna last month."

"So you manage to travel a bit?"

"Yeah," said Howard, "to neutral countries mostly, like Switzerland and Austria."

"How do you find clients?"

"Through advertising. I started with the *International Herald Tribune*, but that was terrible. I only got people who wanted to sell me things. *The Economist* is best."

Howard locked his office, and we walked down the road to a Tex-Mex restaurant called Santa Fe. "They've only been open four months, but they're doing pretty well," said Howard. "It's a good thing we're eating early. It'll be packed later, with a line to get in."

Santa Fe was quiet at five thirty in the afternoon, with only a few barflies. A maître d' seated us and gave us menus printed in English and priced in U.S. dollars. I ordered Heineken; Howard, a tonic. He lit a Doral and chainsmoked his way through dinner: beef fajitas for him, a chicken sandwich for me.

"Your book is going to need some news hooks," I said. "So let's talk about that now."

"Fine."

"First, how about your knowledge of Russian spies inside the U.S. government, beyond Ames?"

"There are plenty of them," said Howard.

"OK, let's expand on that. Start with the American who tipped you off about your wife cooperating with the FBI during your secret trip to the States in '86. Where would he have worked to gain access to the documents he showed you?"

"Probably the Justice Department," said Howard. "The KGB showed me psychological studies that had been prepared by the U.S. government saying that I was suicidal. That would have been done by the CIA."

"Ames?"

"Maybe."

"Or the KGB could have made it up," I said.

"Why?"

"To convince you not to take the trip."

"Uh-huh," said Howard, "I guess that's possible. But I went, and they helped me with false documents and reentry."

"Speaking of Ames," I said, "why didn't the Russians rescue him? They must have known he was under investigation."

"Yeah, they knew he was in trouble," said Howard. "Last September, one of my KGB contacts, a man named Batamirov, showed me a picture of Ames when we were at a restaurant on the river. He asked me, 'Do you know this man?' I said I didn't. I should have known then something was going on. They must've known Ames was in trouble."

"So why didn't they exfiltrate Ames," I asked, "like the Brits did with Oleg Gordievsky?"

"They could have," replied Howard. "It would have been very easy. The KGB wanted to get him out. It went up to Yeltsin for approval, and Yeltsin shot it down."

I almost fell out of my chair. "Why?" I asked.

"Because it would have been too sticky politically," said Howard. "Look, when there was a $400 million aid package for Russia working its way through Congress, some congressman tacked on a rider saying it was contingent on the Russians giving *me* back! Yeltsin didn't want another one like me messing up aid packages. It was more politically expedient to let Ames get caught than bring him here, where he'd become a major political and economic issue. And I'll tell you something else about Ames: he wasn't the incompetent fool they made him out to be in the American press. My KGB contacts say he was a brilliant spy, very professional."

"You wrote in your manuscript that your KGB friends cracked out the champagne when Ames was caught. Why would they celebrate the loss of such an important agent?"

"You have to understand," said Howard, "that these guys had been bashed away at for five years. It boosted their morale to be seen as having put one over on the CIA."

When I asked again about Russian spies inside the U.S. government, Howard said, "Look, the United States has thousands of intelligence officers around the world whose job it is to recruit spies. So does the KGB. With all those people and a big budget, do you think they don't recruit anyone? If they didn't, the money would stop. Of course, they have spies everywhere.

When I was living in Sweden, my KGB contacts told me in advance everything that was coming down on me. They said, 'You're about to be detained and arrested.' They knew! I'll tell you: Igor Batamirov, the man Dick Côté met, was Ames's handler."

As he chewed his fajitas, Howard also confirmed for me what he had told the Dickster: his book was the KGB's idea. "They asked what I wanted in return," said Howard. "I said, 'Just give me a new car.' They said, 'Fine.'"

I ordered a second Heineken; Ed, another tonic. The restaurant had begun to fill up, mostly with expatriate American businessmen. Our talk turned to the new capitalism in Russia, Howard's pet peeve. "In the old days," said Howard, "I had a little book, and in it were special vouchers and phone numbers for getting seats at the Bolshoi Ballet or anywhere else in Moscow."

"You don't have that any more?"

"No one does," Howard griped. "Everything goes for money now."

We returned to the Radisson and ascended the spiral marble staircase to the Business Center on the mezzanine. Howard brought along his copy of Richard Côté's rewrite, which I had yet to edit.

As we walked, I asked, "Do you ever get recognized by anyone, Ed?"

"Only once," Howard replied, "by an American student in Budapest who had just read the David Wise book about me. He freaked out."

We settled at a conference table and set to work on a page-by-page analysis. I noted Howard's corrections, additions, and deletions; Howard chain-smoked throughout. When we finished, Howard went off for a sauna in the hotel's health club. I returned to my room to empty my head again into a pocket notebook.

At quarter of nine, I returned to the lobby, a lavish space with a gargantuan chandelier, beneath which a pianist tapped out musical notes that got lost in the large acoustically challenged room. Howard found me inspecting an arcade of display windows. "What's all this about?" I asked as I motioned to a display of Gianni Versace couture and crocodile shoes.

"The average Russian can't afford this stuff," said Howard with disdain. "He earns about eighty dollars a month. Shall we have a drink at the Press Club?"

We entered the International Press Club, Howard signed a membership book, and we sat our rears on stools at the bar. Howard ordered Pepsis for us both.

"You do pretty well in Russian," I said.

"I do OK. I don't speak it that great, but I understand everything."

On stage nearby, a trio of musicians performed a masterful rendition of the theme from the movie *Once Upon a Time in America*. It was an unexpected pleasure for me, but Howard seemed oblivious to its poignancy.

"So what's next?" I asked.

"What do you mean?"

"After *Safe House* is published. Any plans to write another book?"

"I hadn't thought about it," said Howard. "You have something in mind?"

"Matter of fact, I do." I sipped my Pepsi. "How about *A Spy's Guide to Central Europe*?"

Howard smiled. "Yeah, I like that."

"A tongue-in-cheek travel guide with a spy theme," I continued. "After all, who knows Central Europe better than a well-traveled spy?"

"I could do that," said Howard.

"Budapest, Moscow, Prague, St. Petersburg, Vienna, Warsaw, et cetera. Hotels and restaurants, bars and nightclubs, museums, shopping. . . ."

"And you'd publish this yourself?" asked Howard.

"That's right. I have my own imprint, Enigma Books. Nothing to do with National Press."

"Yeah, I like that."

"You research it," I said, "and I'll write it. You get the byline, because you're the spy!"

Howard smiled broadly. He really, truly loved this idea. We drained our sodas and sauntered out for Howard's nickel tour of Moscow. He parked near Red Square. Young men loitered all around, checking us out. Howard told me his Volvo had been busted into once. "And I had a tire slashed a couple weeks ago," he added. "Some hoodlum knew I was in a Western-style supermarket. He thought I'd put down a bag of groceries to change my tire, and then he'd grab the bag and run."

A young man approached us and said he wanted to sell us old Russian postage stamps. We told him no, but he persisted, following us for five minutes before finding others to harass. Then we wandered around St. Basil's Cathedral. Howard pointed to a viewing stand above the Kremlin wall. "That's where I viewed the May Day Parade with the generals. Most of them are disgraced now." He pointed to another ornate building, now derelict. "That used to be the Communist Party Museum." We returned to where Howard had parked. "My car is still there," he said, as if he expected it to be stolen.

"I guess things have changed here, Ed?"

"Yeah, it's gotten rough."

"Do you see yourself always living in Moscow?"

"No," said Howard. "I don't know. I'd like to visit Chile, Argentina. . . ."

"To live?"

"I wish, but they'd find me."

"How?"

"Through family."

Howard drove to his apartment in Old Town's Arbat district with its narrow and dark roads. Howard exchanged greetings with his concierge, a babushka who lived on the ground floor and observed other tenants and their guests. Up one flight of stairs, Howard keyed two locks.

"Does Moscow have a burglary problem?" I asked.

"It's getting worse."

We entered a long corridor. I followed Howard into the first room on the right, his kitchen, where he put a kettle on a gas fire. "Just as well you decided to stay at the Radisson," said Howard. "During the summer they take turns switching off hot water in districts around Moscow. Mine has been off for three weeks."

He showed me around his pad. On one end, he had a living room with a small, glass-enclosed terrace overlooking some trees; at the other end were two small bedrooms, one transformed into an office. "I guess I'll stay here tonight," sighed Howard. Normally, he would drive forty minutes to his dacha. I was glad to be staying elsewhere; Howard's apartment gave me the creeps. We sat in the living room. "You own this place?" I asked.

"Yeah. Yeltsin gave apartment dwellers a one-time chance to buy their apartments for a token fee. I'm told it's now worth three hundred thousand dollars."

"And the dacha? You own that?"

"No." Howard shook his head. "And I may lose it."

"Why?"

"Budget cutbacks. Two things could happen: one, if some general wants it, they'll take it from me and give it to him. Or two, they'll just shut it down and not let anyone live there."

"Why would they do that?"

"It's expensive to maintain. It needs constant repairs, full-time security. I can see them saying it's too expensive and just shut it down."

"What would you do? Live here?"

Howard shrugged. "I'd have to."

The kettle whistled. I followed Howard back into his kitchen, where he brewed two cups of English breakfast tea. I sat at his small table. Howard remained on his feet. A propos of nothing, he returned to the deal we had touched on earlier in the day—a deal with the U.S. government for returning to the States. "It's awfully tempting to try to make a deal like that," said Howard. "I've made a life here. I've been here nine years. I've set up a business. It would be hard to turn my back on that."

"If that's the case, I guess you ought to stick it out," I said.

But Howard was just rationalizing. "The U.S. government should have to pay me back for these nine years," he continued. "You know, there's something called the Mole Relief Act. I think it means that if I'm proven innocent, the government would have to compensate me for the nine years of misery they've caused."

"Really?"

"Yeah, I read about it recently, the Mole Relief Act." He pulled out a pack of cigarettes. "I'm going to smoke. Let's go out on the terrace." I followed Howard through the living room to his narrow terrace. He grew pensive and then took me through his exchange of faxes with FBI special agent John H. "Maybe you could write something for me I could fax to him," said Howard, "but there'd still be a problem with the Russians."

"Why?"

"My KGB contacts will say, 'Don't rock the boat.' They'll say, '*We're* fine with what you're doing, but if word filters up to Yeltsin's people, it may mean trouble.'"

Howard then wanted to take a walk, so we grabbed our jackets and went out into the light drizzle outside. His street was dark and muddy. "A couple of female news correspondents—one English, one American—rent an apartment above me," said Howard. "I've invited them down for drinks a few times, but they've thought of every excuse not to come."

"Do they know who you are?"

"No, nobody knows around here. I go by the name Ed Janovich. I keep a low profile."

Within a couple of minutes we reached Arbat's main street, a winding pedestrian precinct. Scores of teenagers congregated on the cobblestoned path, blasted on booze. Empty beer bottles were strewn around; broken glass littered the pavement. Vodka and cigarettes changed hands at a busy kiosk. Nearby, a roaring fire in a large trash can warmed whoever needed toasting. They made me think of the *proles* in George Orwell's *1984*. "This is the most fashionable street in Moscow," said Howard. It was hard to tell whether he was being facetious. We strolled past a Baskin-Robbins, which was closed at this hour—about eleven o'clock—and then past a pizzeria. Howard wanted to pop in for dessert, but it was closing, too.

It seemed as if Howard wanted the evening to continue and be in my presence as long as he could. Perhaps he was starved for American companionship. Years later, a scene in the TV series *Millennium* reminded me of Howard that July night in Moscow: the character Frank Black recognized a devil and said, "You must be so lonely." When the devil repeated this line to three other devils sitting inside a doughnut shop, they looked down, recognizing the truth they all shared, and one by one, they skulked out into the night.

Howard and I turned around and walked past the young drunks of Arbat. Ed bought a pack of Dorals from the kiosk, and we trudged through sludge to his apartment building. "You want to come back in?" Ed offered. "Nah, I'm beat. Let's call it a night."

As he drove me to the Radisson, Howard said, "Can you believe this is the best part of Moscow? You can't imagine what it's like in other parts of town."

The next morning, at six fifteen sharp, Howard rounded into the Radisson's forecourt. Punctuality was a trait he shared with his nemesis, John H. I climbed in, and we took off to the airport.

"I really like your idea about a spy's guide," said Howard, as I prepared to launch from his car.

"Great."

"I could take research trips myself. Would you cover expenses?"

"Of course."

"And you think there's money in it?"

I nodded. "I'll pay for your time, at least."

"Would I make a couple of thousand?" asked Howard.

"At least that."

"Then I'll do it." Howard double-parked outside the departures terminal. We shook hands on the *Spy's Guide* project. As I ventured into the building and a gauntlet of exit hurdles, behind me, Edward Lee Howard returned to his life as a defector.

9

LONDON INTERLUDE

Breakfast aboard British Airways lacked flavor, but I managed to wash part of an omelet down with a quarter bottle of champagne. A celebration seemed in order for an assignment well done.

After checking into my room at the Britannia Hotel, opposite the U.S. Embassy on Grosvenor Square, I picked up the phone and dialed 1-6-0.

"Are you here?" asked John H.

"You mean, has the Eagle landed?" I kidded. "Yup."

"How did it go?"

"Swimmingly. I'm in room 137. Come over whenever you're ready."

"You kidding? I'll be right there!"

Minutes later, there was a knock at my door. I let John H. in and then closed the door behind him. "Well?" he asked in high anticipation.

"Did you know Howard was in Santa Fe recently?" I deadpanned.

"Really?" John H. feigned nonchalance.

"Yeah." I paused. "It's a restaurant in Moscow."

John H. laughed, relieved. "I'm expected at the embassy in a little while to make some calls," he said. "What I need from you now is just the *essence*."

Essentially, I reported, Edward Howard was prepared to travel around Central Europe, unguarded, to research the *Spy's Guide* project. John H.'s eyes sparkled, and he smiled broadly. I continued, "And you're not going to believe what he told me about Ames."

John H. hunched over a notebook and scribbled into it like mad as I spoke. Some of his FBI colleagues were in town, and he wondered whether I minded if they joined us for dinner.

"You kidding?" I buzzed the concierge to amend our dinner reservation at Quaglino's from two to four persons as John H. left for the embassy.

A few hours later we assembled in the lobby. Joining me were John H. and Les and Jim from headquarters. We exchanged greetings.

"So how'd it go at the embassy?" I asked John H.

He beamed. "Everyone's satisfied."

We left for dinner. The three G-men climbed into the back seat of a Range Rover while I sat up front with my driver, a Rasputin look-alike I called "Mister Five" because he exhibited all five symptoms of schizophrenia.

The maître d' at Quaglino's led us to a table, and I ordered a vintage Châteauneuf-du-Pape. John H.'s colleagues focused their interest on Aldrich Ames, not least because Les had led the investigation that had busted the CIA turncoat. They lapped up what I'd learned from Edward Howard more hungrily than they had their spiced lamb and garlic mashed potatoes.

We walked out into the night, which was still light at nine thirty. "You guys fancy a nightcap?" I asked.

Mister Five drove us to the Savoy Hôtel while I pointed out Piccadilly Circus, Trafalgar Square, and the Strand. Mike MacKenzie tapped the ivories and ebonies in the American Bar as we strolled in and plunked ourselves at a table next to his grand piano.

"*Sweet Music*, Mike." He obliged me with his own composition.

The others called out tunes including as "As Time Goes By" and "Cavatina." We drank single malt scotch, joked, and laughed. It sure beat Moscow.

10

HICCUP

Back home, I set to work editing Richard Côté's rewrite of Edward Lee Howard's manuscript. It was a vastly improved version but still not publishable.

Inevitably, I had to do what I told the guys at National Press Books I would not do, that is, rewrite the damned manuscript. Côté had organized Howard's written manuscript and injected new material from his interviews with Howard, George Blake, and Igor Batamirov. But he had hardly touched Howard's inclination toward clutter and redundancy, not to mention prevarication. I also excised all references to the CIA operations Howard had compromised, as this information would become an issue sooner or later because of its classified nature. The task took forty-seven hours spread over two weeks in mid-August 1994.

Meantime, taking no chances about what might be considered classified, National Press submitted Côté's version to the CIA's Review Board.

Joel Joseph soon phoned me. He sounded like a walking pinched nerve. "We had a fax from the CIA today," said Joseph. "They say we can't publish Ed's book!"

"None of it?"

"That's what they're saying. They won't even tell us what's classified."

"Why not?"

"Because they say it's too sensitive to even point out to us what's classified," said Joseph. "What do you think we should do?"

"Have you ever seen the movie *Three Days of the Condor*?" I asked.

"Huh?"

"I'd get out of the office for a few days. Sounds like you and Alan already know too much."

I phoned John H. "You know what I just heard?"

"I know, I know," he said. "I only heard yesterday what was coming down."

"So what's going on?"

Blocking the book's publication was just a legal tactic, John H. explained, orchestrated by Bob G., the assistant U.S. attorney. Of course it was not illegal for National Press to publish Howard's book; however, it was illegal for Howard to write his book for publication in the first place. The CIA fax was a first step toward freezing any monies due Howard from National Press. John H. said Bob G. fully expected National Press to figure out it could publish Howard's manuscript. "Will this development cause you any problem with Howard?" he asked.

"No," I said, "because I've already distanced myself from National Press in his eyes. If necessary, I can sympathize with him and offer to make it up with *Spy's Guide*."

My next call was to Howard. I found him at his dacha. His wife and son were still in Moscow, having been to St. Petersburg and back.

"There's been a hiccup with the CIA review process," I said.

"I was expecting something like that," said Howard. "They hate me and I hate them."

"National Press is dealing with it, but I want to keep you updated confidentially."

"That's good of you," said Howard. "I appreciate it."

"It's important you don't go screaming back to National Press, because they'll know the information's come from me. Then they'll stop telling me what's going on, and I won't be able to keep you informed."

"I understand. It's just between you and me."

"It's going to hold up publication," I said.

"I'd really like to get that travel project we discussed going," said Howard.

"Me, too. We should get together again and flesh it out. Maybe go to that city [Zurich] where we first planned to meet?"

"Yes," said Howard. "I may have some business there. We can pony it on that."

"Good. If you can do it, let me know the usual way [Fed Ex]."

John H. was pleased that in our conversation, Howard had evoked *Spy's Guide* on his own, without further prompting from me. John H. was even more excited that Howard agreed to meet me in Zurich.

"You've got a problem, though," I added. "If the CIA and Justice Department come on too strong and National Press kills this book, Howard will probably take it to a foreign publisher, one that would be delighted to publish it *with* the classified passages that National Press would willingly remove."

"I hear you," said John H. "I'll make sure that information gets passed along."

On October 27, I telephoned Howard. "Happy birthday," I said.

"Thank you." Howard was touched. "I'm glad you called. Some people here have asked me to a meeting. They want to know what's happening with the book. Can you check with National Press and get an update?"

I phoned National Press. Joseph had some news: the Justice Department had summoned him to a meeting two days hence. "I think they want to negotiate," he said. "I'm taking someone from the ACLU [American Civil Liberties Union] with me."

I followed up with John H. next. He was intrigued that Howard's KGB friends required updates from him on the status of his book.

Howard and I spoke after his KGB meeting. "What they told me," said Howard, "was that those jokers in Washington just wanted to read my manuscript and find out what I know. Now that they've satisfied their curiosity, they'll stop."

The news from National Press a few days later seemed to corroborate the KGB's spin on this development. "We can publish," Joseph told me. "The Justice Department types gave me a broad outline of what they want deleted, which is about 5 percent. But they won't tell me *which* 5 percent. I'm supposed to figure it out for myself and resubmit the manuscript for further review." That process, added Joseph, would delay the book's publication until spring 1995.

11

SWISS SOJOURN

For a spy no finer city than Zurich in mid-November can evoke a sense of place. Cold, dark gloominess contrasts with warmly lit tearooms and beer cellars and old-fashioned trams run up and down the main drag, past shop windows glittering with chocolates wrapped in gold.

A taxi twisted and turned through the city center, dropping me at Hotel Kindli, as recommended by Edward Howard. The hotel was appropriately veiled by gray plastic sheeting, erected to retain renovation dust. Awaiting me at the registration desk was a handwritten message from Howard: "Meet in reception, 1800."

I asked for Howard's room number and learned he was not staying at this hotel after all (or if so, he had registered under an alias). I peeked into the drab, depressing room reserved for me and returned downstairs. "I need a better room," I said.

"It's all we have."

"Then I need a better hotel. Where's the Savoy?"

She pointed me toward Bahnhofstrasse, and I trudged with my carryall in the pouring rain. The staff of the five-star Hôtel Savoy processed me into their heaven compared to Kindli's hell. And with a vigilant team of receptionists, porters, and a concierge, the Savoy was secure; even the elevator required a key to operate it.

At 5:40 p.m. I made my way back to the Kindli and left a message at reception for Howard to find me in the hotel's restaurant. That's where I planted myself, sipping nutty Swiss white wine.

Howard arrived a few minutes later, just as punctual as he was in Moscow. I waved from across the empty room, and he bounded over. Howard's hair was freshly trimmed, and he looked relaxed in blue jeans, a striped button-down shirt, sneakers, and a brown anorak with a faux fur collar.

I told Howard I'd found the Kindli inadequate, so I hadn't checked in. He confirmed that he, too, was lodging elsewhere—at a Swissair Hotel between the airport and the city's center. Howard had arrived two days earlier on Aeroflot "with some Russians" with whom he had business.

Howard ordered a Coke and proceeded to chain-smoke Salems, a switch from Dorals. "I have to get out of Russia every four or five months," he said, "to keep from going nuts." That's why Howard loved my idea to research *Spy's Guide*: it would allow him to travel out of Russia on somebody else's tab. He dug into his back pocket and produced a fax from Joel Joseph that he'd received just before departing Moscow. It said, in essence, that because of legal problems with his book, National Press would not pay the balance of the agreed advance. Howard was philosophical about it; at least National Press was proceeding to publish the book. He also showed me a fax from ABC News's Moscow correspondent David Ensor, who requested an interview. I took possession of it and asked Howard what kind of business he was doing in Zurich.

"I'm introducing Russians to Volksbank so they can open numbered Swiss bank accounts," replied Howard. The hardest part, he snickered, was convincing Russians to accept Swiss bank interest rates, a paltry amount compared to what they could earn in Russia with their highly volatile rubles. Aside from that, he had two other clients—a German trying to collect a debt from the Russian government and an Austrian trying to establish a life insurance company in Russia. Neither client knew Howard's real name or background. "I'm working at about 60 percent capacity," Howard continued. "It suits me just fine because it leaves me free for book projects like ours."

I asked Howard if he had a favorite restaurant in Zurich. He suggested Mövenpick, part of a high-quality Swiss restaurant chain, around the corner on Bahnhofstrasse. We moseyed over and sat upstairs. Both of us ordered honey-glazed ham and hot tea for Ed, white wine for me.

"Still not drinking?" I asked him.

"I might be tempted to crack a bottle of champagne on New Year's Eve," Howard said. It had been just over a year since he'd touched the sauce. Now he was working on his smoking habit. He'd already invested two C-notes on nicotine patches, to no avail.

I asked after George Blake, the British spy. Howard smiled and told me he had attended Blake's seventy-second birthday party the week before. "About a dozen people were there. I was the only Westerner. George is coming to my place next week for Thanksgiving," he added.

I chuckled to myself. It sounded so pathetic.

Howard told me that, after much effort, he had managed to find a frozen turkey from Arkansas in some Moscow supermarket and that he'd just found a can of cranberry sauce in Zurich. "Now I'm on the prowl for pumpkin pie mix," he said, sounding more like a homesick expat than a "good Russian."

Blake had become a mentor to Howard. He said, "You want to know the secret of Blake's success? Prison. Six years." Howard blew a gust of tobacco smoke. "He knows firsthand what the alternative to Moscow is like. He prefers Moscow. He taught me that when you know your family is OK and taken care of, everything is all right. Relax. Enjoy life.

"My KGB friends love the *Spy's Guide* project," continued Howard. "They laughed. They think it's a great idea, and they want to help. Igor Batamirov wants to help me do Moscow," Howard bubbled. "And we can get KGB people in all the other cities to give us the information we need."

"Yeah, right," I thought. "We'd put KGB officers throughout Central Europe on the FBI payroll."

"All I need to do," Howard figured, "is pop into a city, meet the local KGB guy, pick up his information, check it out myself, and move on to the next spot."

We spent a good hour in Mövenpick developing our *Spy's Guide*. Howard was ready to get cracking on it right after Christmas. I agreed to pay him a five grand advance, with half to start and half on completion. As for expenses, I'd cover everything; Howard would fly cheap on Aeroflot and stay in three-star hotels. We estimated he'd need five hundred bucks per city, including airfare.

Howard added, "It would be nice to be able to pay something to the KGB officer in each city for his basic information."

"How much do you think they'll all want?" I asked.

"More than I'm prepared to offer," said Howard. He guessed five hundred bucks apiece would be sufficient.

"We can work something out," I said, "as long as they're prepared to sign receipts." The bureau had this strict requirement to keep the bean counters happy.

"No problem," said Howard. Then he asked that I wire start-up funds to a numbered account in Zurich, the details of which he scribbled for me. I noted it was not the same account he had given National Press, so now we had information on two. Howard also requested that I prepare a questionnaire for his KGB respondents throughout Central Europe. "They'll need instructions about the kinds of things we want to know," said Howard.

I covered the tab at Mövenpick, and Howard offered dessert at Café St. Gotthard down the Strasse. That's where we short-listed our *Spy's Guide* destinations: Belgrade, Bucharest, Budapest, Geneva, Helsinki, Moscow, Prague, Sofia, St. Petersburg, Vienna, and Warsaw.

Over ice cream sundaes, Howard told me that a couple months earlier he'd visited Lake Baikal in Siberia, one of his favorite places in the world. He'd been tempted to buy a plot of lakefront land to build a house. "Eight hundred square meters [eighty-six hundred square feet] for only five thousand dollars!" Howard's eyes danced. "I should have made a deal, but I got talked out of it by friends in Moscow. They said, 'Why would you want to go way out there?' But they're city people, so what do they know? There's a new air service called Baikal Airlines. You can fly there nonstop in five and a half hours."

Howard then moaned about problems he was having with his dacha. It needed repairs. The management was unsympathetic, so he'd gone to his KGB friends. They, in turn, had leaned on the management to fix the plumbing, heating, and a leaky roof.

"How *are* your KGB buddies?" I asked.

Howard told me he was tired of partying with them because they drank too much and complained about their lives. "It used to be they'd drink and be jovial," he said, "but now they drink and complain."

"Why?" I asked. "What's wrong?"

"Look," said Howard, "these guys earn the equivalent of $750 per month, and that's fine if you don't mind living like a Russian. Though it's three times what a Russian earns, these guys have lived in Paris and Rome, and they're sophisticated. They don't want to live like Russians. So all they do is complain and curse Yeltsin. Morale is very bad." Howard added that the best and the brightest had left the KGB.

"What do they do then?" I asked.

"They either go into international trade or join the mafia." Howard lowered his voice. "What I'd really like is to get some marijuana. But whenever I talk about it with my Russian friends, they're horrified. I try to explain that marijuana is safer than all the booze they drink, but they don't want to know."

I plucked a small 35-mm camera from my pocket and asked a waitress if she'd mind snapping a photo of Howard and me. I wanted a memento, mindful that I was scheduled to make my first appearance at FBI Headquarters upon my return from Switzerland.

The next day, at one o'clock, Howard met me in my hotel lobby. It was raining again. We cut around the corner to a sublevel restaurant called Kropf. When we settled in, I asked, "So how'd it go with your literary agent?"

Howard had planned to phone her after we'd parted the night before to discuss National Press's plan to scrap the balance due on his advance. "Oh, yeah, I want to tell you about that."

After a waitress took our order—two lunch specials of speck and sauerkraut—Howard said, "She tore into Joel Joseph. She told him that she's fed up, that everyone knew there'd be legal problems when we started, and that if they didn't pay up, she'd sue them for breach. Yeah, she was really tough."

"What did Joel say?"

"He said, 'I hear you.' No real commitment. I said to my agent, 'Why were you so tough?' She said, 'It's my job.' Man, all I want is to see my book published. She asked Joel, 'Are you going to publish or not?' And he said, 'I don't want to say anything over the phone because I've been advised by the ACLU that my phones are tapped, so I'll FedEx you.'" Howard shook his head in disgust. "As if the FBI couldn't open a FedEx. It's obvious, Joel has FD."

"What's 'FD'?"

"FD?" said Howard. "Federal disease. I've seen it happen, many times."

"'Federal disease'?"

"Yeah, it happens when the feds turn up. It makes people nervous and jumpy. They get scared. Joel's definitely got FD." He then brought up the subject of the FBI. Howard believed the bureau would still love to capture him.

"After all this time?" I asked.

"It's an institutional thing," said Howard. "I embarrassed the FBI. I escaped before their very eyes. I'll tell you this: the FBI agent who hauls me in will get promoted to GS-16 overnight."

Clear skies greeted us outside Kropf. We walked across the river to Zurich's Old Town. I asked Howard if he thought he was being watched by Russians who were looking out for his safety.

"No," said Howard. "If anyone's following me, it would be Swiss intelligence, to see what I'm up to, but I doubt it. My lawyer once made representations to Switzerland, and the answer we got back was, 'We have no interest in Mr. Edward Howard.'"

We slipped into a tearoom for Viennese cream cakes. Howard voiced a thought about Jonathan Pollard, the American who had spied for Israel and was caught, convicted, and imprisoned. "My KGB friends laughed so hard," said Howard. "They thought the Pollard episode was the funniest thing they'd ever seen."

"Pollard's in the federal pen in Marion [Illinois]," I said. "He hangs out with John Walker and Edwin Wilson."

"I wonder where they'd put me if they had a chance?" said Howard. When I suggested Leavenworth, Howard snickered.

Back at Hôtel Savoy, we found a cozy corner on the mezzanine for a final session on *Spy's Guide*. We worked out an outline. "You've also got to do a chapter on tradecraft for the traveling spy," I said. When Howard concurred, I added, "And one covering all the things every spy should carry on the road."

Howard nodded. "Why not?"

"Do you ever carry a weapon, Ed?"

"Never. I'm not a weapons man. I only know what the CIA taught us at 'the Farm': use a briefcase or anything else you can grab." (Camp Peary, or "The Farm," as it was known, was where the CIA taught tradecraft.)

Next, we discussed false identity documents and how to purchase them on the Russian black market. "I could get you a Russian passport for five hundred dollars," said Howard, "and it would only take a month. You know, I've got another book idea."

"Yeah? What?"

"How to sell government secrets, a handbook for double agents."

I laughed. "Cool. Is that the title?"

"No," said Howard. "I'd call it *Spy's Cookbook*."

"Catchy."

"It would drive the CIA and the FBI nuts." Howard grinned. "I've already worked out the chapters."

"Let's hear it. Mind if I take notes?" I scribbled while Howard dictated his chapter titles:

Chapter 1. Making the Decision to Turn

Chapter 2. Formulating the Plan and Valuing Your Information

Chapter 3. Making the Approach

Chapter 4. How to Negotiate

Chapter 5. How to Hide Your Money

Chapter 6. Secure Communications

Chapter 7. The Weakest Link (a Woman)

Chapter 8. Getting Caught—Deny Everything, Admit Nothing

"Gee, Ed, you've really thought this through."

"Yeah," said Howard. "I'd include cases where guys screwed up: Christopher Boyce, John Walker, Pollard, Ames. Espionage is a dangerous game, like playing with heroin. But if the FBI ever got their hands on me, they'd probably hold *Spy's Cookbook* up in court and say, 'See, he must have done it.' It would probably get me an extra twenty years. Ha, ha, ha!"

Howard rarely laughed, let alone cracked a joke.

12

WASHINGTON CRYPTIC

At precisely seven thirty in the morning, the Monday after Thanksgiving weekend, I found my way to the Badge Room at FBI Headquarters on Pennsylvania Avenue. Moments later, John H. appeared. "Good time in Zurich?" he asked.

"You would not believe."

We crossed the cobblestoned courtyard, punched our badges, and strolled past oil painting portraits of past FBI directors: J. Edgar Hoover, Clarence Kelley, a ghastly one of William Webster. We then went up to the fourth floor, a restricted zone, and down a long corridor to the office of Allyson G., whom I'd first and last seen at the Former Spymaster's house fourteen months before.

A tall, gray-haired special agent in charge named John Q. had just replaced Allyson G. as the headquarters's supervisor on the Howard case. We shook hands and went down another long corridor, where a security guard unlocked a conference room. Jim S. and a bureau employee named Dick A. joined John H., John Q., and me there at a rectangular table. John H. cued me to tell the assembled guests about myself. One-third into my spiel, the bureau's counterterrorism chief, Bob B., slipped into the room and took a seat to my left. When I'd finished, Dick A. spoke. He asked questions about how I might feel when, after spending time with Edward Howard and getting to know him, he got caught and put behind bars.

"You mean, would I suffer a reaction sort of like the Stockholm Syndrome?" I asked. The Stockholm Syndrome is a phenomenon whereby hostages cultivate sympathetic and protective feelings toward their kidnappers.

"Uh, yeah, that's right," said Dick A.

"I'm doing a professional job," I said. "The friendliness I establish with Howard is for one purpose only, for luring him to capture." The difference for me was simple: If I had been a friend of Howard's and someone, anyone, approached me to help capture my friend, my reply would have been negative. But I had conceived and began executing this operation by myself, with the FBI's authorization and support. It was purely business.

Dick A. countered that he understood what I said, but that people never really knew how they were going to feel about this kind of thing until the climax. The bureau's concern was that I might have a change of heart at the last minute. So Dick A. wondered if I would be willing to take a battery of tests for evaluating my state of mind.

I looked around, incredulous. "We've been at this for over a year," I said. "And *now* you want me to take a test?" I almost got up and walked out.

Bob B. spoke up. He had run a few renditions with Middle Eastern terrorists, he said, and seen a couple go south on this very issue. So did I mind if he asked me a couple hard questions?

I thought, *No wonder nobody wanted to spend much time in the J. Edgar Hoover Building.* "Shoot."

"Why do you think Edward Howard trusts you so much?"

"Because I'm good at this." I said. "My legend is fully back-stopped. Howard believes I'm genuine, so he trusts me. On top of that, he likes me. I even telephoned him on October 27 to say happy birthday."

Bob B. nodded and bored his eyes into mine. "How many others know what you are really up to with Howard?"

I raised a single finger. "Just one."

"Who?" asked Bob B.

"The Former Spymaster."

John Q. perked up from across the conference table. "Your wife doesn't know?"

"No."

"Would you be willing to take a polygraph test somewhere down the line?" asked Bob B.

I shrugged. "Why not?"

"You know," said John H., "the president is going to have to sign off on this. And someone from the White House is going to ask if this guy has taken a polygraph. That's why it's important."

"It's not a problem," I said.

Bob B. launched into issues of operational security. "First off, how did you communicate with John H. in Albuquerque?"

"I telephoned him at his office on Silver Street."

"No good," said Bob B. He wanted an anonymous cutout number for me to call with a different area code. Next, he wanted to know where I kept my own copies of reports and notes pertaining to Howard.

"At home," I said.

Bob B. fretted that the KGB might break into my house to check me out. His solution: the bureau would supply me with a safe. Finally, he asked about the rendition itself. "To which destinations would you lure Howard?"

"Bucharest, Budapest, Helsinki, Prague, Sofia, Vienna, Warsaw—take your pick," I said. "He's agreed to visit all these places."

Bob B. nodded, impressed. The list gave him more than enough to work with. "It's better that you are as detached as possible from the actual rendition," he said. "That way, Howard himself won't know your role in this."

I shrugged. "However you execute this is fine by me."

"We'll be on hold," said Bob B., "until the Justice Department gives us a final nod." He indicated Bob G., Jim S., and John H. would deliver a formal presentation two weeks hence. "But whatever our decision," Bob B. added, "you should continue your contact with Howard with a view toward cultivating *positive intelligence* [PI] from your relationship with the defector."

Finally, all in attendance savored the irony of putting the KGB in Central Europe to work on *Spy's Guide*. Then we adjourned.

"About those tests," said John H. as we paced the long corridor, "when . . . ?"

"Tell them to shove their battery of tests up their—"

"Yeah, I figured as much," said John H.

The next morning, we were back at headquarters. This time we ascended to the seventh floor, where the Big Cheese Family resided. After meeting Deputy John Lewis first, John H., John Q., and I walked into the large corner office of Robert "Bear" Bryant, the assistant director for national security. Bryant had a large paunch and a mumbling growl of a voice that was part grizzly and part teddy bear. "So where are we on this?" he asked.

John H. briefed the assistant director. John Q. pitched in, and I did, too.

Specifically, I mentioned Edward Howard's new idea to write *Spy's Cookbook*, a manual for double agents.

Bryant nodded his head and growled his support for our operation. He wanted to haul Howard in, and he ventured his opinion that Budapest would be our best bet. Then Bryant thanked me.

I pointed to John H. "He's the real hero," I said. "This job takes patience, and this guy's got the patience of a saint."

John H. and Bryant had started their careers together as rookie special agents in Seattle. While John H. had settled in New Mexico, Bryant had jumped into the fast lane and risen through the ranks.

We all stood. Bryant shook my hand and gave me his calling card. I now had the confidence of the bureau's national security division at its most senior level.

The following day I met with Joseph and Sultan at National Press. With advance orders of fewer than six thousand copies and a cool reception from sales reps, Howard's book had become more trouble than it was worth.

Sultan favored killing it. Joseph wanted to publish it anyway but only if Howard's literary agent backed off and waived the remainder of his advance. Would I talk to Howard, they asked, and resolve this crisis?

13

A LAME PLAN

I reached Edward Howard at his dacha. He answered, but some-thing appeared to be wrong with the telephone connection. I hung up and dialed again. Howard answered. Nothing was wrong with the line; instead, it was *him*, incoherence squared. "Call me to-mor-row," he finally managed.

When I reached him the next afternoon, Howard was still plastered. He was in the midst of what must have been a colossal binge. Either I could not hear him or he could not talk—I wasn't sure which—so I disconnected and redialed his number. Howard answered after eight rings.

"Is that you, Ed?" I asked.

"Yeah."

"It's me, Robert."

"Yeah. Ro-bert."

"Ed, you don't sound well."

"I'm drink-king."

"Why?"

"I lost my biz-i-nez."

"How? What happened?

Howard lapsed into incoherence.

"When should I call you again?" I asked.

"One day."

"Tomorrow?"

"Yeah. One day."

I tried him again the next day. Howard was no longer drunk, but he suffered from a mammoth hangover. "I was drinking." He said this like a schoolboy caught cheating on an exam.

"For how long?"

"Four days. Man, I need some aspirin."

"What's happening with your business?"

"I lost my office. Had to move out."

"Is that why you were drinking?"

"No. I had a fight with my girlfriend," said Howard.

"Sorry to hear that." I paused. "Look, Ed, here's the deal on your book: National Press will kill it unless you forgo the rest of the advance."

"OK, I'll tell my agent to back off."

"Are you still gung ho on *Spy's Guide*?"

"Yes."

I phoned John H. and clued him in. "For a few minutes there," I said, "I thought Howard was dying."

"That would have put you out of a job," said John H.

"It's not the way this story is supposed to end," I said.

"No."

In keeping with Bob B.'s wishes to improve operational security, John H. gave me a new telephone number, a ghost line with a 202 area code created specifically for my calls to him. "I'm coming to Washington," he said. "We have a new problem."

I met John H. inside Au Bon Pain restaurant on Tenth Street, opposite the Hoover Building, from which only problems emanated. I ordered a latte to go, and we trudged across the street and up to the fourth floor, where John Q. and Jim S. awaited us.

Their new problem in a nutshell was that the Justice Department was waffling, as usual, and holding up our rendition until its people could be certain of the evidence stacked against Edward Howard. Part of the evidence consisted of a financial log Howard had kept that showed how he had laundered cash payments received from the KGB through his wife. John H. possessed a photocopy of the log, but it had been obtained improperly, so a judge might rule that it could not be used as evidence.

The assembled G-men wanted me to travel to Moscow, stay in Howard's apartment, find the log, and photograph it. Then the copy would be acceptable evidence. Their legal rationale was that I would be acting in Moscow as an extension of John H., which, in effect, would serve as a search warrant.

"This type of operation has never been done before," he said. "We're on the cutting edge, setting a legal precedent. The question is, can we serve a search warrant in this manner? Usually, we have to leave an actual warrant behind."

I was incredulous. The G-men wanted me to risk my neck to collect something they already had in their possession! But photographing the financial log was just part one. Part two called for me gaining access to Howard's computers and sucking them dry.

"Uh, let me ask you a question," I said. "What happens if I get caught?"

"Ah," said John Q., "that's between you and him." John Q. then excused himself so that John H. could address this issue.

"I don't have diplomatic cover," I said. "If I got caught, they'd throw me in prison, right?"

John H. nodded. "Our government would negotiate to get you out."

"Yeah, right," I thought. But curiosity propelled me onward, at least to go through the motions before declining this wonderful opportunity. So we went down one floor to the photo lab, where an expert determined that the best camera for this assignment was not a miniature Minox but a run-of-the-mill Olympus Infinity. He showed me the right distance for snapping documents.

Next, I headed for a computer-sucking lesson. For this session, I took a trip to Fort Monmouth in Eatontown, New Jersey, home of the FBI's northeast regional computer center and Tom M., the best computer guru in the bureau. Tom had sucked the hell out of Aldrich Ames's computers. He pulled a rectangular gizmo from his bag and plugged it into a laptop. "This is it," he said. "You just plug it into the parallel port. Then you insert this special laser disk, hit a few buttons, and—bang!—it sucks everything out."

The Former Spymaster gasped when I told him what the FBI wanted next. "This is starting to sound like a shitty novel," he said. "What about your wife and children? Are the feebies planning to look after them if you get thrown into the slammer for twenty years? No, you'll be on your own.

"Just tell them you've lived up to your end of the bargain. You're in this to lure Howard out, not to photograph evidence in Moscow."

Meanwhile, National Press and Howard had resolved their advance dispute. Howard accepted a few extra royalty points—pie in the sky—in lieu of immediate money. They had also resolved their issues with the CIA's review board. So the manuscript had been readied for publication and galley proofs were dispatched to Howard for final corrections. I phoned Howard for a status update on the proofs.

"I have some exciting news!" Howard bubbled, out of character. "Don't tell a soul. It's just between you and me."

"Of course."

"My friends here—you know who I mean?"

"I do."

"They've read the galleys. And they are very impressed with how the book turned out. I told them, this book closes a chapter in my life. And they said, 'No, no, no, we want you to do *more* of this.'"

"Meaning what?"

"They want to get information out through me."

"Go on."

"They have book projects they want me to handle," said Howard, "starting with the man whose name starts with K."

"Vladimir Kryuchkov," I thought, "the former KGB chairman."

"This would be ideal for us," added Howard.

"I'm in," I said.

It was Presidents' Day, a federal holiday, so I found John H. at home. "I just spoke with the author," I said. "He has some interesting news."

"Oh?"

"He told me not to tell anyone," I paused, "but I suppose I can tell you." John H. chuckled.

"His patron, Mr. K. You know who he is?"

"Of course," said John H.

"He wants to write his own book. And he wants the author and me to help him."

John H. sighed. The project meant new administrative hurdles, for sure, but he was game. Anything to keep Howard happy and playing with us until we had a green light to cuff his wrists with cold, hard steel.

14

SPY CITY

It was cold in Geneva in March 1995, just above freezing. Snow flurries were interspersed with occasional bouts of sunshine. Edward Howard arrived at noon for our rendezvous in the Noga Hilton lobby, a contemporary lounge decorated in black leather and chrome. He had gained weight, maybe fifteen pounds, since our meeting in Zurich four months earlier. His mood was glum and downbeat, and his face seemed swollen—symptomatic, I thought, of heavy drinking. He'd given up smoking, he said, and going without nicotine appeared to take a toll on his nerves.

Howard told me he'd taken a train the day before from Interlaken, where he'd spent a week in a rented apartment with his wife and son. It had no phone, no TV. He bitched that he'd never do it again.

I'd brought with me a half-dozen advance copies of *Safe House* hot off the press, which lightened his mood a tad. Howard set to work signing books to me, Joseph, Sultan, and one that was destined for John H. My own imprint's name, an Enigma Book, graced the title page. Howard voiced unhappiness with the cover, however; he felt his photograph did not do him justice.

We settled down to our next order of business, *Spy's Guide*. Howard was full of beans on this project and had begun tackling the spy's destination cities. Moscow was three-quarters done, and he'd been to Vienna on business a few weeks earlier and knocked that one out. He'd decided not to do Budapest himself (as if he *knew* it was Bear Bryant's first choice for a rendition), choosing instead to subcontract it to a KGB officer on site. Geneva he would research this very week.

"This is truly a spy's city," said Howard. "The Swiss don't care what spies do here as long as there is no public scandal." Howard had also decided to delete Belgrade and substitute it with Bratislava, which, he said, was "a good town for covert operations."

"Really?"

"For years," said Howard, "the KGB considered Bratislava an ideal town for a spy on the run who wants to keep a low profile, hide cheaply, and be able to escape to one of three other countries by land within the hour. It is where they used to sneak me across the border into Western Europe as a Soviet diplomat."

"You've convinced me," I said. "Do it."

Also remaining for Howard to tackle were Bucharest, Prague, Sofia, and Warsaw. (He intended to contract out Helsinki and St. Petersburg to local Russian intelligence officers.)

We went to lunch at Tse-Yang, a Chinese restaurant on the Noga Hilton's mezzanine. Over steamed dumplings we explored the new book project Howard had cryptically alluded to over the phone. "Once my first book got cleared, there were some excited, very impressed people in Moscow," said Howard. "I got called to a meeting."

"By whom?" I asked.

"Vladimir Kryuchkov. He summoned me to meet him in a public park."

"Why a park?"

"Because Kryuchkov is under surveillance by Boris Yeltsin's people," said Howard. "He didn't want anyone overhearing us. He was with two others: Igor Batamirov—"

"Wasn't that the guy Dick Côté met?"

Howard nodded. "Yes, he's an old friend of mine and Ames's handler—and Igor Prelin."

"Who's he?"

"A former KGB colonel," said Howard. "Prelin is general-director of the former intelligence officers association. They want to generate works for the Western market. The first one is Kryuchkov's book. It's already written."

"In English?"

"No, Russian. It'll soon be published in Russia. My friends are using their influence to get that stupid jerk Yeltsin out of office."

"So send me Kryuchkov's manuscript," I said. "I'll try to get it translated."

Howard nodded. "I'll see what I can do."

After lunch we strolled the Quai des Bergues and ran into Howard's wife, Mary—a soft-spoken, nondescript woman—and his son, Lee, a slightly awkward prepubescent. The four of us popped into the bar in Hôtel des Bergues for a drink.

Howard's family relationships seemed strained and tense. Earlier, over lunch, Howard had mentioned he was glad to live on his own without family pressures. Now, the twelve-year-old Lee reflected sunlight off his wristwatch into his father's eyes to irritate him.

I pointed out that the bar in which we sat deserved a mention in *Spy's Guide* because it had no fewer than seven ways to get in and out.

Howard chuckled, "You could sneak out without paying."

Lee chirped up, "You did that once, Dad! Remember?"

Howard blushed, suggesting it was true. An embarrassing silence ensued.

Later, after his wife and son had left us, Howard produced his outline for *Spy's Cookbook*. "This manual," Howard had written, "will walk a would-be turncoat through the basic steps of making a decision to steal and exploit secrets, contacting potential buyers, communicating securely with them, and outlining what to do if caught." Following are excerpts from Howard's thirteen-page proposal:

> Selling one little secret is an irreversible step! There is no such thing as being halfway pregnant; likewise, there is no halfway point in espionage. Either you gave out secrets or you did not. It's that simple when the jury meets. You can't plead extenuating circumstances.
>
> Your decision should be made in a cold and calculating manner. Look at the actual costs (operational expenses), potential life-long costs of being caught (jail or being beaten up), and finally the benefits.
>
> Have a plan for a drastic change of life within a specified period of time. It's like playing the stock market. You don't buy into the market thinking it will always go up. You buy at a good price with a target sale price based on analysis. The same way with espionage. Think of it as a short-term business project with some prospect of profit and a good prospect of risk.

Four rules for making the approach: (1) assume the place you might want to make contact [at] is watched and bugged. Leave the car at home, never use the phone, use disguises; (2) make an untraceable offer. Verbal, one-on-one, in an anonymous location; (3) have a plausible excuse (to would-be watchers and interrogators) for making your approach, a credible legend with back-up documents; (4) take your time and be patient. Wait for your opportunity, never rush.

Your dealings will require special forms of payment. The best way is cash or a deposit in a secret account. If they want a receipt, never sign your real name. And unless your spouse is vital to the success of the project and takes equal risk, make every effort to keep your mouth shut.

If caught, don't even give your captors the time of day. Make accusations against the police for false arrest. If you're part of a minority, make that an issue, or paint the case as a political frame. If you were really careful and do not confess, your chances of leaving jail are good.

15

A MOST EXTRAORDINARY
UN-RENDITION

During the first week of June, not long after my trip to Geneva, I met John H. in Chicago. He greeted my United Airlines flight from Washington, D.C., and escorted me to a small conference room in the bowels of O'Hare International Airport.

I had traveled to Chicago to lend moral support to National Press Books during its launch of *Safe House* at the American Booksellers Association's annual convention. Thus far, reviewers nationwide had ignored the title; consequently, sales were dismal. Joel Joseph and Alan Sultan joked sourly that its poor showing must have stemmed from a CIA-plotted conspiracy to bury it.

Meanwhile, John H. and Bob G. had solved their evidence crisis by dragging Howard's wife, Mary, before a grand jury in Albuquerque and questioning her for the first time in ten years. Bob G. had found a legal loophole that precluded her from refusing to testify against her spouse. This time Mary incriminated Howard by revealing that he had laundered cash received from the KGB.

When Howard heard about this development, he assumed it was the FBI's retaliatory response to his book's publication, and he was outraged. "Once again, they're taking it out on my family," Howard ranted to me over the phone. "Mary has to tell them what they want to know to keep herself out of the can. It doesn't matter, because they can't get me anyway. That's our strategy."

John H. told me otherwise. When Howard learned that his wife had been spilling her guts, he demanded that she send him divorce papers. (Divorce followed.)

U.S. Attorney Bob G. now had what he needed. It was time to press the top brass at the Department of Justice for a green light to reel Howard in, especially as we now had him poised to travel to a variety of convenient destinations.

For the benefit of a senior Chicago FBI agent who had laid on the logistics for our meeting at O'Hare, John H. detailed the mechanics of how our extraordinary rendition would play out: Howard would arrive at the airport of our designated location. At Immigration, which passengers had to pass through before officially entering a foreign country (or a no-country zone known as an "international corridor"), Immigration officers would ask Howard to "come with us." They would escort him to a room. John H. would be waiting there to arrest him. He would then escort Howard to a U.S. military jet for a stealthy flight home.

By this time, I had received from Howard a proposal, in English, for Vladimir Kryuchkov's book and what he would cover. It was wonderfully enticing. I passed it along to John H. He was equally intrigued but remained focused on Howard. And why not? We were getting so close, we could practically taste victory.

On July 1, I decamped with my family to Stone Harbor, New Jersey, for a lengthy summer vacation by the beach. John H. phoned on the seventeenth to report excellent progress with the Justice Department. We narrowed down our European capitals for targeting Howard.

Then Washington summoned John H. to present a final plan to the Cheese Family. He told the powers that be that they could choose from three destinations— Bucharest, Sofia, or Warsaw—and we could nail Howard that autumn.

We already knew the techniques and mind-set Howard maintained for low-profile foreign travel, so we knew what tricks to watch out for. How? Because Howard had penned a blueprint for me in a detailed chapter on tradecraft for the traveling spy! Some excerpts follow.

Plan where you're going. Know the area. Check out the establishment you want to meet somebody [at] ahead of time—find the exits, learn the operating hours, and always think about how your opposition would approach you if he found you were there. . . .

Make your travel reservations from a public phone, with a travel alias, use smaller foreign airlines (KGB officers always prefer using Malév, the national Hungarian airline), pay cash for your tickets, change planes. Spend a day or two in another city checking for shadows before going to your target area, make hotel reservations at the last possible moment. And once in a hotel, always approach it as if someone may be waiting for you. . . .

Combine a different hairstyle with a pair of glasses, and you'd be surprised how much your appearance changes. . . .

You just can't trust anyone. No one said it would be easy to be a spy, and this is one of the reasons why.

John H. phoned me from Washington on July 26. Headquarters had trashed our list; instead, they wanted Milan or Rome. "What's your immediate thought on that?"

"Bollocks," I said. "The author might *never* visit Italy! And if he does, it won't be for many months."

John H. told me a new agent, Chris H., had been assigned the case at headquarters, replacing John Q. He said we should all meet, and we agreed to rendezvous in Pennsville, New Jersey, on my side of the Delaware Memorial Bridge. So John H. put Chris H. on the phone for directions. I had no idea where exactly we'd meet, so I planned to arrive first, stake out a decent site, and call Chris H.'s cell phone. I arrived at 2:55 p.m. and settled on Chukkers, a tavern. It just sounded right. And it was empty at that hour. About forty-five minutes later, the G-men arrived: John H., Chris H., and Jim S. Chris H. was sturdy and almost bald. He sported a thick mustache and had intense eyes, and a serious demeanor.

John H. got right down to it: the Department of Justice had ruled out Bucharest and Sofia. As for Warsaw, it was a maybe. It was down to the bureau's legate at the U.S. Embassy in Warsaw to deal with the Polish government and gain its acquiescence. Chris H. expected an update on his cell phone any minute.

"We'd need to know Howard's flight arrival plans," said Jim S.

"No problem," I said. "I'll tell Howard I'll meet his flight." I had a new idea. "If Poland won't work, how about Istanbul?"

Chris H. perked up over his beer. "Istanbul might work."

"I could fit it into the context of the *Spy's Guide* project," I said.

"*Spy's Guide?*" said Chris H. "What's that?"

I put my hand over my eyes and shook my head. When we finished, at about five o'clock, we walked into the hundred-degree sauna outside, shook hands, and said good-bye. As I drove back to Stone Harbor, I felt only sadness in my soul. It struck me that every time the FBI team and I found a new solution, the Justice Department threw up two new hurdles. Its threshold for approval was forever on the rise.

Understanding that the FBI was clearly out of its depth on the potential of playing former KGB chairman Kryuchkov, I had kept the Former Spymaster apprised of this development. At some point, he had met the CIA's Eurasia division chief for a drink to lay it out. Then he phoned me. "I can sum up his reaction in one word," said the Former Spymaster: "*astounded.*"

"Did you explain how all this came about?"

"Sure. He was astounded. He'd never heard any of it."

"Is that what astounded him?"

"The whole thing astounded him. He was astounded that he knew nothing about this. And he was astounded by having a key player like Kryuchkov in this position. He was astounded that the bureau hasn't told CIA about it."

John H. phoned me. "Chris has been busy," he said. "He's gotten a positive response on Warsaw."

We were on course to rendition Howard. As the momentum built, a countdown began. Then Washington again summoned John H.

He phoned me from headquarters on Wednesday, August 30, and asked that I make a dinner reservation at O'Donnell's in Bethesda. He was waiting there with Chris H. and Jim S. when I arrived just before seven o'clock.

A pall had been cast over the assembled G-men. John H. and Jim S. explained that a "related conflict," which they would not identify, had suddenly arisen at headquarters. Consequently, there was no longer a big hurry to rendition Edward Lee Howard. Thus, the operation to nail him in Warsaw had been scrubbed at the eleventh hour and indefinitely postponed.

"We've been put in a holding pattern," said Jim S., "for maybe as long as six months."

Somehow, I wasn't surprised that our operation had evolved into a most extraordinary *un*-rendition. It seemed that the notoriously politicized Justice

Department, from the beginning, never really had the gumption to go through with it. We had met every demand the powers that be had made to legally justify a rendition, but they scrapped it at the eleventh hour anyway. They were worried about embarrassing the Russian government even while corrupt Russian leaders were laundering billions of dollars and the Russian intelligence services were taking advantage of eased tensions with the West by teaming with organized crime groups and doubling their espionage efforts worldwide.

Edward Howard did indeed travel to Warsaw to research *Spy's Guide*, arriving November 5 and departing two days later. I still have his expense receipts. Given the go-ahead, we could have apprehended an American traitor who prided himself on being the only spy to have been taught his tradecraft by both the CIA and the KGB.

The boys from the bureau asked me to "hang in there," that is, to keep Howard greased until such time that their "related conflict" could be resolved. In the meantime, we would plod on with *Spy's Guide* and Kryuchkov's book, and I would be given leeway to cultivate positive intelligence, as the bureau's counterterrorism chief, Bob B., suggested that November.

I knew then, in my bones, that it was over and that the Justice Department would never green light the rendition of Edward Howard. More time would pass, making it more difficult to prosecute Howard for espionage. It was always a tough charge without the culprit's admission, and Howard's mantra on this point was an unwavering (and smartly reasoned) "Deny everything, admit nothing." The silver lining beneath this dark cloud was at least I'd get a crack at Kryuchkov, the former KGB chairman.

16

DOING MOSCOW WITH
ED AND THE BOYS

I was amused the moment I began reading Vladimir Kryuchkov's chapter summary for a book he wanted to title *A Life Devoted to the Cause.* "I was in Stalingrad when the Great Patriotic War broke out in 1941," he had written. "It was a hot summer day, June 22, and my dream had come true: my parents went to town to buy me a bicycle. As they prepared to pay for it, loudspeakers announced the start of war. I did not get the bicycle." The passage spoke volumes to me about this man and about his whole life: he didn't get the bicycle.

On page 84, Kryuchkov discussed how Edward Lee Howard had assisted the KGB: "With Howard's help we were able to cut off channels through which information vital to the security of the USSR was being leaked." The KGB's own former chairman admitted what Howard had always denied!

I now managed the two books simultaneously—Howard's *Spy's Guide* and Kryuchkov's memoir, for which Howard was the designated point man. For more efficient communications with Howard, the FBI's computer whiz, Tom M., had set me up with the newest Compaq laptop computer with Internet capability for exchanging e-mail with Howard and for receiving downloadable material from him.

The bureau's Russian translators went to work on Kryuchkov's manuscript. I zapped Howard numerous e-mails, which he would carry to Kryuchkov, in which I urged the former KGB chairman to spice up his prose with revelations and anecdotes. Kryuchkov, in turn, promised to write material that did not appear in the Russian version of his book.

One year later, I was still waiting. Finally in January 1997, the new material arrived. And so did the time for a face-to-face encounter with

Kryuchkov. The idea was to pump him with questions about spy riddles the FBI hoped to solve. I scheduled my trip for mid-June 1997, more than two years after I had last seen Edward Howard and three years since I had first met Howard in the Russian capital.

The FBI's Russia specialists supplied me with a shopping list of subjects I would broach ostensibly to "improve" Kryuchkov's dead horse of a book. Their questions were designed to shed light on past spy cases and other unresolved issues. For his part, Special Agent John H. wanted an update of Howard's doings and state of mind.

As my Swissair jet neared Sheremetyevo Airport, the clouds thickened, then darkened, and what had been a smooth cruise became rocky and un-certain. I listened to the soundtrack of *Russia House* on my Walkman as we bumped into a final approach.

This time Customs was a breeze, but Edward Howard was not waiting in the arrivals area. A dozen-plus cab drivers descended on me, circling again and again like sharks. (Choose the wrong driver and you'll end up mugged or dead.) I found a wall and leaned back in the dark, cavernous terminal.

Howard finally appeared, dressed in a suit and tie, looking ten pounds heavier and cursing traffic. He took my bag and led me to the battered blue Volvo. Its odometer now clocked 106,670 miles.

As we drove, Howard told me the plan: Kryuchkov would arrive at my hotel at nine o'clock the next morning accompanied by Igor Prelin, the gen-eral director of the retired intelligence officers association. Prelin's last job at the KGB, explained Howard, was as its public relations chief. Now he acted as the front man for the old-guard KGB-in-Exile, an informal group of diehard former intelligence officers. Lena Orlova, also known as Larissa, would be on hand to translate. Howard said he would make the introductions and then let us get on with the project. He might return for dinner at Kryuchkov's home.

Howard filled me in on news of himself. From traitor to trader, Howard had become a stock market analyst affiliated with a firm called Rye, Man, and Gor Securities. As director of its analytical department, he was bullish on Aeroflot stock. Howard also told me he'd been to Cuba two months earlier and was considering buying a sea-front apartment in Havana. "Come meet me there," he said. "I'll introduce you to some Cuban intelligence people. Who knows, maybe there are some books in it for you."

"The more the merrier," I thought.

Howard had worked out how to retire in five years, based on investments in the Russian stock market. He'd already mapped out his future: winters in Cuba, summers in a cabin at Lake Baikal, and part-time consulting by fax and e-mail. Five-year plans are a Russian tradition.

Ninety minutes later we arrived at my hotel, the elegant Baltschug Kempinski. I checked into my room and returned to the lobby for further chitchat with Howard. A woman plucked a harp while young Muscovites juggled cell phones, Russia's newest status symbol.

I asked Howard if he wanted to manage money for new clients. Damn right he did. He could set up fiduciary accounts in Cyprus, he said, and, as some Russian stocks did not require conversion to rubles, he could buy and sell them in U.S. dollars. What's more, he'd take only a 2.5 percent commission instead of the normal 5 percent. "I'm close to the market," said Howard. "I'm constantly on the phone to publicly traded Russian companies to assess their activities."

"Sounds good," I said. "Are you willing to travel to meet prospective clients?" Although the FBI was still in a "holding pattern" on luring Howard to capture—twenty-two months had passed since we'd been told it might take "as long as six months" before we could try a rendition—John H. and I continued to scope out such opportunities in the event that we might one day get a go-head.

"Sure," replied Howard. "I'm traveling widely." But, he added, he didn't want to talk about travel on the phone, fax, or Internet. So I suggested we establish a code to make communications possible. We both made identical notes:

Gorki = Geneva and the Hôtel Les Armures
Kharkov = Zurich and the Hôtel Savoy
Minsk = Warsaw and the InterContinental
St. Petersburg = Prague and the InterContinental
Samara = Havana and the Hotel Nacional

Always meet at noon in reception, one day past the date stipulated in communication.

Howard then told me he had also cultivated a relationship with a Moscow-based insurance company called Rosegal, 49 percent of which was owned by the Great American Life Insurance Company. Howard wanted to get into automobile insurance, which, he said, was virtually nonexistent in Russia.

"What happens when cars collide?" I asked.

"The drivers fight it out."

Howard departed for a business appointment, and I retired to my room. The view of the Kremlin and St. Basil's Cathedral was so grand, I opened the french windows and ordered room service: Beluga Malassol caviar 56g, buckwheat blinis, and a glass of Stolichnaya vodka, all for 65 deutsch marks, the currency this hotel used. On my desk I plopped a copy of the *Washington Post's* Sunday book section, *Book World*, backstopping my "legend" should anyone pay a visit while I wasn't around.

The next morning, Howard and his special guests arrived on time. I descended to the lobby to greet them; we went straight back up to my room after seeing Howard off.

Vladimir Kryuchkov had the cherubic face of a kindly uncle. You would never know, looking at him, that he had been one of the most powerful men in the Soviet Union. The seventy-four-year-old former KGB chairman dressed like a Communist Party apparatchik in a charcoal wool suit, a white shirt, a navy blue tie with a white vertical stripe, and a woolen sweater-vest. His round, apple-cheeked face was dominated by large spectacles with heavy amber-colored frames. A wisp of gray hair atop his bald pate stood on end. It was hard to believe that this short, smiling man had personally ordered the executions of spies given up by Aldrich Ames. As KGB chairman, he had visited their cells the night before their executions and asked, "Are you comfortable?"

Kryuchkov's sidekick, Igor Prelin, was dressed—comically, I thought—in black slacks, a black silk shirt, a black striped tie, and burgundy shoes. He wore his hair slicked back, heavy on the grease, and had a trim gray beard. "Al Capone meets Red Mafia," I thought.

Lena Orlova, or Larissa, was also a KGB agent and now Howard's fallback date. Plain with ivory skin and observant eyes, Orlova had an odd physical trait—a bobbing Adam's apple. Females normally do not have them. Was it left over from a sex change? Chernobyl radiation?

I opened the meeting and explained my position on Kryuchkov's book: the memoir would have to focus on his intelligence career instead of being a full-fledged autobiography. The American reading public would not sit through the two long volumes the Russians had just published. The memoir also needed jazzing up, a little color. But more important, it needed major revelations as well. Kryuchkov had to include things nobody had ever known before. He had to give his audience the sort of thing they called "gee-whiz moments" at the *National Enquirer*.

Orlova translated.

"Ah," said Prelin, "silver bullets."

"Right," I said. "Silver bullets." I said solemnly, "We need to solve some of the great spy mysteries of the second half of the twentieth century."

Vladimir Kryuchkov had begun his government career as a diplomat. Posted in Hungary during that nation's repressed rebellion in 1956, he caught the eye of Ambassador Yuri Andropov, a rising star who would, in time, become chairman of the KGB and, finally, succeed Leonid Brezhnev as the Soviet Union's top banana. Andropov became Kryuchkov's mentor, first transferring him from the foreign ministry to the KGB and then nurturing Kryuchkov's career to the top.

In all, Kryuchkov spent twenty-four years in high positions at the KGB, including as the chief of the First Directorate, where he became the spymaster responsible for Soviet espionage and covert operations worldwide. In 1988 Mikhail Gorbachev crowned Kryuchkov chairman of the KGB. And in August 1991 Kryuchkov showed his appreciation by conspiring to unseat Gorbachev in a failed putsch.

I asked permission to tape-record our session. Kryuchkov agreed, and we began.

"I trusted Gorbachev," said Kryuchkov. "He swore that he would not permit disintegration of the Soviet Union." Now Kryuchkov had only profound scorn for his former boss. "The date of the downfall of the Soviet Union can be precisely marked to the day Gorbachev took power in 1985," he said.

Kryuchkov was convinced—"A silver bullet," Prelin interrupted—that Alexandre Yakovlev, one of Gorby's closet advisers, worked secretly for the CIA and that Yakovlev had been recruited in 1959 while an exchange student at Columbia University in New York City. "I brought this to Gorbachev's attention," said Kryuchkov. "I suggested that we commence an official investigation. What did the president of the USSR do? Nothing, absolutely nothing."

With hindsight, Kryuchkov now questioned Gorbachev's allegiance to the Motherland. "Gorbachev was praised by American and German leaders. He liked everybody in the West," said Kryuchkov, attempting profundity. "So here is the question: did Gorbachev work for the East or the West?"

Kryuchkov believed that the CIA's strategy of destabilizing the Soviet Union from within is what led to its collapse. "The KGB received trustworthy information on this point," said Kryuchkov. "We knew that they had created a network of influence in Soviet society, a long-term program that influenced our intelligentsia and demoralized our military. We must pay tribute to Western strategists," he added with sarcasm. "They did not make a mistake backing Gorbachev."

"How do you know these things?" I asked. I realized the former KGB chairman *should* have known these things, but Maurice Buckmaster, the late chief of Britain's Special Operations Executive during World War II, whom I had met in the mid-1980s, had taught me always to play the skeptic when talking to sources.

"It all started with Philby," replied Kryuchkov. Kim Philby, the infamous British MI6 operative who spied for the Russians over three decades and did untold damage to the West. "The materials Philby passed to us were of extreme tactical and strategic importance."

"Did you ever wonder if Philby wasn't a *triple* agent?" I posed.

"When Philby first arrived in Moscow, we watched his apartment, monitored his telephone conversations, and opened his mail," Kryuchkov admitted. "He did not understand everything about our Soviet reality, and many things upset him, particularly our way of life. But during his last ten years, Philby enjoyed the unlimited confidence of his Soviet friends, and there was nothing about his behavior to doubt his loyalty to communism and the Soviet Union."

But it was another Western spy whom Kryuchkov ranked as "one of our most brilliant achievements," Aldrich Ames, the CIA mole who reported to his masters in Moscow for almost ten years. "Until Ames joined our side in the mid-1980s," said Kryuchkov, "we had very limited success in the hunt for foreign penetrations in our service. During my chairmanship, Ames's security was of paramount importance." But Kryuchkov took no responsibility for

Ames's arrest. Other former KGB officials, however, believe Kryuchkov's treatment of those Ames fingered—that is, recalling them from foreign posts and swiftly arresting and executing them—convinced the FBI and the CIA to launch a spy hunt.

On the subject of famous spy cases, I asked the former KGB chairman about Vitaly Yurchenko, the KGB officer who had defected to the United States while in Italy in 1985 and then redefected to the Soviet Union. Yurchenko had given up "Robert" to CIA debriefers, who included Aldrich Ames. That code name and the description of Robert's circumstances traced immediately to Edward Howard.

"During a walk in Rome," said Kryuchkov, "Yurchenko suddenly felt sick. He sat down for a rest and passed out. When he regained consciousness, Yurchenko saw strangers bending over him. Everything else was a fog: an airplane, an isolated house, the United States."

The real fog, in this instance, Kryuchkov had created. His tale was fabricated for internal Soviet consumption. "Nobody believes that," I said, shaking my head.

"No?" said Kryuchkov. "Then how about this: Yurchenko knew what he was doing. It was a self-appointed mission to embarrass the CIA."

"Better," I said, "but I've been hoping your book would be *truthful.*"

As Orlova translated, Kryuchkov stiffened. Even after many months in the can, the former KGB chairman was still accustomed to sycophants who said *da*, not *nyet*.

We moved on to the case of Nicholas Shadrin, a Soviet naval commander who defected to Sweden in 1959 and went to work for the CIA. In 1975 Shadrin disappeared while on a trip to Austria.

"Yes, we did kidnap Shadrin," Kryuchkov conceded. "He had violated his oath, defected to the West, and worked against the USSR. For this crime, he was tried in absentia, convicted, and sentenced to be shot. In the early 1970s, our service located Shadrin in Washington and established contact with him. He agreed to make amends and work for Soviet intelligence. I believed he was truly remorseful and could be useful to us. But he became too enthusiastic, and we found his behavior suspicious. Then we received reliable information that the Americans were behind this game.

"So we decided to lure this traitor out and bring him home. Oleg Kalugin, a First Directorate colonel, was put in charge of the operation. In meetings, we discussed how to deal with Shadrin's resistance and transport him from Vienna to Prague. We decided to use chloroform. But Kalugin had his own agenda.

"The result was a fiasco. Drugged unconscious, Shadrin was pulled a thousand yards in the snow at the Austrian-Czech border, then left to lie in the icy cold for twenty minutes because the car that was supposed to carry him got stuck in the snow. Shadrin died.

"My deputy flew to Prague to assess the failure of this operation. He reported that our receiving team was upset—all except Kalugin, who appeared satisfied by the outcome. An autopsy determined that Shadrin had liver cancer at an advanced stage, so he would not have lived more than six months anyway."

During a short break, Igor Prelin engaged me in conversation. He told me he had written a novel, published in Russia, based on a true story. "It's about a CIA officer I ran for eight years. He died tragically in Lebanon."

"When?" I asked.

"April 1983—the embassy bombing."

I was surprised by the casualness with which Prelin laid such a bombshell on me. Perhaps he wanted to track where it might travel with me. Instead of jumping on this topic, I asked Prelin if Kryuchkov had been followed to my hotel.

"They've been called off for one day." Prelin winked. "We have professionals in charge again." Prelin then told me that he represented thirty-six hundred retired KGB officers.

"Who has better counterintelligence," I asked him, "the Russians or Americans?"

"We do," replied Prelin. "America only catches agents through betrayal. We catch them through hard work."

Stopping once again only for room-service sandwiches, coffee, and tea, my session with Kryuchkov went on till four o'clock in the afternoon. I filled three ninety-minute cassette tapes. One topic we covered was Kryuchkov's leading role in the attempted putsch to unseat Gorbachev, for which the former KGB chairman went to prison. "How did you feel to be so powerful one day and in prison the next?" I asked.

"It is like existing in another dimension," replied Kryuchkov, "a nightmarish dream, except you don't wake up. The first night, the first few days, I wasn't feeling anything. Different emotions were fighting within me. I felt weightless, had no physical feeling within myself. I was not thinking personally. I tell you, I thought very little about my family—my wife and children and grandchildren. My main concern was the state problem. I was a Komsomol member at fourteen and a party member at eighteen, so I was brought up in an atmosphere of heroic ideas. When I entered the cell, other prisoners there for other things were shocked. It was five in the morning. They gave me hot tea and let me go to bed. At six when they turned on the lights, nobody woke me up, so I had a chance to sleep. The first thing I did when I woke up was my morning exercises. It's been a habit for sixty years now. I exercise for one hour. The guards and other prisoners looked at me with shocked eyes. I had decided to do my normal thing."

"I hear that you are now under surveillance," I said. "How does it feel to be subjected to the kind of treatment you once supervised yourself?"

"I'd be offended if they were not watching me," snapped Kryuchkov.

"I have to ask you about Ames," I said.

"Have you read what I wrote?"

"Yep, and I need more. So far, five books have been written about Ames. You, the former KGB chairman, must address it in depth for anyone in the West to take your book seriously." When Kryuchkov obfuscated with vague generalities, I attempted specificity, broaching something Edward Howard had laid on me a few years earlier. "Could the KGB have rescued Ames?"

"This problem started when I was already out of the business," replied a terse Kryuchkov. "This is a game, a war, without any rules."

I was getting nowhere fast. I took another stab at it: "Why did you act so quickly to arrest and execute spies identified by Ames when this would probably arouse suspicion that someone in the CIA was tipping you off?"

Igor Prelin jumped into the fray, changing the subject. "Why only Ames?" he protested. "Some agents were identified without his help. We had to act. Big secrets from the KGB and the Ministry of Defense were being given out. This was a danger and threat to our people."

"Who was the worst CIA director?" I asked, changing the subject to ease tension.

"The worst for *us*?" said Kryuchkov. "[William] Casey was the worst for us."

"Why?"

"Casey did more than anyone else," replied Kryuchkov. "First he strengthened them, and then he widened them—with more personnel. And he protected them from too much control. He raised their spirit."

"What kind of contact did you have with the CIA?"

"The first contact between representatives of Soviet and U.S. intelligence took place in December 1987, between me and Robert Gates, who was deputy director of the CIA," said Kryuchkov. "We met in Washington, an unofficial meeting in a small restaurant. Gates knew which brand of whiskey I drink, Chivas Regal. We spoke in generalities about Soviet-American relations. A couple of years later, Gates visited Moscow, and we had a meeting at a KGB guest house in Kolpachny Pereulok. Gates asked me if I wished to know the CIA's view of what would happen to the Soviet Union in the year 2000. I said yes. In a few carefully chosen words, Gates said he doubted the Soviet Union would still exist. He asked if I would like to see the CIA's analytical report on the future of my country. I said I would be grateful to accept such material. And though we later reminded Gates about his offer, we never did receive the CIA report. I thought about Gates's tragic forecast. And then, with some mortification, I watched it happen ten years ahead of schedule."

"Ah," said Prelin, "a silver bullet."

"Let's shoot for another silver bullet," I said. "Oleg Kalugin has written that John Cairncross is *not* the fifth man in Britain's Cambridge spy ring. If not Cairncross, who was it?"

Kryuchkov snarled at the mention of Kalugin's name, but Prelin got excited. "Why not ask for the sixth and seventh? There were lots of agents in Britain. Somebody invented this 'five.'"

"OK, who were the sixth and seventh?" I asked.

"Aha!" said Prelin, as if that were an answer.

"OK, how about this: why wasn't the KGB able to prevent Gorbachev from giving up Eastern Europe?" I asked, feeding them another question from the bureau's shopping list.

"We have instilled a feeling among KGB officers that they should respect the laws," said Kryuchkov. "We were very upset with Gorbachev's actions already, but it was not of an organized character. I don't write this in my book, but I am telling you now: I was offered to take all the power into my hands as the KGB chairman. I refused this, though it was possible, because it would have been a real coup."

"What do you want your epitaph to say?" I asked.

"Just my name, date of birth, date of death." His summation was the essence of Kryuchkov. Except to students of Sovietology and espionage, his conversation and ideas were as tedious as his pen.

Just as Howard had forecast, Kryuchkov invited me to be his guest for dinner. Prelin, Orlova, and the former KGB chairman discussed logistics. Then Prelin turned my way. "I come here for you at six." He winked. "The KGB will take care of you."

At six o'clock on the dot I found Prelin in the lobby. He relieved me of a bottle of Ridge Geyserville, a California zinfandel I had brought as a gift for Kryuchkov. "I give him for you," said Prelin.

Prelin drove a BMW. He told me he was born in Siberia and came to Moscow in 1966 for intelligence school. He worked five years in counterintelligence before joining the KGB's First Directorate and then had tours in Angola, Mozambique, and Senegal. On my return to Washington, my report to the FBI included Prelin's comment about running a CIA officer for eight years, allegedly one of eight CIA officers who had died in the U.S. Embassy bombing in Beirut. I suggested the bureau should determine who among the deceased CIA officers had previously served in Angola, Mozambique, or Senegal and where precisely such an officer had been stationed in 1977. I doubt anyone ever did.

The pompous Prelin prattled on self-importantly until we arrived at Edward Howard's apartment. This arrangement was illogical, however, for Lena Orlova drove with Howard in his car and I was still stuck with Prelin for company, at his insistence. When we reached Kryuchkov's apartment building, Prelin instructed me to join Howard in his car while Prelin went up to fetch the boss.

Five minutes later, a chauffeur-driven Zhiguli pulled out with Kryuchkov and Prelin in the backseat. We would not be dining in Uncle Vlad's apartment, as Howard had thought.

"Kryuchkov has a car and driver again," Howard commented. "The Duma Committee on Security, run by the Communists, made Kryuchkov a consultant, and that qualifies him for a driver."

"Prelin's a piece of work," I said.

Howard cursed under his breath. "These First Directorate colonels all think they're hot shit. They all drive BMWs."

We followed the Zhiguli to Taganka, a Moscow suburb, and parked in the lot of a restaurant called Fairy Tale. Inside, the owners greeted Kryuchkov warmly. They had closed the restaurant's larger room off to all but our party.

"This is K.'s favorite restaurant," Howard whispered to me.

In the dark dining room, a long table was spread banquet-style with three kinds of smoked Baltic fish and other appetizers. Howard acted blasé about the whole affair. He could not have cared less about being present; he had joined us only at Kryuchkov's insistence. In an ironic twist of "post-usefulness syndrome," common to defectors once fully debriefed, now that Howard had become a hotshot stock analyst, surfing the wave of new Russian capitalism, *he* appeared to have no further use for his former handlers. But although Howard did not seek the company of these old-guard KGB officers, he remained charmed by Kryuchkov's obvious affection toward him.

Kryuchkov gave me as a gift the two-volume, hardcover Russian edition of his autobiography. He autographed it in Cyrillic: "To Robert, good luck with your creative pursuits." If only he knew how creative they were!

My new friends and I ate by candlelight and drank what Kryuchkov called "Stalin's favorite wine," a Georgian red called Kindzmarauli. Talk of Joseph Stalin cheered the former KGB chairman. He recalled a special moment, in 1953, when he realized he stood only a hundred feet from the tyrannical dictator. "It was the happiest day of my life," said Kryuchkov, a tear welling behind his thick glasses. It pleased him to report to us that a Stalin revival was taking place in Moscow. Whenever Stalin's name was invoked at the ballet or the theater, said Kryuchkov, people broke into applause.

In contrast to his adoration for Stalin, Kryuchkov despised Nikita Khrushchev. But, he added, "Khrushchev, to his credit, never would have tolerated Gorbachev. When I go out, I have no bodyguards. I walk the streets alone. If people come up to me, they are kind and sympathetic. But Gorbachev dares not step one foot out of his home without five bodyguards. The people taunt him. They throw tomatoes at him."

Over appetizers, we agreed on a title for Kryuchkov's English edition of his memoir: *Spy Lord: Secrets of the KGB Chairman.*

"What will Washington think," Prelin said to me, "when the Soviet Union reemerges?"

"Is this something you expect to achieve militarily?" I asked.

"No," Kryuchkov answered. "It's what the people want."

"So you're going to reunite through public referendum?" I said.

"Yes," Prelin and Kryuchkov replied in unison.

"Everyone seems to be in favor of big nation-states," I said, "like a unified Europe. But just the same, I don't think I'd use the word *Soviet* if I were you. Nor *Union* for that matter." My tongue was planted firmly in cheek. "Maybe you should call yourselves the Democratic States of Eurasia?"

Prelin concurred while I struggled to keep a straight face.

"The problem," said Kryuchkov, "is that your country interferes with the popular vote."

"Ah," I said.

"It's not right for your country to do this," added Prelin.

"OK, here's what you do," I said. "We have secession groups in Texas and California and elsewhere. Alaska has a whole political party devoted to breaking from the federal union. You should retaliate and give these groups your support."

"Ah, yes!" Prelin lurched forward. "We tell Vladimir Alexandrovich [Kryuchkov] to do this when he was KGB chairman! But he does not listen!"

And I sat there thinking, "What am I doing in this asylum?"

Kryuchkov launched into another complaint against the United States. "You have too many laws, so you're not free. We did not repress people with laws. So we had real freedom."

This dinner was a surreal cartoon. I'd come through the looking glass and landed at the mad KGB chairman's dinner party, as painted by Salvador Dali.

Then Prelin jumped into his greatest gripe of all. "The American IRS is now teaching the Russian government how to collect taxes," Prelin complained. "I have to pay 104 percent tax on one of my projects."

I countered, "I don't understand how this could be possible. You'd lose money."

"Da," Prelin shrugged to make his point. "But I make special arrangements, so it turns out OK."

Thankfully, the conversation reverted to publishing. I explained that the spy genre was not doing well. "Nobody cares," I said. "Everybody in the States says the Cold War is over."

Prelin shook his head sadly. "Da, that's what they say here, too."

The main course—small dumplings with meat (of what origin, I dared not ask)—was served as we chatted. Then dinner ended abruptly without any offer of dessert or coffee. And Prelin had still not given Kryuchkov my gift, the bottle of wine. When I asked him about it, he said, "I take care of it, KGB honor." Which meant, I suppose, Kryuchkov never got his bottle.

I mentioned this matter to Howard on the drive back to my hotel. Howard shook his head and obviously had no time for Prelin. "He's like a student council president," said Howard. "He plays his role as head of the former KGB officers association to the hilt. He crashed my last birthday party."

Birthdays in Moscow had always been a bone of contention with Howard. "It's tradition that all your Russian friends drop by," he told me. "You're supposed to give them food and vodka." With his tightwad character, it wasn't exactly Howard's idea of a good tradition.

17

I SPY

By autumn, Vladimir Kryuchkov was growing anxious. Why had I not yet found a publisher for his book? In fact, with the bureau's knowledge, I had genuinely submitted a manuscript entitled *The Kryuchkov Konfessions* to senior editors at several publishing houses in the United States and Britain. (The bureau had no interest in whether Kryuchkov's book was published in the United States; it was only concerned that I do whatever felt natural to further the ruse.) The various editors I approached unanimously assessed the former KGB chairman's tome for what it was—dull and uninteresting.

To placate Kryuchkov and to keep the ruse going, I put my imprint, Enigma Books, back into action and dummied a contract for him to sign. Kryuchkov's modest advance on royalties would come from the FBI's coffers. On November 13, Kryuchkov sealed the agreement with his signature.

Two months later, I returned to Russia with my designated "editor," Rick K., a trusted publishing colleague whom I had recruited as a witting FBI asset. Rick had played roles in some of my private-sector intelligence operations and had proven invaluable as an insertion agent and a second set of eyes.

"Don't bring your address book to Moscow," I said, preaching to Rick what I myself practiced. "Get an index card, scramble whatever numbers you might possibly need on it, and carry it in your wallet." I cautiously assumed that the Russian Federal Security Service (FSB) perused my possessions while I was away from my hotel room. "And bring a copy of *Publishers Weekly*," I added. "Maybe a *New York Review of Books*."

By this time, the FBI had become accustomed to my flying habits. Its accountants squawked about my Delta BusinessElite fares and four-hundred-dollar-a-night hotel rooms. But it was the price they had to pay for this production. So Rick and I flew from New York's JFK Airport to Moscow in style and toasted our partnership in espionage with champagne. Then I took a pill for a good night's sleep, knowing it was essential to hit the ground running on four-day spy jaunts eight time zones away.

Many hours later, Moscow welcomed us. Rick, who met Edward Howard for the first time in the arrival area, later said he was struck by the deep sadness he detected in this traitor's eyes.

Howard led us to his brand-new Volvo sedan, dark blue with black leather interior. Either the Russian stock market had been kind to him, or he had finally received the new car Kryuchkov had promised him for publishing *Safe House*. I sat back and let Rick do most of the yakking, breaking him into the spy game. Bright sunshine reflected off a fresh snowfall and bestowed upon the Russian capital a clean, fresh radiance. Rick commented on the construction going on everywhere.

"That's democracy for you," said Howard, sardonically.

He dropped us at the Baltschug Kempinski. Rick and I checked in and then hoofed through slush to Red Square, stopping at GUM, a department store, for a beer. We spent the rest of the afternoon and evening goofing off; drinking bottles of Schneider Weisse, first at the Baltschug Bar, then in the lobby; and chuckling over whoever might be deployed to keep tabs on us.

At 9:55 the next morning, Rick and I found Kryuchkov and Prelin sitting stiffly on wing chairs in the lobby. The hotel staff seemed to recognize the former KGB chairman. Kryuchkov wore the same navy blue tie with white vertical stripe. We went up to my room, where Lena Orlova arrived a few minutes later.

As Rick set glasses before everyone and poured mineral water, I provided a status report on the book. "The [dummy] publisher was not happy," I said. "We need more—to use Igor Prelin's phrase—*silver bullets*." Also, I had a final volley of questions for Kryuchkov to answer, as provided by the FBI.

The former KGB chairman stirred, smiled, and drummed his fingers on the arm of his chair. He had a few comments to make. "Why was it necessary to answer more questions? According to simple logic, based on what you sliced from my original manuscript, from the interview transcripts, and the new material I had written, why, it all added up to four hundred pages. Wasn't that the precise number of pages you wanted this book to be? So why more questions?"

I replied, "A number of gaps still remain. Plus we have a few new subject categories to consider for inclusion, to satisfy the publisher."

Kryuchkov turned to Prelin, who had been scratching rashy patches of psoriasis or eczema on his arms. They conversed in Russian. Lena Orlova did not translate, her loyalty transparent.

Kryuchkov and his stooge left the room to continue their discussion. When the Russians returned ten minutes later, Kryuchkov thanked me politely for my hard work, but he declined to answer any further questions.

When Prelin argued with him, Kryuchkov acquiesced. "OK, ask a question," Prelin instructed.

"In our last interview," I said, "you referred to the First Directorate as the 'White Bone.' Why 'White Bone'?"

"We were called White Bone by other directorates of the KGB," replied Kryuchkov.

"What does it mean?"

"It is Russian for somebody of noble origins," said Kryuchkov. He looked at Prelin, snapped a few words of Russian, and rose, ready to leave. What should have been *The Kryuchkov Konfessions* had become the *Kryuchkov Kop-out.*

I gave the old goat bags of Tootsie Roll Pops and Hershey's Kisses for his grandchildren. It sweetened him a little but not much as we descended to the lobby. While Prelin searched for Kryuchkov's car and driver, the rest of us sat and waited. I made small talk about U.S. politics with the former KGB chairman. He expressed a fondness for Colin Powell, whom, he said, he once met. But, he added, "a black man could never be elected president of the United States."

Prelin returned and told Kryuchkov the car was ready. Kryuchkov got up from his chair and departed. Prelin remained behind. He, Orlova, Rick, and I returned to my room.

"That went well," I muttered. My mind, however, was already focused on the upside: Kryuchkov had thrown a tantrum and failed to cooperate after I'd flown all the way to Moscow. Now the dummy publisher could bail from publishing his dull, dogmatic book without offending anyone except Kryuchkov himself, who'd already been milked for all his worthwhile information. Howard and Prelin would understand.

Prelin dismissed his boss's behavior with a backhand wave, said something derogatory about "old people," and announced, "*I* will answer your questions." His implication: I could us Prelin's words in the former KGB chairman's book as Kryuchkov's own.

I shrugged and thought, "Why not? Let's grill this scaly weasel."

"There is no such thing as ugly women," Prelin began. "Sometimes, there is not enough vodka." He laughed hard, with a pretentious self-confidence betrayed by the rash that had broken out on his face, neck, knuckles, and arms. Then he opened himself up to interrogation.

I began by reminding Prelin about the CIA officer he had supposedly recruited and handled before the officer's untimely demise in Beirut. Prelin refused to identify this alleged spy by name, saying only that he was divorced, he didn't have any children, and his parents were deceased. He suggested that I read a novel he'd published, which he said was a thinly veiled fictional treatment of that case. "Intelligence services worldwide study my novels," said Prelin.

"In his dreams," I thought. Then I continued, "Bill Clinton visited Russia in 1970. Have you ever seen his KGB file?" Information about President Clinton was *not* on the FBI's shopping list; I asked this question out of my own curiosity.

"I was offered a hundred thousand dollars by American television for information on Clinton's visit to Moscow. But we wanted Clinton to become the president in 1992, because he was better than the other candidate [George H. W. Bush], from the Russian point of view."

"You mean, what you knew about Clinton might have led to his defeat if publicly known?"

"Yes," said Prelin. "That's why we did not give this information."

"A girlfriend?"

"There were some things," said Prelin. "I wouldn't respect him if he did not have affairs with Russian girls."

"So just sexual adventures?"

"You should have come to Moscow when you were twenty-two or twenty-three and the KGB was in good shape. You'd be sitting with Ames, in the same prison maybe. I can only tell you that our information could have influenced the election."

"Would it be enough to get him into trouble today?"

"Da, it could," said Prelin, "but we're not interested in anything bad happening to Clinton. With his problems now, the combination would finish him." He was referring to the Monica Lewinsky scandal.

"What about Princess Diana's death? Was it an accident?" I asked, again out my own curiosity.

"Ha! It's a great motive for an assassination, for the royal family to have somebody in the family with an Egyptian husband, which means the young princes would have brothers and sisters of different origins. Diana was going to become a Muslim, so she'd have Muslim children. That doesn't strengthen the lot of the British monarchy; it is a strong point against it. So if you examine, as Sherlock Holmes taught us, and ask yourself a question: Who gains? You get the answer—the Royal Family."

"Is the British intelligence service capable of doing this kind of thing on the Royal Family's behalf?"

"Ha! Better than any intelligence service in the world. I consider the British the most cruel of the white population. They are the most cruel nation."

"With your understanding of intelligence," I continued, "is this something British intelligence would take upon itself to execute, or would it require instruction from the royal family?"

"You think during the Stalin era we shot anybody without instructions? You think that Martin Luther King or [John F.] Kennedy was assassinated without instructions from a higher echelon?"

"What higher echelon?"

"[Lyndon] Johnson knew about Kennedy."

"Is that what the KGB believes?"

"Our organization thinks it was a plot," said Prelin.

"You are familiar with the circumstances of Princess Diana's accident. How could that have been a staged assassination?"

"Why not?" said Prelin. "A few days ago the same thing was tried with a Russian provincial governor. He was driving on a two-lane highway, and they detonated a fifty-gram explosive. It's nothing to damage a car, just a simple explosive, but they were counting on a psychological effect. The whole idea is to scare the driver."

"Where would the explosive be?"

"In our case, the thing went off too early," said Prelin. "The driver got scared, but he had time to react. Now, about Diana, as far as I know, the experts were considering this. Some people were blaming the paparazzi, that somebody was taking pictures in front of the car with a flash—no. I can put something on the windshield of your car that will have the same effect. It will flash in an instant, and when the car is moving, when it's dark in the tunnel, such a flash will make you blind."

"What kind of flash?" I asked.

"Some chemicals, manganese and selenium. It will not burn, just cause a bright light. The thing is so weak, it leaves no traces. It would be a tiny thing, magnetic, where the wipers are. At the right place, by remote control—flash!"

"Has British intelligence used this method before?"

"Ha! They've done things better than this. The British service was intensely trying to recruit a Soviet scientist. It was 1976 or '77—he went to London on a delegation—when they tried to recruit him. He was there a month. They started following him. He went to our embassy and reported it, and they told him to go to Berne, Switzerland. The British followed him there, tried to recruit him again in his hotel room. They gave him a drug, but they gave him too much, and he died. And they just threw him out of the window. The Swiss gave the body back. We examined it. We found traces of the drug and proved he was dead before he went out the window. So we know very well about the British."

Here was the old-guard KGB's (big) mouthpiece, telling me in the space of fifteen minutes that the KGB had a file on Clinton that could have prevented his election and reelection, Lyndon Johnson had conspired to assassinate President John F. Kennedy, and British intelligence had murdered Princess Diana on instructions from the British monarchy. He was a conspiracy theorist's dream.

At six o'clock that evening Howard arrived at the Baltschug Kempinski with his new girlfriend, Mila, to take Rick and me out for a "real Russian dinner." Howard had requested that I not mention Mila to Lena Orlova; he juggled both women. Howard had met Mila at a party, he said, on March 8, 1977, International Women's Day in Russia.

Mila was a blonde knockout divorcée from the Ukraine and had a twenty-two-month-old son. She was young, curvy, vivacious, and the kind of trophy rich cretins like to show off in Monte Carlo. Mila apologized, in excellent English, for wearing sunglasses. She wanted to hide a bad case of conjunctivitis.

"Or," I wondered, "was it recent plastic surgery? Or a black eye?"

Howard found a parking space outside Le Romanoff. I thought to myself, "You wouldn't call a decent restaurant Le Stalin or Le Khrushchev, not unless its specialty was boiled potatoes and cabbage."

At dinner, Rick focused on Mila and I on Howard, as we had prearranged. By chance, Howard told me, he had bumped into a woman from the U.S. Agency for International Development whom he'd known when they both served in the Peace Corps in Colombia many years earlier. When she met Howard a second time, she told him that she'd had to report their encounter to the U.S. Embassy. As a result, the embassy's legate had made Howard a new offer: come home, admit espionage, and spend two years at a minimum-security prison.

"Sounds like a fair deal to me, Ed," I said. "Why not go for it?"

"First off," said Howard, "who knows what could happen to me in prison? And after I got out, I'd probably wind up back in Moscow because my experience and contacts are here. So why bother?" He paused. "Maybe in a couple years they'll offer me a better deal."

When I asked him if he still wanted to sneak back into the United States for a visit, Howard puffed on a Salem—he was back to chain-smoking—and smiled. "Yeah, I'd like to take a Greyhound bus tour and see the Grand Canyon. But I'll have to be careful. One of my KGB contacts told me, 'They have given up on you. They'll only get you if you show up on U.S. territory.'"

As far as I knew—and I knew a great deal—Howard's KGB contact had it right. From where had the Russians gotten such good intelligence? The current spy hunt back in Washington had focused, erroneously, on a CIA officer named Brian Kelley.

As we ate our meals, a trio of Russian musicians performed traditional tunes. Howard was so cheap, he wouldn't order a second bottle of wine, so I took control of ordering and paying the tab. This change cheered him significantly, and he opened up with an interesting tidbit on George Blake: the British traitor had finally been venturing out of Russia for vacations abroad.

Blake had marveled at the ease with which Howard traveled so freely around Europe, so the previous summer he'd taken his wife on a Mediterranean cruise.

I asked Howard about his business. "My KGB contacts like to point me out as a success story," said Howard. "Doing well, making money."

But he was not as buoyant as the summer before. The Russian stock market had petered out and was losing money, not making any. Howard, with his accountant mentality, defined himself by his financial worth and fiscal growth. His enthusiasm for meeting new clients had waned in this declining market, so I needed a new lure. Since Howard was no longer flush with cash, I ventured he would probably be willing to meet a "movie producer" to discuss a hefty sum for film rights to his book *Safe House*, wouldn't he?

"I'm there," said Howard. And speaking of books, he told me his old KGB handler Igor Batamirov was thinking about writing one and asked if I was interested in the project. Indeed, I was.

The next day Rick set off with Igor Prelin to meet a couple of old fogy generals about their own memoirs. Then Rick returned to the hotel and joined me for a six o'clock meeting with Batamirov that Howard had arranged. Howard had also cautioned us not to tell Prelin about it because "he wants a piece of everything."

Igor Anatolyevitch Batamirov, at about five feet eleven and 180 pounds, cut a formidable presence in a sport coat, a V-neck sweater, slacks, and English driver's cap, overcoat, and woolen scarf. His large, doughy face sat heavily upon a wide-girth double chin. Batamirov also wore a six-piece, gold puzzle ring he had acquired in Kuwait. When I mentioned I'd once bought a similar ring, an eight piece, at the souk in Beirut, Batamirov smiled. His best years, in the early 1970s, he said, had been spent in Beirut. His other foreign postings had included Iraq and the United States.

This former counterintelligence chief exuded a low-key self-confidence. As head of the American section in the KGB's Penetration Unit, Batamirov had handled both Howard and Ames. He was, he knew, a master of the kingdom. Unlike Prelin, he had no need to toot his own horn.

Batamirov gazed into space as he spoke decent English, lapsing into quiet, reflective moments that added to his authoritative air. He told me he'd spent twenty-nine years in the KGB and retired from active service in 1994, after five years as counterintelligence chief. Then he divorced his wife of many years and married a woman with whom, he said, he'd enjoyed an intimate relationship for twenty-two years. "It was always my plan to marry this woman," said Batamirov. "But two things had to happen first: one, my children had to grow up, and two, I had to retire. Otherwise, it would have ruined my career."

Batamirov knew I'd come to town to see his former boss. He'd read Kryuchkov's book, as published in Russia, and found it "very dull." As for his own book, Batamirov told me of his fascination for what he called "the phenomenon and psychology of betrayal." He said that betrayal is a very complex issue and that he had seen it all, from both sides.

"Excellent," I said. "Sounds like a whole chapter or maybe a book unto itself."

Batamirov said that the United States and Russia should offer a one-time "pardoning" to traitors.

"You mean amnesty?" I said.

"Yes," replied Batamirov. "I've seen so much damage done to our side, the American side, all sides. Something should be done. An amnesty." This idea seemed heartfelt on his part.

Batamirov responded to my questions in a deliberate, thoughtful manner, avoiding eye contact until strategic moments, when he would use such contact to conclude an important point or assess its impact on his listener.

When I asked about Ames, Batamirov confirmed his involvement as Ames's handler "at the beginning." Then I asked about Yurchenko and told him that Kryuchkov seemed to believe Yurchenko's version of his defection. "Yurchenko is a liar," said Batamirov, "and Kryuchkov is a fool."

I asked him what else he would write about in his book. Batamirov knew many interesting tales and offered one: President Jimmy Carter had requested a secret meeting with Leonid Brezhnev before the Soviet invasion of Afghanistan. Batamirov said he was intimately involved in trying to make this meeting happen, but, ultimately, Brezhnev declined.

I coached Batamirov on the basic elements of a book proposal. He listened intently and said he would do his best with it. When I asked if he would be willing to visit the United States and meet prospective publishers, he said yes. I knew the FBI was going to love this one.

Edward Howard drove Rick and me back to the airport the next day. We agreed that our next meeting would take place in Havana, where Howard promised to introduce me to his Cuban intelligence pals.

Rick and I were the only passengers flying BusinessElite back to New York, so we had a whole cabin to ourselves. Hearing the aircraft door clunk shut was, for me, a golden moment.

PART II
CONNING THE CUBANS

THE MEMBERSHIP CARD ISSUED TO THE AUTHOR BY THE KGB'S FOREIGN INTELLIGENCE VETERANS ASSOCIATION (FIVA). SAID FORMER KGB COLONEL IGOR PRELIN TO ERINGER: "ONLY TWO OTHER NON-RUSSIANS HAVE HONORARY CARDS LIKE THIS—GEORGE BLAKE AND EDWARD LEE HOWARD."

EDWARD LEE HOWARD WITH THE AUTHOR IN ZURICH IN NOVEMBER 1994.

All photos © Robert Eringer.

ROBERT ERINGER   4-91

1510

65-7198/2550
51

Pay to the
Order of _Edward Howard_ $ 7,500.00

Seven thousand, five hundred ∞ 1,00   Dollars

Oct 7   19   95

CHEVY CHASE BANK FSB
CHEVY CHASE, MARYLAND 20815

For _____

1510   ⑆00007500000⑆

PAID CHECK FROM THE AUTHOR TO HOWARD.

Warsaw Expense Report

Dates of Travel: November 5-7, 1995

Rates used: $1.00 US = 2.30 new zloty= 4500 Russian roubles

From: Edward Howard

To: Robert Eringer

Nov 5
Visa form $3
Taxi home to airport $20
Aeroflot ticket 1,894,000 roubles= $419
Airbus into Warsaw   3.50 zloty
Dinner   70- zloty
Tourism books   63.70 zloty

Nov. 6
lunch   20 zloty
coffee   5 zloty
dinner   40 zloty

Nov. 7
Hotel Intercontinental with reduction   698.62 zloty
Airbus to Warsaw airport   3.50 zloty
Transport home in Moscow $20

Totals $462   904.32 zloty=$393

Grand Total for trip $855

HOWARD'S EXPENSE REPORT FOR TRAVEL FROM MOSCOW TO WARSAW
ON NOVEMBER 5–7, 1995.

INSIDE FAIRY TALE, THE KGB CHAIRMAN'S FAVORITE MOSCOW RESTAURANT: EDWARD LEE HOWARD, THE AUTHOR, KGB COLONEL IGOR PRELIN, AND KGB CHAIRMAN VLADIMIR KRYUCHKOV. JUNE 1997.

THE AUTHOR AND KGB CHAIRMAN VLADIMIR KRYUCHKOV. MOSCOW, JUNE 1997.

THE AUTHOR FLANKED BY KGB COLONEL IGOR PRELIN AND KGB ANALYST
ALEXEY SOKOLOV, IN LONDON, ENGLAND. FEBRUARY 2000.

Dinner in Hemingway's Havana haunt, *La Bodeguita del Medio*, in March 1999: Howard, the author, Lena "Larissa" Orlova, and Cuban intelligence officers Salvador Perez and Rolando Salup.

IRA EINHORN TRYING TO HYPNOTIZE THE AUTHOR.

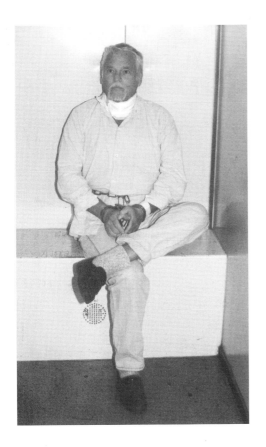

"THE UNICORN" IN CUFFS EN ROUTE TO JUSTICE. EINHORN'S NECK IS BANDAGED FROM HIS ALLEGED SUICIDE ATTEMPT.

OCT 24, 2001

R,

I DID GET YOUR NOVEL, BUT WHATEVER YOU SENT NEXT WAS CONFIS-
CATED. BOOKS MUST BE NEW & COME FROM BOOKSTORES DIRECTLY - NOW
THAT I AM HERE THEY CAN BE EITHER HARD OR SOFT.

ACCORDING TO A., YOU HAVE JUST DISAPPEARED & FRANK DOES
NOT ANSWER HER E-MAILS.

WHEN WE LAST TALKED YOU SAID YOU WOULD WORK TO GET C.D.
PUBLISHED & LOOK AFTER A. SOME.

IF SOMEONE HAS SPOKEN TO YOU THAT IS INFORMATION WE SHOULD
HAVE. IF YOU ARE JUST RUNNING FOR COVER, SAY SO. JUST DISAPPEARING
ISN'T... - YOU FILL IN THE WORDS.

I'M ABOUT TO DO AN ARTICLE - BIG ONE - WITH THE
NEW YORK TIMES MAG. & IF THE WAR EVER COOLS DOWN VANITY
FAIR WILL DO SOMETHING ON A. PERFECT SPOTS TO TALK ABOUT
C.D. PEOPLE HERE WANT IT & OTHER PEOPLE WILL DEMAND IT IF WE
CREATE THE KIND OF NOISE NOW POSSIBLE. THE SILENCE - MINE -
HAS GENERATED LARGE INTEREST.

GET BACK IN TOUCH WITH A.

NEED AN ADDRESS & TEL. NUMBER, SO WE CAN TALK.

IF YOU ARE PARANOID, SAY SO. YOU CAN WRITE & PUT A
FALSE ADDRESS ON THE LETTER. MY OUTGOING MAIL IS SAFE.

ENJOY THE ☼.

Ira

P.S.: ENVELOPES COMING IN MUST HAVE COMPLETE ADDRESSES,
THOUGH THEY CAN'T TELL IF THEY ARE CORRECT.

THREE MONTHS AFTER HIS EXTRADITION, LANGUISHING IN STATE PRISON,
THE MAN WHO THOUGHT HE WAS SMARTER THAN ANYONE STILL DOES NOT KNOW
THAT HE WAS STUNG BY THE AUTHOR.

18

CUBAN INTEREST

One week after leaving Moscow, I zapped this e-mail to Edward Howard: "The publisher does not accept that Prelin's answers can be used to fill gaps in Kryuchkov's book. They feel that if Kryuchkov cannot open up, we don't have a book. So what now? You might put this question to Kryuchkov."

Howard responded the following day, February 4: "Kryuchkov had a heart attack three days ago and is in the hospital. He's out of the picture for many months."

"Had I upset the poor bastard?" I wondered, but then I reminded myself of the men he'd had executed.

John H. was in Washington on my return, eager to debrief Rick K. and me. We met him over libations and crab cakes at Clyde's in Chevy Chase. John H. was pleased to hear I still had the command to draw Howard out of Russia, but since a rendition remained on hold, what really excited him, as I had expected, was Igor Batamirov's willingness to pen a book and visit the United States. The requirement was not terribly complicated: lure the former counterintelligence chief to Washington so FBI special agents could make a pass at him.

But first, Batamirov had to follow my format directions and draft a book proposal. His progress was slow, according to Howard, who was playing intermediary, because Batamirov was tending to his terminally ill mother. In September, Batamirov confirmed to me in a telephone call that he had written a book proposal and had passed it to the "censorship office" of the Foreign Intelligence Service (SVR), successor to the KGB. The censors had apparently objected to "some paragraphs." Then I asked Batamirov how he was surviving Russia's financial crisis, and he replied, "It's bad."

However bad it was for Batamirov, it was worse for Howard. After greedily investing almost all his money in the stock market, he then watched it disappear, along with his five-year plan and his dreams for homes in Havana and Lake Baikal. The collapse of a five-year plan is another Russian tradition.

Batamirov had just seen Presidents Clinton and Yeltsin on TV, in the wake of the Monica Lewinsky scandal. Commented the veteran KGB chief, "Clinton looks like he's had his balls cut off, and Yeltsin looks retarded."

Come October 27, I phoned Howard as I did every year to wish him a happy birthday. A few weeks later, Howard met with the Cuban intelligence station chief in Moscow for lunch and a discussion about me. The result was positive, and Howard asked that I send him a packet of material about myself for dispatch to Havana. I obliged him with clippings I had written as a journalist and details of books I had represented as a literary agent.

A month later, Howard confirmed that the Cubans would welcome my presence in mid-March and that I should make reservations at Hotel Nacional. On February 9, 1999, Howard sent this instruction by e-mail: "I should arrive 11 March and must work 1 day with them. You should arrive evening 11 March, then I will work with you and them 12–14 March."

Aeroflot flew nonstop to Havana once a week. This schedule meant we could easily establish the precise plane upon which Howard would be traveling. So I laid this idea on John H.: we could plant an agent on his aircraft. Seven hours into the flight, as the plane cruised the northeast corridor of the United States, our agent could appear to suffer a heart attack (drugs exist to harmlessly induce such symptoms). The pilot would likely land at the nearest airport—Boston, New York, or Washington—to "save the dying passenger." FBI agents could then enter the aircraft, on U.S. soil, and remove one Edward Lee Howard.

John H.'s response after checking with FBI Headquarters was that he didn't have a warrant to arrest Howard in Massachusetts, New York, or Virginia. He wondered if there was any chance we could divert his plane to New Mexico. Aside from suggesting that no federal warrant for espionage existed against Howard, someone at the Department of Justice must have thought continually derailing Howard's rendition was funny. In fact, on September 25, 1985, an arrest warrant had been signed by U.S. Magistrate Sumner Buell charging Howard with violating Title 18 of the United States Code, Section 794: espionage, a federal crime. Four days later, a second federal warrant had been issued charging Howard with unlawful interstate flight in violation of probation from his aggravated assault plea.

(When I later met with John H. on March 16, at Washington's Marriott Wardman Park Hotel following my return from Cuba, he conveyed the JusticeDepartment's new concern: Edward Howard was said to be on the sauce again. While drunk, he would apparently do stupid things, such as phone people he knew in the United States and apologize for his bad behavior. The concern at FBI Headquarters was Howard might, while intoxicated, board a U.S.-bound plane. Said John H., "He could turn up at JFK Airport one day, and we wouldn't know what to do with him."

"Does this mean our *new* mission is to ensure Howard never comes back?" I couldn't resist asking, but John H. did not laugh.)

Then I received a telephone call from Luis Fernandez, who identified himself as the first secretary of the Cuban Interests Section in Washington, D.C. Because Cuba and the United States do not have formal diplomatic relations, the Cubans operate through the protocol of the Swiss embassy. Fernandez had received instructions from Havana to issue me a visa, and this direction puzzled him. He asked that I come over and complete a visa form.

I jumped into my car and drove to 2630 Sixteenth Street, NW, arriving within the hour. A receptionist inside the stately building summoned Fernandez, a short, barrel-shaped Cuban in his mid-forties with a paintbrush mustache and balding crew cut. Sweating and harassed, Fernandez ushered me up a marble staircase to a large, sparsely furnished visitors' room.

Sitting across from me in coat and tie, Fernandez consulted a notebook and said he needed to know who I was and what I wanted to do in Cuba. I affably outlined my generic background and explained that I wanted to explore potential book deals and business opportunities. When Fernandez asked me how this trip had been orchestrated, I explained that it had been a couple years in the making, through a Moscow-based friend whom I would meet in Havana. "Aside from whatever opportunities it may provide, Cuba is closer than Moscow for seeing my friend," I pointed out.

"So close yet so far away," sighed Fernandez. Then he went into a diatribe about the harsh treatment Cuba endured by the United States. He said it made him happy that I would see for myself the truth about Cuba. "We have sent six hundred doctors to Central America to give humanitarian aid after [hurricane Mitch hit Honduras]. Does the U.S. press corps care about this? No. They prefer to write about prostitution. There is more prostitution in France than in Cuba." With a pained expression, Fernandez went on to say that the United States would not lift its economic embargo of Cuba because of the efforts of a small group of Cuban émigrés who had a stranglehold on a handful of politicians. I shrugged, feigning sympathy.

Fernandez took my completed application form, promised to issue me a Cuban visa, and invited me to remain in contact with him. "We need all the help we can get," he said. "Life is very difficult for us in your country."

19

HANGING IN HAVANA

"You shouldn't be going to Cuba, sir," growled the check-in clerk at Baltimore/Washington International Airport. She gave me a scorching look after examining my Air Jamaica ticket: Baltimore–Montego Bay–Havana. "You're an American citizen," she stated, motioning irately at my U.S. passport in case I hadn't noticed.

I could not exactly tell her I was working on behalf of FBI foreign counterintelligence. And I didn't feel like flashing my press card (working journalists are exempt from the U.S. Treasury Department's ban on travel to Cuba). Besides, I was curious to see what would happen.

"I don't know if I can check you in." She stalked off to consult a supervisor, returning a minute later. "I can only check you in for Montego Bay," she sneered triumphantly. I shrugged.

An Airbus 320 cruised me to Jamaica in two hours, fifty-two minutes while I lunched on jerk chicken. Upon arrival, the terminal building at Sangster International Airport stank of sweat and stale tobacco smoke. Customer Service issued me a boarding pass to Havana and for fifteen dollars sold me the Cuban visa that Luis Fernandez of the Cuban Interests Section never delivered. Inside the first-class lounge, the bartender recommended Appleton Estate V/X Jamaican rum. A belt of this rum with ginger set me up for the one-hour hop to Havana.

Even from on high, Cuba looked barren and beat up, with its roads oddly vacant of vehicles. By contrast, José Martî Airport was fresh, modern, and colorful, though it was almost absent of travelers.

As the first passenger to disembark from the MD-80, I traversed

Immigration and Customs in five minutes. My bags were X-rayed, and a young Customs agent scanned me with a metal detector. Then he frisked me and gestured at the bulges in both front pockets of my blue jeans. "What is?" he asked.

"Money."

"Let me see."

I dug into my pockets and produced two wads of Yankee dollars. In my left palm, I showed him all hundreds.

His eyes popped. "How much?" This query was more out of curiosity than about official business.

"About four thousand dollars," I replied. I had to carry cash because U.S. credit cards are not accepted in Cuba and U.S. credit card companies are prohibited from dispensing money to Cuba. Plus I had cash expenses for Edward Lee Howard.

He looked at me in amazement. To him, my traveling money was sixteen years' salary. "Go on." Official Cuba welcomed me, and especially my money, into its grubby mix.

State-run taxi drivers hovered everywhere. One scampered to his South Korean car and raced to greet me at the forecourt. I asked him, "How much to Hotel Nacional?"

"It's meter." In U.S. dollars.

"Do it."

Beneath a sunny blue sky, I studied the carnival of poverty around me. Giant billboards proclaimed *Socialism or Death!* In passing buses, cramped passengers appeared to be opting for the latter in the stifling heat and no air-conditioning. The taxi's radio blared twenty-year-old hits from Paul McCartney and Billy Joel. In thirty minutes, or by quarter of three, we reached the Nacional.

Quickly processed with an eclectic compost of foreign tourists, I ascended to my suite, or rooms 705 and 706. It was drab and dowdy, but I'll assess what it was not: with its dirty windows and stained carpet, it was not a five-star deluxe accommodation, as designated by Cuba. Yet, all things being relative, it was probably luxurious by contemporary Cuban standards. As the bellhop said with pride, "It have hot water." It had not only hot water but *red*-hot water, red from rust. The most irritating feature of this room, though, was its odor. It smelled like Poland. If one could break down the main ingredients of this smell, foremost would be stale tobacco smoke, followed by low-grade building materials (probably including asbestos), and poor ventilation. It had the B.O. of communism.

I washed my hands and went downstairs to look for Al Lewis. The actor who played Grandpa Munster on the 1960s' television series supposedly lurked in Havana hotel lobbies. And why not? Cuba is spookier than his TV haunt, 1313 Mockingbird Lane.

The Nacional's lobby is a long, high-ceilinged hall, policed at either end by a pair of security men in suits, with receivers in their ears, and on heightened alert to ensure that only foreigners visit the state-owned hotel and its dollars-only facilities. Cubans with pesos or even with Yankee dollars are barred from entering and treated as second-class citizens in their own country. I inspected a display case of jewelry crafted in tortoiseshell and black coral, both banned everywhere else in the world as endangered species. A souvenir shop nearby peddled cheap key chains that were made in Spain and bore Che Guevara's likeness. It did not have much of a book selection, except for stacks of one title, *CIA Targets Fidel*.

Al Lewis wasn't in the lobby, so I strolled into the Nacional's serene grounds overlooking the Malecón (sea wall and promenade) and the sea. Outside, beneath swaying palms, the smell still reminded me of Poland. It could not be evaded. This rummy island was Poland-on-the-Caribbean. (Or as Edward Howard later put it, "Cuba is where Eastern Europe and Latin America meet.") I rested my bones in a white wicker chair on the grand portico. Even the cushions reeked of rancid tobacco.

I did not see Al Lewis, inside or out. Neither did I see Ed Howard, who, in any case, I did not expect until much later in the afternoon. He was somewhere in the city holed up with his buddies from the Directorate General of Intelligence (DGI).

I sauntered out of the Nacional and went one block to the Hotel Capri. Its lobby was even more like Poland than Poland. No, that's not fair—to Poland. It more resembled a drab Intourist Hotel I once visited in Kharkov, the Ukraine, in 1980. And still no Grandpa Munster.

I returned to my shabby suite for a snooze. My telephone snorted at 4:40 p.m. Edward Howard awaited me downstairs.

Howard looked heavier than when we'd last met, fourteen months earlier. Not only was he chunky, with a paunch, but his face was thick and bloated.

Later, I caught a glimpse of his tongue, which was yellow-green. Howard was a picture of poor health, but then he'd just spent twelve and a half hours flying overnight on Aeroflot in economy class.

Howard wore stone-colored shorts, a knit shirt, and sneakers. He insisted we immediately go and meet the chief of some entity called Centro de Prensa Internacional (CPI)—Minrex (Ministry of Foreign Relations), whose office, in the Vedado district, was around the corner. Howard's DGI pals had decreed that an officer of theirs named Juan Hernandez should work with me.

Dark skinned and handsome, Hernandez had a fast, easy smile and twinkling eyes. Although the Cuban spoke reasonable English, Howard eased our dialogue with fluent Spanish, which he had learned while serving as a Peace Corps volunteer in Colombia. Hernandez had his hands full with the upcoming Baltimore Orioles exhibition game in Cuba. That, combined with the Cuban all-star team's visit to Baltimore, was his operation. Four years later, while posted to the Cuban Interests Section in Washington, D.C., Hernandez would be expelled for "undertaking activities inconsistent with official duties."

After introductions, Hernandez lit a cigarette and leaned back in his chair. "What do you want?"

I said I wanted Robert Vesco to write a book. A fugitive from U.S. justice, Vesco was an international financier and crook who had settled in Cuba.

Hernandez smiled and shrugged. "Vesco is in jail. He stole a million dollars from the Cuban people."

"OK," I said, "I want Joanne Chesimard to write a book." Chesimard was a Black Panther who had been serving a life sentence for murdering a New Jersey State trooper when she escaped from prison in 1979. She then fled to Cuba, which, of course, granted her political asylum.

Hernandez said he'd try to get a message to Chesimard.

Then I went for the crown jewels. I told Hernandez I wanted Fidel Castro to write a book.

Hernandez smiled, blew cigarette smoke at the ceiling. "This one is difficult."

"Of course," I said. "The things most worth doing in life often are. But I'll settle for his brother Raúl. In some ways, Raúl's memoir may be more interesting, if less marketable."

Hernandez nodded, smiling, and then told a joke, which Howard translated: "Raúl's generals brought to his attention that he was smoking women's cigarettes. Raúl replied that if he was smoking them, they were definitely for men." Hernandez laughed.

I waited for a punch line, but apparently we'd already heard it. This seemed like a good time to move from book projects to business opportunities. When Hernandez asked what I wanted to do in Cuba, I answered, "I'd like to own a bar with him," and pointed to Howard.

Hernandez hooted. "I have people come in here and say they want to invest one hundred million dollars in Cuba. And you just want to own a bar?" His eyes twinkled. "I like that."

I hoped he liked it enough to hand me the keys to a bar.

"I will make you a meeting," he said. He gave me Castro's business card, not the Bearded One's, but one for *Elvira* Castro, director of something called the Investments Promotion Center.

As Howard and I walked back to the Nacional, I glanced around the lobby, checking out sofas. "Looking for someone?" asked Howard.

"Yeah. Al Lewis."

"Who?"

"Never mind."

"Come on, I'll buy you a drink," said Howard. He led me through the back portico to a bar adjacent to the Salon de la Historia whose walls celebrate those colorful characters who had stayed at the Nacional in more convivial times, including Meyer Lansky and Santo Trafficante. We occupied a pair of stools at the bar and ordered a mojito for me, Fanta orange soda for Howard.

"Mind if I smoke?" Howard produced a pack of Salems. "At least I've switched to Lights. Busy day," he added. Upon his arrival that morning, Howard went directly to see the Cuban DGI. So though he was jet-lagged, Howard spent most of the day at a safe house in Havana's Miramar district.

"I was with Señor Deema," he said, "chief of the North American division. He's jet black, trained in Leningrad. They all were back then. His first love was a Russian girl. I don't think he ever got over her. Deema asked me lots of questions about you. I told him about your working with Kryuchkov and Prelin, that the Russians like you. It didn't seem to matter. They don't

care much about the Russians anymore. They want to know you for themselves. Deema has an idea for a book."

"Everyone has an idea for a book," I thought. I sipped my mojito. "Yeah?"

"In 1989 the Cubans rolled up a CIA spy ring. Every one of the twenty-
eight agents the CIA recruited turned out to be doubles working for the Cubans. The DGI is disappointed nothing big ever came of it in the media. They
consider it one of their major coups and would like to see more made of it.
Maybe a book."

I shrugged. "That's what I'm here for. What did they want to see *you*
about?"

"Oh," said Howard, "most of today was spent on all the exams and
interviews you have to take if you want to join the CIA. They wanted to know
every detail."

"Why?"

"Obvious, isn't it?" said Howard. "They'd like to get one of their people,
somebody from Miami, into the agency. I told them everything I knew. They
laid on a pretty nice lunch, a buffet. Surprisingly good food."

Howard was exhausted from flying overnight and then jumping straight
into a day-long debriefing, but he agreed to join me for dinner at El Floridita.
We taxied to Old Havana, but El Floridita's staff refused to seat us in the
restaurant, a wiggy affair, because Howard's shorts defied their dress code.
So we grabbed a bar table and ordered the "Cuban sandwich"—a concoction
of ham, cheese, pork, butter, and mustard—and a garnish of near-rancid
coleslaw. The daiquiri, supposedly invented there by Ernest Hemingway, tasted
weak and bland. I pushed it aside and ordered a mojito.

At the next table, a repugnant sixty-something-year-old Spaniard held
hands with a teenage Cuban girl. I turned and asked Howard about Mila, the
girlfriend I'd met when last in Moscow.

"It's an on-again, off-again relationship," said Howard. "Currently it's
off. She wanted to come to Cuba with me, but I nixed that. She was here with
me a year ago, so to hell with her."

Howard then told me a KGB officer named Vladimir Popov had first
introduced him to Havana ten years earlier. Popov, who had spent six years
in Cuba after getting the boot from Washington for "activities incompatible
with his diplomatic status" (spying), taught Howard the lay of the land.

Early on, Howard had considered settling in Havana with his former wife and son. The Cubans offered him a house in the Miramar district for a thousand dollars per month, but he and Mary had declined because of the dissatisfactory schooling Lee would have received. Howard was equally happy his son had *not* been brought up in Moscow. "I have a friend with a thirteen-year-old daughter," Howard told me. "One day she did not arrive home from school. Police were called, and a search began. They found the girl in a brothel five days later. What happened was, when the girl was walking home from school, a car pulled over, two men jumped out, and they dragged her in. They beat her, sold her virginity for a thousand bucks, raped her, and put her to work as a sex slave."

Outside, El Floridita's colorful neon sign contrasted with the otherwise low wattage of Old Havana.

My sleep that night was punctuated by sudden consciousness and odd sounds. I heard a drumbeat at three o'clock, probably produced by a power generator outside. Later, two synthesized female voices hollered, "We don't understand—noooo!" And then a strobe light penetrated my brain. Was it from the mojitos? I still haven't figured it out.

I awakened at dawn. From my window I witnessed a clear sunrise over the sea, but to my right, Old Havana was enveloped in a smoggy haze. I parked myself in the Nacional's cafeteria when it opened for complimentary breakfast at seven o'clock.

Howard joined me soon after. The buffet featured abundant, if unappetizing, choices. Howard gorged himself, making the most of the Nacional's bedlam-and-breakfast deal.

Suddenly, I had a surprise: Lena Orlova appeared. Turns out, she'd flown in with Howard and slept all the previous day. This trip was her first time in Cuba, she said. Howard acted sheepishly about Orlova's presence. He mumbled something about paying her way himself and that the trip was a bonus for her work as his assistant.

Howard and I talked about travel, always my favorite subject with him. Where had he been? Where would he go? For one thing, Howard had visited Santiago and "got Chile out of my system." He had also visited Egypt and taken a cruise down the Nile with his son. He'd spent Christmas in Vienna with his ex-wife and son, and he had been to Germany, Luxembourg, and Paris, France. "I go anywhere in Europe," Howard boasted, "except the United Kingdom."

Next, Howard laid out his plan for the day. At eleven o'clock, we would meet his friend Rolando Salup, a DGI officer who had spent seven years in New York City under United Nations (UN) diplomatic cover and six years as an intelligence chief in Moscow. Howard knew Salup from Moscow, where he had become personal friends with the Cuban and his wife and entertained them at his dacha. Howard told me that Salup's father had owned the famed Copacabana in its heyday, before the state nationalized it. "Rolando wants to get it back," said Howard.

It was only nine o'clock, so I hired a taxi to take Howard, Orlova, and me on a tour of Havana's neighborhoods. We drove as far as the Marina Hemingway on Havana's outskirts, double backed through Miramar, and stopped at an artisans' open-air market.

"My mother always gets mad when I tell her I've been to Cuba," said Howard, for whom this was the sixth visit. "She has a Cuban refugee friend, who's convinced her the Cubans will sell me back to the Americans for a few dollars. The Cubans would never do that." Howard paused. "But some Russians might." Howard's greatest fear was the FBI would make a deal with the Red Mafia for his safe delivery to the States.

Salup appeared in the Nacional at eleven o'clock sharp. He seemed easygoing but with an edge. I sensed he had a mission. It was probably as simple as making a buck, getting a dollar percentage for brokering a deal.

I'd expressed an interest in native art. So that's where we headed, in a Lada driven by Eric, the boyfriend of Salup's daughter. Barreling along the Malecón, Eric engaged in "accelerate-and-brake," a game Cuban motorists play with the many police officers who stand at street corners to wave down and ticket speeding motorists.

Our first stop at gallery number one, in Old Havana, was a mishmash of overpriced, low-quality contemporary schlock-art and bric-a-brac masquerading as antiques. We cruised over to gallery number two in a suburban Miramar neighborhood. There, a hub of middle-aged men brokered Cuban family heirlooms to moneyed foreigners. Up and down the squalid street, private enterprise flourished: from stalls outside private houses people hawked ice cream, pizza, and, in the back alleys, young women.

Next we journeyed to Eric's apartment, which doubled as a warehouse for his inventory of merchandise. There wasn't anything I needed or wanted.

Howard admired a glass duck. He collected ducks, had a thing about ducks, and possessed more than fifty ducks in his dacha, he confided. As a kid, whenever Howard doodled, he doodled ducks. But he didn't buy this duck.

We then went on to the home of a deceased Cuban artist, allegedly of some renown. An old woman sat fixated in front of an ancient black-and-white TV set as her family tried to sell me their few remaining possessions of value. I liked a few watercolor paintings, but I begged off a decision, feeling sad for this family and disgust for Fidel Castro for the indignity he had forced upon his people. Salup calmed down because I was at least considering a purchase.

When it was time for refreshment, we drove to the Copacabana and sat by the pool. We ordered Cuban sandwiches all round—except for Howard, who opted for tuna—garnished with lukewarm fries. Salup told me that he'd spent much of his childhood around the Copacabana. After Castro took over, the state transformed it for a while into housing for medical students and never paid his family a single peso. I asked Salup if he felt bitter about it.

"No, no." He looked both ways. "It's now valued at $35 million," he said. Salup then announced his three stepbrothers had moved to Miami.

"Do you stay in touch with them?" I asked.

"No, no."

Meanwhile, Howard telephoned Juan Hernandez, who confirmed a meeting with Elvira Castro at three o'clock that afternoon. "We have to pose as reporters for the *Washington Times*," said Howard.

"Why?" I asked.

"It's the only way Hernandez could organize a meeting for us at short notice."

I marveled, "These people were pulling a ruse on each other just for access."

And so, posing as a pair of *Washington Times* reporters, Howard and I appeared at the Investments Promotion Center at the appointed time for our "interview." Castro was accompanied by an interpreter, who translated her overview of foreign investment in Cuba. In a nutshell, she wanted foreigners to provide capital to Cuba so the state could lure and accommodate greater numbers of foreign tourists to fuel its decayed economy. She fed us the numbers: in 1998, 1.3 million tourists visited Cuba; in 1999, 1.7 million were expected; and in 2000, more than two million. She projected that seven million tourists would visit Cuba annually by 2010. So the state needed hotel rooms—eighty thousand of them, she said—and it wanted foreign investors to pay for them. "Bars, nightclubs, and small hotels are not available to foreigners," said Señora Castro. "We can do those things ourselves."

So much for my bar.

We returned to Hotel Nacional. Up in my room, the B.O. of communism had dissipated. No, it had not gone away; instead, it had seized me. Now I was part of it. Once you are within its grip, it takes a half-dozen hot showers and four bars of soap to scrape it away. But I'd barely washed my hands when Howard called. "We're going back to see Hernandez," he said. "He's got news."

I grabbed a bottle of Macallan scotch, one of three I'd brought along as gifts for helpful Cubans. I gave one to Hernandez when we met.

"Why you give this to me?" he asked.

"Because you're such a nice guy."

Hernandez laughed. He leaned forward. "I have something interesting. A friend of mine has written a biography of Fidel Castro." We thrashed this around. Apparently, Castro had cooperated with the project. The manuscript, in Spanish, had not been published anywhere.

"When can I see it?" I asked.

"It would be sent," said Hernandez, "by diplomatic pouch to the Cuban Interests Section in Washington."

"Get it to Luis Fernandez," I said.

"You know Luis?" Hernandez smiled.

I returned his smile as if to imply, "Do *I* know Luis!"

"Luis and I worked together in Venezuela," said Hernandez.

Howard brought up the book idea that Señor Deema had laid on him about the Cubans rolling up a CIA spy ring.

"Yes." Hernandez nodded. "A very good story." He agreed to consult with Deema and follow up on this.

As we walked back to the Nacional, Howard told me that the cost of the scotch I'd given to Hernandez represented a month's salary.

At seven o'clock, I planted myself at the Salon de la Histoiria bar and sipped a mojito while Cuban mariachis strolled, strummed, and sang with a power and passion unique to this people. I just knew that the fifty-something bandleader was a heart surgeon by day who had to moonlight in the tourism trade to put food on the table. He could feed his family (if there was any food to buy) on his music because, in the absence of its Russian Big Brother, no longer as supportive as in days gone by, Cuba now catered to tourists, commercializing Che Guevara on T-shirts and selling key chains made in Spain. But the music, ah, the music! Aye, Cuba, it's all they had left.

After Howard and Orlova arrived, we taxied to La Bodeguita del Medio, Hemingway's haunt in Old Havana. The fifteen-minute ride cost $4.40. We paid in dollars, of course. Nobody in his right mind wanted Cuban pesos, except dumb tourists who bought Cuban banknotes with Che's likeness on them. I handed the driver a fiveski and told him, "Keep it."

"Sixty cents is a whole day's salary to a Cuban doctor," admonished Howard, who did not want the natives spoiled.

"Damn, a line," I said when we saw the crowd of people gathered in front of La Bodeguita. But the maître d', recognizing us as Americanos, hauled us into the bar. "What about them?" I asked, motioning at the throng behind me.

"Them's Cuban," he replied.

"So what?"

"These tables are reserved for *foreigners*," he said. "We have only few tables for *Cubans*." If Mr. Cuban Restaurateur thought this state of affairs ironic, he did not let on. Hell, at least *he* was making a little moola.

In La Bodeguita's small, graffiti-bedecked bar, I asked Howard what his DGI buddies had to say about who would succeed the Bearded One. Would it be his brother Raúl? Howard whispered that Raúl had been caught in a drug-trafficking scheme a few years earlier. Although a few generals took the rap and Raúl's role was hushed up, his chances to succeed Fidel had been trashed.

Howard and Orlova were not getting along. She wanted a gin and tonic, and making a face, he snidely said they didn't do that kind of thing in Cuba (i.e., it was too expensive for this tightwad). Orlova stormed out; Howard went after her. I sipped a mojito and studied the bar's photographs of Hemingway, whose visits were this dive's claim to fame.

Howard and Orlova returned and brought with them Rolando Salup and his "former" DGI pal Salvador Perez. The maître d' escorted us to a corner table upstairs and handed us menus. All prices were in U.S. dollars.

"For someone who hates the United States," I commented, "Fidel sure likes its monetary system."

"He not dislike United States people," said Salup. "He dislike U.S. government. You like nice traditional Cuban meal?" We deferred to Salup's judgment, and he ordered pork, rice, black beans, fried bananas, and a cucumber salad.

I'd heard the official line on foreign investment from Elvira Castro. Now the thirty-three-year-old Perez would tell me the unofficial truth: don't waste time or money investing in this Poland-on-the-Caribbean. "You want to make money? Trade." He meant as in embargo-busting with private entrepreneurs (read: DGI) like himself.

"We need things all the time," said Perez in good English. "One day it might be rice; the next day, paint; the day after, something else. If we're there to meet the market, to fill the gap, we make money. I call you, tell you what's needed. You find it, and we make the deal." Perez told me that one reason foreign investment in Cuba stinks is because foreign investors are not allowed to hire their own labor force; instead, labor is provided by the state and paid state-controlled wages. "A Cuban labor force is a waste of time," Perez continued, "because it has no incentive to be productive."

Salup, of all people, nodded in agreement.

"Are you saying," I cupped my hand over my mouth and leaned forward, "that socialism doesn't work?"

"No, no, no!" Both men shook their heads, mortified, with their eyes popping out of their heads.

"So how do we commence doing business?" I said.

The embargo-buster laid it out: "First step, establish a business entity— a trading company—in Panama or Mexico. Cost? A few hundred dollars.

"Second step, register the entity in Cuba. I could handle that. Cost? A few hundred dollars.

"Third step, open a bank account in Cuba. Cost? Nothing. Then start trading."

I asked why Che Guevara's likeness was everywhere—on statues, murals, T-shirts, key chains—but the Bearded One's face was nowhere to be seen.

"Ah," said Salup, "Fidel is against cult of personality. That is why no statues. For Che it is OK. He's dead."

I had another theory but kept it to myself: Castro long ago decided that the best way to instill fear among Cubans—and to stay alive—was to remain mysterious and elusive. In parting, I gave Salup a bottle of Macallan and Perez a Morgan silver dollar as a "good luck" coin. They gave me their calling cards.

The next morning, Howard and I strolled Old Havana for a final chat. Occasionally, we passed a dog in the street, and I was struck by how awful and peculiar the canines looked in this town. They were either diseased or sick with worry.

"The FBI will know you were here," warned Howard. "You may get a knock at your door, and they'll want to know what you were doing in Cuba."

"What should I do if that happens?" I asked. "Just tell them you can't afford to talk because it would cause complications with the Cubans on future trips. They can't do anything to you. But they fooled Mary that way."

I bought a red star revolutionary beret from a market stall. "I'll wear this when the G-men come a-knocking," I said.

Howard laughed. Then he unveiled his new book idea, *How Not to Do Business in Russia*. He wanted to feature all the kinds of swindles the Russians pull off so well. Howard had learned the hard way. "My KGB friends won't like it," he added, "but I don't give a damn."

I encouraged Howard to get cracking. "Screw the Russians."

Back at the Hotel Nacional, I settled my account with Howard. He was on my payroll, an FBI asset. I handed him my last bottle of Macallan. "Give it to your concierge at Veradado," I said. Howard and Orlova had planned a week's vacation on Cuba's best beach.

"No, I'll give it to Edouard Prensa," he said, "the Cuban DGI chief in Moscow."

"Perfect."

Howard gave me a jar of caviar he'd brought from Russia. After he departed, I opened it for lunch, as I sure as hell wasn't eating another Cuban sandwich. Howard's caviar was oversalted and too compressed. I ate some just for nourishment and dumped the rest. Knowing Howard, it was the cheapest black-market jar he could find.

After settling my tab with Hotel Nacional, I killed an hour sitting on a wicker chair in the garden and sipping one last mojito. A lone peacock strutted the grounds, occasionally piercing the serene setting with a horrible shriek.

"Yeah, I feel the same way," I muttered under my breath and kept one eye peeled for Al Lewis.

Departing Cuba was as easy as arriving, even a greater pleasure. There was no traffic leaving the city (few cars) and no line at the airport's first-class check-in. My only hurdle was a twenty-buck rip-off "exit Cuba fee," which was worth a thousand times that to Cubans who risk their lives to flee the country, sometimes in a rubber raft. And then I saw some decent shops.

I bought a bottle of Havana Club rum and a Che Guevara Swatch watch for the Former Spymaster to wear at his next dinner party. And finally I found something with Fidel Castro's image on it—not any old something but a half-ounce commemorative gold coin. It was overpriced at $375, but I sprang for it and rewarded myself for a job well done. Waiting for my jet to board, I plucked the proof coin from its protective case and mixed it with the other coins in my pocket. I wanted Fidel to get beat up by Jefferson, Lincoln, and Washington. I wanted to tell people, tongue in cheek, that I had the Bearded One in my pocket.

When I arrived in Montego Bay, the same bartender was right where I'd left him in the first-class lounge of Sangster International Airport. He poured me another belt of Appleton Estate V/X rum and ginger. With Cuba behind me, it tasted better.

20

CUBAN COVERSION

As usual, John H. was already in Washington, awaiting my return. On this occasion, he brought the FBI's Cuba contingent from the Washington Field Office into our dealings. It was by necessity, as this was their turf. And while Special Agent Anna M. was intrigued by my doings in Havana, she was much more interested in Luis Fernandez of the Cuban Interests Section. Her primary responsibility was to learn as much about Fernandez as possible. And thus far, she knew precious little, except this bit: he was an overworked intelligence officer who had arrived in Washington, D.C., as a temp; became a permanent employee; and was now expected to remain under diplomatic cover for a five-year tour. Hence, I had a new mission—to befriend Fernandez. I was to find out what he was working on, with whom he had contact, and assess his recruitment possibilities.

I asked about penetrating Cuba's embargo-busting stratagem. After all, the Cuban DGI had just invited me to participate in illegal commodity trading, but no, apparently it was not the Washington Field Office's concern. The CIA would have been interested. However, when I later pitched the agency on a sting penetration of Cuban intelligence's embargo-busting, its interest waned after the FBI put up a fuss. The G-men did not want the CIA encroaching upon my activities.

When I telephoned Fernandez at the Cuban Interests Section and told him I had had a wonderful time in his country, he sounded puzzled. "Really?"

"Yeah," I said. "And I met somebody you know—Juan Hernandez."

"Oh, yeah, I know Juan!"

"You worked together in Venezuela, right?"

"That's right!"

"Juan and I had some meetings," I said. "The upshot is he's supposed to send something to me via diplomatic pouch. I don't think we want to get into this over the phone. Maybe we should discuss it over lunch?"

"Sure, we should."

Two weeks later, on April Fool's Day 1999, I met Luis Fernandez at his favorite Vietnamese restaurant. We both ordered chicken curry and Kirin beer. Then I gave Fernandez a copy of *Safe House*.

"Wow!" he said. Fernandez was even more impressed when I told him I'd just met Howard in Havana. The revelation worked like a can opener; Fernandez began to spill the beans. I've always felt that a person never learns much when he does the talking, and on top of that, most people love a good listener. So I listened while Fernandez blabbered his life story.

He studied international relations at Havana University (a class of fifteen); served in British Guiana, Venezuela (four years), and Mexico (five years); and had never been to Europe or Russia. He was surprised to be given a post in Washington, "a high honor for anyone," but for him especially, because he had no North American experience. Fernandez wasn't boastful but bewildered, one of his innate characteristics.

He told me he'd been in town eighteen months and had no clue how long his tour would last. "I went to my ambassador last week to ask about this," said Fernandez, "but I did not get an answer." Fernandez confided that he would much prefer to be back in Cuba, "with family, my neighbors, and my sea wall." In addition to the stress of long hours, he worried about saying the wrong thing and landing himself in trouble with Havana. Fernandez told me that his dual role in Washington was to track everything that appeared in the U.S. media about Cuba and to promote positive media coverage of Cuba. Regarding the latter, he gave me a manila envelope stuffed with good news about Cuba.

When I told him I enjoyed the food at La Bodeguita in Old Havana, Fernandez invited me to his home for a Cuban meal cooked by his wife. He seemed starved for a social life and appeared in no hurry to break from our lunch as we enjoyed hot tea and snifters of complimentary hazelnut liqueur. I finally signaled for the check and paid the tab, courtesy of the FBI.

A dinner invitation duly arrived by fax. Three weeks after our lunch, I appeared at the Fernandez home, an apartment at Kenwood Condominiums on River Road in Bethesda, with a bunch of flowers in one hand for Mrs. Fernandez and a fine bottle of Ridge Geyserville zinfandel in the other for my host. But my host was missing, delayed at the office. And Mrs. Fernandez, a reluctant hostess, spoke no English. She ushered me to the other on-time guest, Chip B., a former CIA officer who said he had recently led a delegation of political cartoonists to Cuba. Chip B. told me he had served with the agency in Beirut, El Salvador, and Vietnam and that he wanted to write a book on "the truth" about prisoners of war (POWs). He told me the Cubans were helping him research the POW issue.

Fernandez bumbled in about twenty minutes late, and suddenly his shoe-boxy, sparsely furnished apartment came alive with Cubans. One of them, Luis Abierno, latched onto me within thirty seconds.

An affable man, Abierno was of medium height, slender, and balding with dark hair and a trim mustache. He told me he was attached to the Foreign Relations Ministry and had just been separated from his wife and young child for a six-month tour in Washington. In contrast to the flaky Fernandez, Abierno seemed to be fast-track material. He took an armchair next to mine. He knew about my trip to Havana to meet Edward Howard and said that he would have met me there, but this posting—his first time outside of Cuba—had come up. "We've talked about you," said Abierno.

"You mean I'm famous in some circles?" I said.

Abierno nodded, smiling. "Yes, your name is around." He asked a few probing questions about publishing Howard's book.

"National Press had to remove a whole chapter," I said.

"Why?"

"The CIA insisted."

"Do you still have this chapter?" asked Abierno, who was too young to appreciate subtlety.

I shrugged. "Probably. Somewhere."

"Maybe you will give it to us." A smarmy smile crossed Abierno's face. "Maybe if we help you with a few things, you will let me see it."

"Maybe," I said.

Abierno asked what book projects I desired from Cuba.

"Robert Vesco," I said.

"But Robert Vesco is in prison," said Abierno.

"Yeah, I heard that from Juan Hernandez. You sure it's true?"

Abernio nodded and winked. "Jail in his house. But it is real prison, very strict. Why is Vesco's book of interest?"

"Books have been written about him," I said, "but he's never told his own story."

Abierno countered, "I doubt it would be good for U.S.-Cuba relations to bring attention to him." Vesco's presence in Cuba was a sore point between the two countries.

"Here's how we solve that sucker," I said. "Get Vesco to write his book for me. Then hand him back to the U.S. government just before it's published. Good for U.S.-Cuba relations, great publicity for the book. We sell a million copies, and everybody's happy, except Vesco. But who cares about him, right?"

Abierno studied me, amused. Chip B., listening in, regarded me with astonishment.

"If we can't do a Vesco book," I said, "what about Fidel Castro's memoirs?"

"Many writers want to do this," said Abierno.

"Of course," I said, "but how many can pull it off? Your biggest problem is finding somebody you can trust." I patted my chest. "And now *that's* solved."

Abierno said, "The timing is tough because of tense relations between our countries."

"You want to talk tension?" I said. "Try working with former KGB chairman Kryuchkov in Moscow while Yeltsin's trying to find any new reason to lock him away again. In any case, I'm in no hurry. Take your time with Castro." I then told Abierno of my interest, sparked by my meetings in Havana, in pursuing a book idea about a CIA spy ring of double agents.

"That would be interesting?" he asked.

"Sure," I said. "Sounds like a great story."

Abierno said he would check into this possibility and help me if he could. He added that he loved to read nonfiction espionage books and that he had just read David Wise's book about Aldrich Ames and also *The Blond Ghost*, David Corn's biography of Ted Shackley. When I told him that five or six editors produced 90 percent of all espionage nonfiction published in the United States, Abierno was riveted. "Do you know them?" he asked.

"Some of them."

Abierno processed this information quickly and made an astute remark about how such editors must possess tremendous knowledge. Looking piercingly into his eyes, I could tell little cogs in his brain were putting this idea to work. He then advanced two proposals of his own for me to chew on: "Maybe you could help us edit books written by Cuban writers, and maybe you can investigate things in America?"

Point two snagged my attention. "What things?" I asked.

"Black holes of information," said Abierno.

"My specialty," I said, "but right now I need to fill the black hole in my stomach." Abierno followed me to the buffet, where we filled our plates with Cuban delicacies and cut plans to meet again for a discussion on what information he needed.

I spoke with Luis Fernandez only briefly, during the last ten minutes of my visit to his home. He told me how very much he would like to visit Moscow, if only to see Lenin's Mausoleum in Red Square before the reformers snatched his embalmed corpse and hanged it from the Kremlin clock tower.

21

CUBAN COVERSION II

The Luis duo—Fernandez and Abierno—was sitting beneath an artificial palm tree in the men's favorite Vietnamese restaurant when I arrived to share curry with them.

Abierno drilled his eyes into mine. "So what have you been doing lately?"

"I've been to London and Monaco," I said. "It's sort of my beat."

"What were you doing there?" asked Abierno.

"Books."

"What kind of books?"

"Intrigue and lunacy."

"Not current events?" said Abierno.

"You have to be careful with current events," I said. "There's so much news these days that people overdose on what's going on from TV, newspapers, news magazines. Who needs to read a book about it? You've got to find offbeat subjects, the *hidden* truth, to make a book. And it's all about forecasting. You have to predict what will interest readers two or three years down the line, because that's how long it takes to research, write, and publish a book."

"What about those five editors?" asked Abierno.

"Excuse me?"

"The ones who publish spy books?"

"Ah, you have a good memory, Luis!" I looked at Fernandez. "At your party, I told Luis that only a handful of editors publish something like 90 percent of all nonfiction espionage books."

"I would like to meet them," said Abierno. "Maybe you can introduce us."

"Maybe," I said. "We need something to sell them first."

"The spy-ring book," said Abierno, "about the CIA and double agents in Cuba."

"I'm ready." I shrugged. "I'm still waiting to hear from Juan Hernandez about that and about that authorized biography of Castro."

Thus ensued a rehash of my book project meetings in Havana. But just as *my* instructions from the Washington Field Office had been diverted to focus on them, *their* instruction from Havana was apparently to focus on me and how I might be of use to the Cuban DGI.

"But you can investigate the Cuban spy-ring story in America, no?" said Abierno. The implication was that *I* could dig up information from the U.S. side and give it to them.

"Sure, that part's easy," I said. "But there's no point doing it until I'm assured access to the right material from Cuba."

"OK, we see," said Abierno.

A waiter took our order for three chicken curries, and Fernandez launched into a tedious spiel about how books like this one might only enflame tensions between our countries. This possibility, he said, contradicted Cuba's policy to promote normalization and not enflame tension.

"It doesn't matter," I said. "There won't *be* any normalization of relations till Castro's gone."

Fernandez gasped. "But nothing will change after Castro," he said with a vehemence I did not know he possessed. "Raúl will take over. Everything will be the same." My misconception, he insisted, was a result of propaganda disseminated by Cuban émigrés in Miami.

"Wishful thinking, amigo," I thought. "So what's the message you guys want to get out?" I posed. "Write it down, and maybe we can carve a book out of it."

"It's not so simple," said Fernandez.

"Then you're not doing your job right," I said. "You're in America. You've got to simplify the issues to get your message understood. Aren't you familiar with sound bites?"

A waiter served our food. Abierno attempted to follow my example and eat with chopsticks. He quickly tossed them aside.

"Tell me your objectives," I pressed.

"The problem," said Fernandez, "is three congressmen have put a lock on normalizing U.S.-Cuba relations. Wouldn't it be grand," Fernandez continued, "if somebody investigated them and exposed their back-door financial contributions?"

I nodded.

"Could you help us do this?" asked Abierno.

I plucked a notebook from my back pocket, tore out a page. "Write down their names."

Fernandez scribbled: *Ileana Ross (FL), Bob Menendez (NJ), Diaz-Balart (FL).* The Cuban DGI was asking me, an American, to investigate three U.S. congressmen.

"I need starting points," I said. When Fernandez and Abierno exchanged glances, I pressed, "Presumably, your country has already investigated these congressmen. Give me some leads."

"You can go to Cuba." Fernandez nodded knowingly. "They tell you a few things."

"OK," I said, "but before I go running off anywhere, show me what you've got so I know it's worth doing."

The Luis duo shared another glance. Abierno said, "We talk about this. and see what we can do. And remember, you owe me a chapter."

"A chapter?" I said.

"From the Ed Howard book."

"Luis, you do have a good memory!" I looked at Fernandez and pointed my thumb at Abierno. "He's going to be famous one day." I returned to Abierno. "That chapter is a funny story."

Abierno was all ears.

"We hired a ghostwriter to help Howard write his book," I said. "After the CIA ordered the classified stuff cut out, our ghost was so spooked, he burned his copy."

"And your copy?" said Abierno.

"Yeah, it's still around somewhere," I said. "I don't spook easily."

"What's in the chapter?"

"CIA operations in Russia."

"And Howard did not care that he had to lose this chapter?" asked Abierno.

"Ed was happy just to get his book published."

The check arrived. I grabbed it. Both Luises objected, but when I insisted, they said the next meal would be theirs. Fernandez handed me a copy of something called *Cuban Banking and Financial System.* "You will find this interesting," he said. (Wrong.) "You have friends in the media?" Fernandez wanted to expand his contact list.

"Plenty."

"You can introduce me?"

"Of course," I said. "We'll have a dinner party at a restaurant, your treat."

My next meeting, two months later, was one-on-one with Luis Abierno at Biddy Mulligan's, a bar inside the Doyle Washington Hotel at Dupont Circle. Abierno had received his marching orders and would soon return to Havana. I told Abierno I wanted to know about Felipe Pérez Roque, who had just become Cuba's foreign minister. Pérez Roque was the flavor of the season to succeed Castro one day.

Abierno confided that he had attended technical college with Pérez Roque and that Pérez Roque had scored a five, or the highest rating, in every subject, every term. They'd also worked together in youth groups and knew each other socially as well as professionally. Abierno questioned the notion of a Pérez Roque succession, not because the foreign minister lacked intelligence, but because he lacked charisma. "He knows how to put all the right words together," said Abierno, "but he cannot deliver them effectively."

"Is there a book in Pérez Roque's story?" I asked.

Abierno said it would be difficult to ask Pérez Roque to participate in anything that highlighted himself. Self-promotion, he confided, was the kiss of death in Castro's Cuba.

22

THE DINNER PARTY

Meanwhile, so far as the Edward Lee Howard case was concerned, things looked bad—not for Howard, but for the United States of America: FBI special agent John H. opted for early retirement, effective the first week of September 1999. He would not have folded ahead of schedule had headquarters not signaled that the Justice Department would never lift the "related conflict" holding up Howard's rendition. John H. had intended to remain at his desk until the Howard case was resolved.

But a couple years earlier, John H.'s boss, Jim S., who had provided enthusiastic support for capturing Howard, had left Albuquerque for a U.S. Embassy legate position in Athens, Greece. Not long after that, Jim S. had retired from the bureau. Bob G., the gung ho assistant U.S. attorney, had also left public service and gone into private practice. Once John H. retired, he would be out of the loop, too. He'd be exempt from learning anything more about the Howard case, which would be absorbed by another Albuquerque-based special agent for whom Howard would only be a nuisance and not a priority. Although I did not realize it at the time, I would become the de facto advocate for keeping the Cheese Family aware both that the Howard case still existed and that it was still important.

The day I could no longer phone John H. with new developments evolving from the Howard case was terribly sad for me. We had made a good team. He was an extraordinary special agent. Till I started working with other agents, I did not appreciate just how skilled John H. was in what he called "Bu biz." In his low-key manner, John H. knew how to work the system with finesse. He could walk the labyrinthine headquarters, take the knocks, and get back up for a return bout with never a sour word about anyone. He was one of the few who knew how to operate within a bureaucracy that had become ridiculously disconnected. Everyone I worked with thereafter paled in comparison to the soft-spoken but savvy John H.

But life goes on. So did my Cuban operation. It was still administrated by the FBI's Albuquerque office but managed by the Washington Field Office.

At Luis Fernandez's request, I organized a dinner party on October 1 to introduce him to news media people: a British journalist of Indian descent, and a producer from NBC News—both of whom were unaware of my FBI role—and Rick K., whom I'd signed on as an asset in my Cuban coversion. The venue, as usual, was Fernandez's favorite Vietnamese restaurant. Luis Abierno had left Washington and returned to Havana. So in his place Fernandez brought along Reuben de Wong Corchou, who had arrived one week earlier from Cuba. Corchou was better dressed than Fernandez was, but he was so somber in his Soviet-era spectacles and slicked-back dark hair, I almost asked if I could hire him out for Halloween to scare the kids.

Corchou's grim and dour personality was totally devoid of humor. He did not smile and seemingly could not laugh. Within two minutes it became clear this guy was the dinner guest from hell. Getting him to talk was harder than pulling teeth; it was more like enduring a root canal.

Under pressure from me to loosen his tongue, Corchou divulged that he had studied English and Cuban history at Havana University. Then he taught these subjects for ten years at the same institution before joining the foreign ministry and working there through the 1990s. As for foreign travel, Corchou had taken a grand tour of the Soviet Union in 1981 and spent much of 1998 in Tokyo, during which time he also visited China. This tour in Washington was his first time in the United States.

Although he professed to be a staunch Marxist ideologue, Corchou wore a Rolex Submariner wristwatch. I reckoned this extravagant timepiece was a counterfeit bought on the cheap in Asia.

I asked Corchou and Fernandez to speculate what Cuba would be like five years from now. Both men seemed at a loss and didn't respond. When the British journalist asked Fernandez what he thought of Castro, Fernandez choked up. After he composed himself, he said, "He is my father." ("Does this mean we should add Luis's name to the list of Fidel's illegitimate children?" I flippantly tacked onto my FBI report.) I sensed that Fernandez was showing off for Corchou, as if he thought the new guy was in town to audit his behavior.

The British journalist, a loquacious chap, asked both Cubans, "So what's your problem with the United States?"

Fernandez straightened up and said, "Two words." As Fernandez poised to continue, I thought, "This should be good. What two words could possibly sum it all up?" But, alas, Fernandez had mistaken this expression to mean something else, because what actually spewed from his mouth was a two *thousand*–word diatribe on how Cuban people are deprived of food and medicine because of U.S. policies.

"Why don't you do what China does and hire Henry Kissinger to lobby in Washington?" asked the British journalist.

Fernandez did not understand the question. The Brit rephrased it, but Fernandez still didn't get it. I re-jiggered the question myself.

"Ah," said Fernandez, "we have no money for this. We are effective in our own way."

The British journalist then asked about Che Guevara's standing in contemporary Cuba. Corchou, the historian, fielded this question by reciting Che's birthday: "June 14, 1928." For a moment, I thought he might stand and sing "Comandante Che Guevara," but, mercifully, this did not happen.

I privately asked Fernandez if my package from Juan Hernandez had arrived. Earlier, Hernandez had confirmed by e-mail from Havana that he had finally sent by diplomatic pouch the material he had promised seven months earlier. Fernandez said he had talked to Hernandez on the phone, and the material had been sent to someone in the United States named Pedro. When I asked who Pedro was, Fernandez shook his head. He did not know. Nor did he know whether Pedro was going to contact me or what.

When the bill came, Fernandez did not remember that this dinner party had been his idea nor that it was his turn to treat.

I next met Fernandez, whom I'd code-named Flakester, four weeks later, on October 30, at a Starbucks in Chevy Chase. He trudged in bleary eyed, wearing a Nike windbreaker and a black polo shirt and sporting a freshly trimmed crew cut. He launched into another harangue about how a small minority of anti-Castro Cubans in Miami and three congressmen could

"Can't chew?'

"His mouth is a mess," said Howard. "Not because of rotted teeth, but because of rotted gums. He's not socializing much. He didn't even join me for Thanksgiving."

I then asked after Mila. I'd learned from the bureau—not Ed—that Howard had married her.

"We had a fight two weeks ago," said Howard. "I have a calendar, and whenever we have an argument, I write *MF* in the day's square. Of course, a lot of squares are filled with MF. Mila found the calendar one day, and she asked me, 'What does MF mean?' I told her it stands for 'mind fuck.' And, of course, that was grounds for a whole new argument." Howard told me he preferred Lena Orlova for company, and he continued to juggle both. "Mila's father is retired KGB," Howard continued, "and her mother works for the FSB [internal security]. I came home once and found Mila on the phone with her father's SVR contact, and I got annoyed. I think she might be reporting on me."

Howard briefed me on his KGB friends' latest intelligence on how a former KGB agent named Vladimir Putin had managed to succeed Boris Yeltsin as the president of Russia. Putin had escaped a scandal when he was a top aide to the mayor of St. Petersburg, then decamped to Moscow, and cultivated a close relationship with Yeltsin through Anatoly Chubais, a financial whiz who had bilked the World Bank out of billions of dollars. Yeltsin's family members had grown to like and trust Putin; they promoted the notion of a Putin presidency as an insurance policy for the ailing Yeltsin. Their primary concern was who would best protect their fortune and safety after Yeltsin's term. Putin gave the right assurances, and a deal was struck.

I then asked Howard for news on Igor Batamirov, the former counterintelligence chief who had been so keen to write about "the psychology of betrayal."

"It's the current climate," said Howard, meaning the Putin regime. "Batamirov sees shadows behind shadows. He's very cautious." Howard told me Batamirov would not visit Washington "at this time" (on the heels of NATO's involvement in Serbia) because of how his former employer might perceive such a trip. "He'll meet you again," said Howard, "but only in Moscow."

"And Prelin? Any new book projects?"

manipulate U.S. policy toward Cuba. Again, he implied that they were funded by a mysterious source.

"I sent your earlier request for leads," said Fernandez, "to Havana." His boss's reply: instruct Eringer to get started, show him results, and then he'd help fill the holes. "You go to Cuba," he said. "We give you facilities. But I have to be careful because the Cuban Interests Section is not supposed to assist writers."

As we parted, I said, "Happy Halloween. Go spook a few people tomorrow."

Almost six weeks later, I still hadn't heard from "Pedro." I phoned Fernandez, who was sick with flu.

"Who's Pedro?" he asked, preempting me.

"Exactly," I said. "What have you heard?"

"Nothing, man. Who was that guy who was supposed to send that package?" Fernandez was flakier than a dandruff attack in a blizzard.

"Juan Hernandez."

"Right, Hernandez," said Ferndandez. "I will phone Hernandez."

"Excellent," I said. "Phone Hernandez. Find out who the hell Pedro is."

23

CLOAK AND CORKSCREW

I set off again in November 1999 cloaked in a black raincoat and carrying a Laguiole corkscrew in my pocket. It could be useful as a weapon, being more versatile than a dagger, but more important, it could uncork a bottle of Château Lafite-Rothschild.

My driver slyly cut around Thanksgiving Sunday traffic at Dulles International Airport, detouring through the long-term car park and dropping me at the arrivals area instead of departures. This move had the added benefit of complicating any possible surveillance. Not that I thought anyone would be watching me this early, but surveillance would likely kick in sooner or later, based on the scope of my operations, some of which are not revealed in this book.

I found the Swissair desk and checked in for the nightly transatlantic flight to Zurich. When making a connection in Europe, there is no better hub than Zurich, where devoted Swiss timekeepers ensure strict adherence to schedules. Its airport is uncomplicated compared to, say, London Heathrow or Paris Charles de Gaulle (CDG) International Airport, where one must jog three miles for a connection after landing thirty minutes late because of dense air traffic.

I settled into Swissair's club lounge. True to national character, the Christmas tree was bedecked in gold. I boarded the Airbus 330 and took my first-class sleeper seat, replete with an eiderdown quilt. Then I slid into a solid four-hour slumber before the jet glided into Zurich at 8:35 a.m.

Not twenty minutes later, on an earlier flight than that posted on my ticket, I belted myself into a second aircraft destined for Geneva. It is always a pleasure to alter flight arrangements at the last minute while on

spy missions. So, ahead of schedule, I hopped the Swiss Alps whi[...] on my Walkman to my personal rallying cry for sub rosa tasks[...] *Bouncy* by the High Llamas.

Geneva was as gloomy and austere as its Calvinist founders. Th[...] ing featured the kind of cold that seeps into your bone marrow ar[...] your soul from within. By contrast, the elegant Hôtel Beau Rivage st[...] comed me warmly. A fifty-foot Christmas tree decked in red and gol[...] ments adorned its atrium lobby, which offered gracious hospitality c[...] with soft, comfortable furnishings.

A message awaited me at the check-in desk: "Welcome! I shall be[...] to see you and plan to come to the BR reception at 12:30. Edward."

I unpacked in room 223, showered, and ventured into Geneva's clam[...] shades of gray. First, I ventured to Fina for a fistful of Cuban Montecristo[...] 5 cigars. Then I went to the Chocolaterie des Bergues for a mug of the worl[...] creamiest hot cocoa.

This respite set me up for Ed Howard who, as always, arrived at m[...] hotel on the minute, the one characteristic he shared with John H. To m[...] surprise, Howard had lost about thirty-five pounds. He said he felt good, but[...] I thought he looked like a corpse. His face was gaunt and drawn, with a pasty[...] complexion and dull eyes. You need bulk for a life in Russia, not just as[...] insulation from the cold, but also because you never know where your next meal is coming from. In Howard's case, this insecurity was a reality: he'd lost most of his money in Russia's stock market collapse, and his mood reflected his appearance. As a result of the weight loss and without money to spare for a new wardrobe, Howard's clothes—blue jeans, a brown sweater, and a trench coat—were two sizes too big on him.

As we set off along Quai du Mont-Blanc, surveillance cut in—a pair of Swiss or Russian young men of military disposition in plainclothes. I made them; Howard was oblivious or, more likely, didn't care.

We crossed the Quai des Bergues pedestrian bridge over Lake Léman and entered Mövenpick Restaurant. I ordered filet de perche, a Geneva specialty, and crispy shoestring fries while Howard chose vegetarian lasagna and chain-smoked Salem cigarettes throughout.

"How is George Blake?" I asked.

"He can't chew," said Howard.

"I asked him before coming here," said Howard. "He said, 'What about Kryuchkov's book?'"

"It's coprolite," I said.

"What?"

"Petrified shit."

Howard chuckled. "The KGB is back with a vengeance under Putin. Prelin's gotten busy and has a job with the Duma."

We moved on to the Cubans. Howard was surprised and disappointed that I had not received any material from Juan Hernandez in Havana. On a trip to Cuba two months earlier, Howard had talked to Señor Deema of the DGI about my project. "Deema will be outraged to hear you're still waiting," said Howard.

Aside from a ten-day trip to Mexico City and Cancun in May, Howard said he wasn't traveling much. More and more, he liked to spend time at his dacha, and he had converted one room into a gym. Plus Howard's ruined finances and declining business had turned him reclusive. "I'm going to give it three months," he said. "If I can't salvage my business, I'll dissolve it. And I may take you up on your offer to do another book, this one about a grand tour of the United States."

"How's that?" This definitely caught my attention.

"We'll meet at a prearranged hotel in Ciudad Juárez, Mexico," mused Howard. "About ten o'clock on a Saturday night we'll cross the border into El Paso, Texas. That part's easy." Once inside the United States, we could take a cross-country jaunt and write it up as a humorous travel book, *Wanted Spy Fools FBI!* "There's no other place I'd like to visit but the States," continued Howard, "for one final look at my old haunts *and* to see the Grand Canyon."

Early that evening, we met in the bar of my hotel. Sitting in an overstuffed armchair, sipping white burgundy, I glimpsed Howard through a window as he approached the hotel entrance. Beneath a streetlamp, in his baggy clothes, Howard looked like an old man, a shadow of his former self. He sauntered in and ordered a Coke.

"Have a real drink if you want," I said. "You don't have to stay on the wagon for me."

Howard declined. "I only drink on my birthday and New Year's." Howard then told me he'd heard that "the guy running my case, John H., has retired."

"What does that *mean* to you?" I asked.

"The FBI doesn't want me anymore," Howard replied. "It would cost forty thousand a year to incarcerate me." Howard said he'd heard this information from his KGB friends who, in turn, had gotten it from American sources. "But they're out there," Howard added, "like that old movie *Butch Cassidy and the Sundance Kid*. You ever see that?"

I said, "Yes, I have."

"There's a point in the movie," said Howard, "where Robert Redford looks back at the people tracking him and he says that classic line about those Pinkerton detectives: 'Who *are* those guys?' That's me. I'm saying, 'Who *are* those guys?'"

One of *those* guys was not out there, but in here, right next to him, noting Howard's every word. It pleased me that an American traitor felt his trackers would never give up. And more so, his trackers were running circles around him.

We then taxied to Geneva's Old Town, to the clubby eaterie Les Armures and ordered raclette.

As Howard dipped pieces of bread into molten cheese, he recounted an experience from his recent business trip to Rome. "I took confession at the Vatican. I told the priest I'd broken just about every rule. The priest asked, 'You haven't killed anyone, have you?' When I said no," Howard's voice quavered, "the priest told me there's still hope." Howard was obviously in denial over Adolf Tolkachev's execution, a direct consequence of his treachery. This moment was the nearest Howard ever came, in my presence, to showing remorse.

Afterward we strolled down to the "spy bar" inside Hôtel des Bergues. I smoked a Cuban cigar and sipped Armagnac. Taken together, it was my favorite jet-lag remedy. Howard finished his pack of Salems over hot chocolate.

The next day, Howard came by the hotel mid-morning for money. He signed a receipt, as usual, for "services rendered." "At what point," I wondered, "would the Russians suspect him of *tripling*?"

We went back to Mövenpick for an early lunch, and Howard confided to me about a stock market scam in which he participated with some Australian friends. It worked like this: the Sydney-based broker would choose a penny stock and put the word out to Howard and other international friends that the stock was hot. Suddenly, orders would come streaming in from all over the world. The Australian financial community would take note and start investing in the stock. "I've seen this work four or five times," said Howard.

I plucked a Morgan silver dollar from my pocket and gave it to Howard. "For good luck," I said. He appeared touched.

We strolled across a bridge to a souvenir shop where Howard bought a CyberTool Swiss Army knife as a Christmas gift for a Russian friend. That's where we parted, in rue du Mont Blanc. I did not know it then, but it was the last time I would see Edward Lee Howard.

24

THE BEDMATES

John H. would have seized upon Edward Lee Howard's plan to steal into the States for a surreptitious visit to his native New Mexico, but John H. was gone. And no one at the Washington Field Office or FBI Headquarters wanted to do anything more about Howard than pile paper, the bureaucrat's favorite pastime. In fact, FBI Albuquerque had so little interest left in Howard's case that the folks there breached protocol and transferred administration of me to the Washington Field Office, which had a greater stake in my other operations.

Enter Mike S., a well-meaning, hard-working special agent charged with processing the product of my various sting operations. He and I met on January 8 at Chef Geoff's, a restaurant on New Mexico Avenue in the leafy, affluent northwest Washington neighborhood of Wesley Heights. The special agent summed up the current thinking in his field office about Edward Howard: "Nobody's going to get into trouble for not doing anything on this, but somebody might if he does something and it goes wrong." He was conveying the bureaucratic sentiments of his Big Cheese, James "Tim" Caruso, the national security chief at the Washington Field Office. To me it stank like overripe Camembert.

"I thought the FBI always got its man," I said.

When Mike S. shrugged, I thought, "Guess not." Then I presented my case: "The bureau should catch Ed Howard. It sends the right message to any future would-be traitors: 'it may take us fifteen years, but we'll never forget you and we'll nail your ass.' So what if some U.S. attorney can't win in court? That's his problem, which he's trying to shirk. The bureau's job is to catch

Howard and throw him in the clink. If he walks later, like O. J. [Simpson] did, at least we did our part."

Mike S. shrugged again.

If the Washington Field Office smelled cheesy, Igor Prelin reeked even worse, and that was just by e-mail. Prelin had harnessed a new book and asked me to meet in London with him and the book's author, a former colleague named Stalian "Alexey" Sokolov.

When I checked with the FBI about a meeting, the agents said, "Sure, why not?" By this time, I managed a cluster of ever-evolving operations without geographic restraint and earned enough clout to set my own agenda. And so I was off again, to London, just two months after my Zurich rendezvous with Edward Howard.

Prelin and his friend Sokolov waited for me in the small lobby of the old Coburg Hotel on Bayswater Road. I'd made dinner reservations around the corner at the Royal China restaurant.

We sat, studied the menus and each other, and ordered hot sake. I congratulated Prelin on his foresight: he had predicted a Putin presidency two years before anyone could have known.

"Yes," Prelin chuckled, brushing modesty aside. "I got your message from Edward. You remember our conversation. I say it will be a name nobody knows. We at KGB engineer Putin to power."

"How?" I asked.

"Finally, a deal with Yeltsin," said Prelin. "Yeltsin receives immunity from corruption. But after he dies, we go after all Yeltsin relatives."

"Another Russian tradition lives," I thought.

Said Prelin, "Putin's power base is from GRU [Main Intelligence Directorate of the armed forces] and FSB. He will increase intelligence presence around him from 40 to 80 percent."

I asked about my old uncle Vlad Kryuchkov. Prelin said that the former KGB chairman had been in the hospital for knee surgery. He had become an unofficial adviser to Putin, counseling the new Russian president to take strict control of the government and build a strong Russia.

Alexey Sokolov nodded. At sixty-nine years of age, or eight years older than Prelin, Sokolov had a saggy horse's face and a perpetually gloomy expression. This trip was Sokolov's first visit to London.

Hot sake arrived. I poured, we toasted. Soon after, three bowls of wonton soup appeared before us, followed by prawns with honey and black bean sauce, scallops with asparagus, stir-fried Dover sole, and two bowls of steamed rice. Following my example, both KGB veterans attempted to use chopsticks. They fumbled their food and turned our table into a war zone. When they finally gave up on the chopsticks, the two Russians did not request cutlery but switched to using their soup ladles. I concluded competency in using other cultures' eating utensils should be a prerequisite for spy work.

In between swallows, Prelin raised the reason for their trip, Sokolov's book. They pitched it as a nonfiction exposé of Oleg Kalugin, the former KGB First Directorate chief who had settled in the United States.

"Cool," I said. "What's the story on Kalugin? Why won't he return to Moscow?"

"If he comes back to Moscow," said Prelin, "he will be executed within twenty-four hours."

Sokolov looked quizzically at his buddy. "But we no longer have death penalty, Igor."

"No matter." Prelin was vehement. "Execution within twenty-four hours."

"So you'd like to kill Kalugin?" I said.

"Of course," Prelin said matter-of-factly.

"Do you know where he lives?" I asked.

"Washington," said Prelin. "Vienna. It is in Virginia, near Washington, no?"

"Do you have his address?"

"Of course," said Prelin. "He lives with two daughters."

"Would you ever try to kill him in the United States?" I asked.

Prelin shrugged and smiled. "Who knows?"

Back to Sokolov's book, he told me it was already written and published in Russia. In it, he claimed Kalugin was personally responsible for every Russian spy case, including that of Aldrich Ames, that went south on the KGB over a forty-year period.

"Oh, come on," I said.

"I tell you," Prelin whined, "Kalugin gives Ames up. We know this."

Sokolov nodded. This KGB veteran had done one four-year stint in Washington in the late 1960s, then spent the rest of his career at headquarters in

Moscow analyzing the U.S. intelligence services. He did not tell me—I already knew—why he never served overseas again: Sokolov's superiors had discovered he was a closet homosexual, and they did not wish to see him fall to honey-trap blackmail scenarios. Kalugin apparently outed Sokolov, thereby ruining his career.

Sokolov told me that he had personally recruited John Walker, the NSA spy, and that the English-language version of his book would detail this case. "I once recruited American couple working for the State Department in one elevator ride," Sokolov boasted. "Twelve floors. By the time we reach bottom, in one minute, I recruit."

As for the mechanics regarding Sokolov's book, Prelin offered George Blake's services as a translator. "Ah, but we have MI5 behind us," said Prelin, looking over his shoulder. "I know them!"

Sokolov, who was facing me, craned his neck. "Where, Igor? Where you see?"

"This is like a Bullwinkle cartoon with Boris and Natasha," I mused to myself. I didn't even turn around.

Seated next to me, Prelin said with glee, "I am kidding!"

I settled the check. Prelin requested that I walk them to their hotel, about fifteen minutes away, where they had some gifts for me.

As we walked along Bayswater Road, Prelin occasionally slipped his arm through mine. Soon we arrived at the Lancaster Court Hotel. When Prelin suggested we go up to the room the Russians shared "to drink vodka," I declined. Instead, I offered to wait in the small lobby while they grabbed their gifts and to take the party to my hotel, the Lowndes, which had a cozy lounge and a decent bar.

Fifteen minutes later, a taxi deposited us on Lowndes Street. Inside the hotel lounge, Prelin ordered a cocktail of his own creation: gin, Campari, and tonic. He instructed Sokolov to drink the same. I opted for Armagnac and went to my room to find a Cuban cigar. On my return, Sokolov reached into a plastic bag from a duty-free shop at Sheremetyevo Airport and handed me my gifts: a copy of his Russian book, *Spy Story*, in which he had written "To Robert Eringer, who are going to know more about spies than I do, with the best regard of the author . . . ," his signature, and the date; a bottle of KCTOK vodka (best for cleaning ovens); and a jar of caviar.

"Gee, thanks, Alexey." I snipped the tip of a Montecristo No. 5, lit it, puffed, and then consulted my Armagnac. That's when Prelin offered me two million dollars for the CIA's file on Aldrich Ames. "How could I possibly get the Ames file?" I laughed.

Prelin shrugged. "Any way you can. If you get, two million dollars."

I asked Prelin, "Are you still chief of the retired KGB officers association?"

Prelin confirmed that he remained head of this association and that it had more than four thousand members. He whipped out a red, faux leather, gold-embossed card. "This is my membership."

I studied Prelin's card, membership number 259, with a twenty-year-old photo of himself. "Nice."

"You want?" asked Prelin.

"What do you mean?" I asked.

"I make you honorary member of FIVA, retired KGB association. For services to Motherland."

"Really?"

"You will receive card exactly like card carried by Edward and George," said Prelin.

"And you get nice badge, too," added Sokolov. "Five stars."

"Is that how many years in prison I'd get if the FBI finds out?" I said.

"No more than twenty years," cracked Prelin.

Sokolov suggested that I share with him the byline of his Kalugin book.

"But you've already written it," I said. "You've done all the work."

Prelin jumped in. "It would be better for the book to have an American author, no?"

"No, you moron," I thought, "no Western author is going to give your crap book credibility on my watch." I said, "I'll think about it."

The next day, I hosted a lunch for Prelin, Sokolov, and Nicholas Davies, a British nonfiction book author. All I'd told Davies, whom I'd known since he was the foreign editor of the *Daily Mirror* years earlier, was that I was developing book projects with this pair of Russians. Davies had sponsored them, at my request, on their visa applications to visit Britain. We met at the Lowndes and walked to Zaffarano, a high-class Italian restaurant two doors away.

Prelin deliberately sat with his back to the wall. "Ah, this is good," he exulted. "I can see the door!"

"Tell me if anyone from MI5 comes in," I deadpanned, but my sarcasm was lost on him.

We got off to a faltering start. Davies spoke too fast for the Russians, though they pretended to understand him when they obviously did not. Clearly we needed lubrication. I ordered a bottle of pinot grigio.

Conversation centered on Davies. The Russians had done their homework and knew he'd written a slew of books on British royalty, primarily about Princess Diana. Sokolov, sitting across from me, said little. He looked at me steadily. A propos of nothing, he said, "It is true you join Ku Klux Klan?"

"Yep," I replied. "I still have my robe and hood. Of course," I added, "I did it to expose the Klan in a British newspaper."

Another question from Sokolov: "What is meaning 'dream bed'?" Apparently, Sokolov had thought the term meant twin beds. Consequently, he and Prelin had to double up as bedmates in a standard-size double bed. Such imagery was most unappetizing. And then our meal arrived.

Digging into salmon over a bed of spinach, Prelin reported gleefully that during his career he had never worked with a female KGB agent. He said women were no good to work with. Sokolov nodded in agreement.

After Davies departed, my two Russian guests and I retired to the Lowndes lounge. I coached Sokolov regarding what to write as an addendum to the English-language edition of his book. For his American readers, I told him to cover four points. First, he had to address the Aldrich Ames case. Second, if, as he said, his job was to analyze U.S. intelligence services, he should state what his assessments were. Next, because no one, I pointed out, had yet written a book on Russian intelligence since the KGB's disintegration, he should explain how the new services—the SVR and FSB—worked. Finally, he had to include a strong chapter on how the Russian intelligence apparatus engineered Vladimir Putin's ascension to the presidency.

Sokolov agreed. Prelin concurred that this would help the book. All that remained was determining the payment for George Blake's translation services. They promised to check with Blake and let me know the cost.

"And I will send you KGB card," said Prelin.

Six weeks later a large envelope arrived by FedEx. It had been opened and resealed with U.S. Customs tape. Inside was my own red, faux leather, gold-embossed KGB card, membership number 4038, and a five-star badge. It was official. I'd been adopted by the KGB.

25

GET SMART

Alexey Sokolov sent me an e-mail saying that George Blake had agreed to translate Sokolov's published book plus 180 pages of additional material—topics of interest to me and, by extension, the FBI—for nine thousand dollars. (A few years later, Blake told me that he had actually declined this opportunity, because he had wanted nothing to do with Igor Prelin.) But then there was a hiccup on my end. The FBI's Washington Field Office was experiencing a budget crunch. And *I* was the one they wanted to crunch. I heard about it from Special Agent Mike S. over lattes at Starbucks in northwest Washington on March 10, 2000. I could scarcely believe my ears.

The problem was the Washington Field Office was funding my operations, but aside from my Cuban coversion excursions, the office did not benefit directly from my work. Word was the office's national security chief, James Caruso, had gotten tired of subsidizing data destined for headquarters (that is, positive intelligence from Russia), for Albuquerque (information on Edward Lee Howard), and for Philadelphia (another sting operation in the works). Mike S. told me the Washington Field Office considered me "too diverse." So without consulting headquarters, Philadelphia, or Albuquerque, Caruso's solution was to terminate our arrangement. "You're expensive," said Mike S.

"I'm good," I pointed out. "And you guys knew the cost when you took me over from Albuquerque."

Mike S. shrugged.

"Am I supposed to stand everything down now?" I asked.

"I've been instructed to tell you to stop billing hours effective immediately," said Mike S., "so that would be the obvious result."

"That's ridiculous," I said. "Am I supposed to just ignore everybody I've been rusing?"

Mike S. agreed it was ridiculous, but the Washington Field Office had to expect that a comprehensive stand-down would necessarily result from cutting off my funds.

I considered the situation. "Here's what we'll do," I said. "The Sokolov op is killed, because George Blake wants nine grand to translate, and you don't have nine grand. The Batamirov lure is killed, too, because he's expecting me to pay for his trip to Washington, once he decides to visit. As for the others, it's just my time. I'll keep everything running in passive mode, and I'll keep track of my hours. If your budget 'un-crunches,' you take care of me. If it doesn't un-crunch by October 1 [the beginning of the new federal government fiscal year, six months off], I'm done, and you're under no obligation for my time between now and then."

Mike S. said the arrangement was cool with him but would have to be at my own discretion.

"Trust me," I said, "everything I do is at my own discretion." Truth be known, that's part of what irked the Washington Field Office.

I plodded on in passive mode. But I had my own back come summer, when I lunched with the House Intelligence Committee's chief investigator. He was an old friend who, of course, had no idea I'd been working secretly for the bureau. I asked him, "What would you say if we could have caught Edward Lee Howard and didn't?"

My friend was appalled. "Do you mind if I go see FBI director Louis Freeh and see what he has to say?"

"Do I mind?" I said. "It's about time *somebody* came up with a straight answer." And I thought to myself, "Why not take this to the Biggest Cheese?" After all, Director Freeh had experienced sting and undercover operations up close and personally. As a young FBI special agent in the mid-1970s, he had infiltrated the Mafia in New York and had been nicknamed "Mad Dog" because he liked to buck the bureaucracy.

At four thirty in the afternoon of September 8, my friend and the Intelligence Committee's chief counsel buttonholed Freeh. The FBI director told them he'd heard that somebody from his shop had gotten close to Edward Howard, but no one had ever told him Howard wanted to visit New Mexico.

In principle, Director Freeh expressed both great interest in capturing Howard and surprise that his organization did not actively pursue this lead. Director Freeh, my friend later told me, went on to say that he knew how his bureau treated those who went around the back door and did not follow the chain of command, however disconnected. He was also appreciative that my friend had dealt with this matter in a positive, nonpartisan manner. For that reason, the director promised to handle this situation with great discretion.

The opposite occurred. Director Freeh flushed at the top and sent sewage scudding everywhere. Neil Gallagher, the assistant director for national security, caught it full in the face (as deserved) before it cascaded downward. Freeh's response also soiled James Caruso (equally deserved) and mystified middle managers. Then Special Agent Mike S. caught some crap and brought it to my attention at our usual Starbucks. He wanted to know if I had—horror of horrors—disclosed my relationship with the FBI to somebody on the House Intelligence Committee.

"Yup," I replied. "Sure did."

"This isn't good," said Mike S. "Some of our middle managers will take this to mean you're not a trustworthy guy."

I looked Mike S. squarely in the eye. "Tell your middle managers to go fuck themselves. They should do their jobs and catch Ed Howard."

From my experience, the middle managers' role at headquarters was to hammer down special agents. First, they made them travel to Washington and walk the labyrinthine corridors to try and find the right new person who must sign off on some aspect of a new twist. Then they had to endure several rounds of cynical meetings designed to make any new initiative appear somehow to put the bureau at risk of—egads!—embarrassing itself. And even if the plan survived the first dozen hurdles, the managers then sent the special agents back to the boonies and gave the plan to a gaggle of Justice Department attorneys to quash, just so they would have one less risk to worry about.

I had watched John H. walk this walk. With exceptional patience and savvy, he had been the sole advocate for keeping the Howard case alive.

"You're looking at the new advocate," I told Mike S.

26

CUBAN COVERSION III

Despite Edward Howard's best efforts with the Cuban DGI's Señor Deema in Havana and Edouard Prensa in Moscow, I neither heard from the mysterious Pedro nor received written material from Juan Hernandez in Havana. And since I'd been operating in the passive mode, I hadn't pushed it.

In December, my landline Caller ID tagged an incoming call as "Cuban Interests." I picked up the phone.

"Hello, man," said Luis Fernandez. "Where are you?"

I rolled my eyes. *He* was calling *me*. "Fernandez wasn't just a flake. He was a *fluke* of nature," I thought. I said, "I'm in Washington, the entertainment capital of the world."

Fernandez howled with laughter. Then he got down to business. "Can you meet me tomorrow?"

I supposed so.

Flakester looked heavier than when I'd last seen him, ages ago. In his black blazer, white shirt, and navy blue slacks, he looked like a penguin as he waddled toward me in a Starbucks near his home on River Road. The first problem with Fernandez is that he's a bore. The second problem is that he's whiny. But the FBI was paying again, retroactive to when they'd crunched me nine months earlier, so I had to endure this Cuban. This time, however, Flakester did not immediately jump into a tirade about the United States. Instead, he told me he'd had a communiqué from Luis Abierno in Havana. They were ready for me.

"Ready for what?" I asked. So much time had passed, I'd forgotten.

"To do your books," said Fernandez. "Abierno asks you to come to Havana for few days."

I told Flakester, "I'm busy now with other projects."

"Pity," said Fernandez, because he wanted me to help him whip the U.S. media into a frenzy over an anti-Castro Cuban named Luis Posada Carriles.

"Who?"

"He's a terrorist!" cried Fernandez. "We want him extradited to Cuba." Flakester worked himself into blathering apoplexy over Carriles's alleged connections to the anti-Castro Cuban conspirators in Miami, the CIA, and the Iran-contra affair, in that order.

Six weeks later, Fernandez wanted to see me again. He'd gained another ten pounds since Christmas and had morphed from a penguin into a walrus. I bought him a fattening latte.

"Luis Abierno asks when you come to Havana."

"Why?" I said.

"They are very interested in the project you suggested."

I told Fernandez, "I'm busy, but maybe I'd send Rick K. in my place."

"But we don't know Rick," Flakester whined. "We know *you.*

"Sure you know Rick," I said. "You met him at that dinner party we had. He's a good writer. I'd assign him anyway, so it's better if he makes the trip and evaluates the material you have in Havana."

"Maybe I meet Rick again," said Fernandez.

Next, on the Flakester's agenda was the real reason he had phoned me three times to arrange this rendezvous. He handed me a photocopy of an invitation to an evening reception inaugurating the Washington, D.C., offices of a brand-new outfit calling itself the Free Cuba Embassy. It was going to take place February 6 at seven o'clock. Flakester launched into a spluttering fit about the audacious absurdity of such a so-called embassy. Then he made his pitch: "We'd like you to attend this reception, meet some people."

"What people?"

"Jorge Garcia," said Fernandez. "He is boss of this group." Flakester also requested that I ingratiate myself with Garcia and infiltrate the Cuban American National Foundation (CANF). "Identify the guys," he said. "Get to know the environment."

Fernandez recounted the story of a recent flight he took to Washington from Miami, and he had found himself seated near Jorge Garcia. "I prepared myself psychologically," said Fernandez, a solemn expression on his droll face. Garcia had recognized Fernandez from the Cuban Interests Section and struck up a conversation. Flakester probably stained his shorts.

Once he had my tentative agreement to spy on the opposition for him, Flakester agreed to provide me with the names of others, beside Garcia, whom I should target. That very afternoon, Fernandez included them in an e-mail to me:

1. Jorge Mas Santos, Chairman
2. Denny Hays, Executive Director in Washington
3. Joe Garcia, Vice President
4. Feliciano Foyo, Treasury
5. Alberto Hernandez Sarduy, Staffer
6. Jose Hernandez Calvo, President of CANF
7. Ninosca Perez Castellon, Speak Person
8. Rick Menendez, Staffer
9. Abel Hernandez, New Jersey Directive

Of course, the FBI went nuts. A Cuban intelligence officer was asking me, a U.S. citizen, to help him spy on other U.S. citizens on U.S. soil. His request was most incompatible with his status as a diplomat. If the bureau had not been so intent on assessing Flakester for possible recruitment, it would have sent his butt back to Cuba, persona non grata (PNG). On some "bureau"-cratic level, though, someone decreed that I should attend the Free Cuba Embassy's reception.

I did not.

When Special Agent Mike S. telephoned late that evening to see how I'd made out, I explained my reasons. "I didn't go," I said, "because as far as I can tell, we have no plan, no objectives—just an approval for me to waltz in there and start spying on Americans, ostensibly for Cuban Intelligence. Then I would've had to figure out what to tell Fernandez about the people I met and what we discussed. If I made it up, we would've run the risk of pissing him off if he caught me out. If I told him who I'd met and what they said, it could've ended up in a Havana newspaper to expose these Free Cuba folks, and we'd piss off the good guys. If we had an end goal, I'd do it. Otherwise, we're just pissing in the wind."

My old friend the late Walt Perry had been an ace investigator for the Internal Revenue Service. He was a chief proponent of the sting operation, or "illusions," as he liked to call them. Walt always told me: "Define your mission, establish objectives, determine timescale, decide a budget, do it, win. And always have an exit strategy."

I heeded his advice.

The chicken curry had gotten so bad at Fernandez's favorite Vietnamese restaurant, we could have been chowing down in Havana. The date was March 6, 2001. The "we" was Luis Fernandez and me. The chicken may have been rabbit. Or cat.

Flakester had already been seated and was scribbling in a notebook when I arrived. When I sat down, I told him I'd been conceptualizing a TV situation comedy based around a spy bar called *Spooky's Safe House*. "Above the bar," I explained, "I'd put a sign that says 'Fake ID Accepted.' The only public phone would have a plaque that says 'Secure Line.' Of course, it'd be bugged by the management."

Fernandez's eyes bugged out of his head. Talking about espionage made him nervous.

"And Ed Howard says he's going to give me the raincoat he used when he escaped from the FBI in 1985," I added.

Flakester's round head bobbed around in all directions, his eyeballs nearly popping from their sockets. Then he chuckled about Robert Hanssen, a senior FBI counterintelligence official who had been arrested for espionage two weeks earlier. "The Cold War never ended," said Flakester. He then lowered his voice and asked if I had attended the Free Cuba Embassy reception.

I told him, "I had planned to attend, but I was called out of town at the last minute. I missed it, sorry." I added, "Receptions are terrible places for making meaningful contact with people. If you're really serious about this, I could phone one or more of the names on your list, go see these folks, and really talk to them."

"You could do this?" Flakester's eyes brightened. He agreed that receptions are impersonal and blamed that stupid idea on Luis Abierno. "I would like you to meet Jorge Garcia."

"What is your objective for my making contact with Garcia?" I asked. I wanted to see if these buggers were any better with real goals than the middle managers at the bureau.

"We'd like to expose how they orchestrate terrorist operations against Cuba," said Fernandez. "They plan assassinations of our leader and economic espionage. They have a paramilitary branch. Follow the money," he added, as if this were an original phrase.

"OK," I said. "Supposing I go see Garcia. What's in it for me? I think I deserve a box of Cuban cigars, at least."

"Of course!" Fernandez bubbled with joy. "I get you cigars."

Clinched: I'd spy for the Cubans in exchange for cigars. It would be the Double Ruse: while pulling a ruse on the Castro Cubans for the FBI, I'd ruse the Free Cubans for the Castro Cubans, but I'd really be rusing the Castro Cubans.

"When will you go to Cuba?" asked Fernandez. "Abierno is waiting for you."

Because of Hanssen's arrest, the second-to-last place I wasn't going anytime soon was Havana—Moscow was first—especially when, all of a sudden, the Cubans were pushing the idea. Nobody knew what or whom Hanssen had compromised, and everyone at the bureau was paranoid as hell.

"I don't know," I said. "I'm busy with things. Maybe Rick K. will go instead of me. He's coming into D.C. next week. Would you like to see him again?"

"Yes, of course."

Fernandez cleaned his plate. And this time, for once, he picked up the check.

When I met Fernandez a week later with Rick K., he made another pitch for me to travel to Havana.

"Coming on a bit strong," I thought. Then I told him, "I've already spent enough time and expense on Cuban project development. Luis Abierno should get his butt to Washington with all the material he promised me long ago." I sipped my dry martini—Beefeater with olives—and puffed on a Hemingway Short Story, the flavorful Arturo Fuente cigar. Fernandez insisted they needed something more from me.

"Like what?"

"I'd like you to meet Hays," said Fernandez.

"Who? I thought you wanted me to meet Jorge Garcia?"

No, the plan had changed. "We'd like you to talk to Hays." From Flakester's e-mail, Denny Hays was the executive director of the Cuban American National Foundation.

"What do you want me to talk to him about?" I asked.

"We want to know about his motivation and plans." Most astonishing, Flakester said this in front of Rick K, whom he barely knew.

I asked him, "Have you brought my payment—like, my cigars?"

"No, I forgot," said Fernandez. "You drive me back to my office?"

This move was calculated on his part, the first sign of cleverness I ever discerned in Flakester. He wanted a free ride back to his car. So I drove Fernandez to Sixteenth Street but declined to enter the building with him for my "payment" at this late hour. The bottom line was he thought he'd recruited a spy, but no cigars.

I never did try to see Denny Hays, and I never saw Luis Fernandez again. This operation no longer had legs. Because of the Hanssen case, I would not visit Cuba, and the FBI would not sanction such a trip, for the same reason. Without a well-conceived, forward-thinking game plan from the bureau, I wasn't about to place myself between Cuban intelligence and the anti-Castro Cuban community. The FBI discussed bouncing Flakester's butt back to Cuba but ultimately decided he was so ineffectual, it wasn't worth the trouble.

PART III

BAMBOOZLING BEELZEBUB

27

RUSING THE DEVIL

On June 13, 1997, armed French police burst into an old mill house in Champagne-Mouton, a village in a cognac-producing region in southwestern France known as the Charente. There, acting on a tip, they found Ira Einhorn, an American hippie guru who was wanted in the United States for murder.

Almost twenty years earlier, Einhorn had bludgeoned to death his thirty-year-old girlfriend, Holly Maddux, when she dared call their relationship quits; stowed her body in a trunk; and locked it inside the closet of his Philadelphia apartment. That's where her mummified corpse remained, until homicide detectives discovered it eighteen months later, on March 28, 1979. When detectives turned around and told the naked Einhorn (he didn't like wearing clothes) what they had just found in his closet, he replied, "You found what you found."

Out on bail, the self-professed founder of Earth Day bolted a few weeks before his trial was to begin in January 1981. Einhorn moved from Ireland to England, then to Sweden, and to France, living under assumed names as a fugitive from justice. It was a far cry from his days as a high-profile antiwar and ecological activist who rubbed shoulders with Abbie Hoffman, Jerry Rubin, and Barbara Bronfman.

In 1993, Philadelphia prosecutor Joel Rosen tried Einhorn in absentia. Based on forensic evidence, the jury took just two hours to convict him of first-degree murder. Einhorn was sentenced to life imprisonment, if he was ever found.

A Philadelphia district attorney named Richard DiBenedetto persevered and finally tracked Einhorn to France after his Swedish wife, Annika Flodin, applied to renew her driver's license. The French took Einhorn into custody and put him in prison. Thus began a fight by the U.S. Justice Department to extradite the so-called Unicorn Killer back to the United States. (Einhorn means "unicorn" in German.)

The French balked, raising an objection to Einhorn's extradition based on their opposition to the U.S. death penalty. When the U.S. attorneys pointed out that the death penalty was not an issue in Einhorn's case and that his sentence was life imprisonment, the French objected to the concept of trials in absentia. To mollify French sensitivities, Pennsylvania's state assembly quickly passed a special law so that Einhorn could be tried again.

Yet the French continued to waffle. After six months, they released Einhorn from prison and set him free, pending extradition hearings. It became a long, drawn-out process with many levels of appeal.

In early 1998, when John H. was still on the job, I told him I knew the French. They were not going to give Einhorn to the United States any time soon, maybe never, and when Einhorn saw that they might relent, he'd flee again. I asked John H. to let me take a stab at him. I knew I could insert myself into Einhorn's existence and could get a grip on him from the inside.

Ever the good soldier, John H. phoned his colleagues in Philadelphia to say he might be able to help with their Einhorn problem. Their response was, "Thanks but no thanks. We've got it under control."

FBI field offices are run like little fiefdoms. The agents don't like headquarters telling them what to do, and they especially don't like *other* field offices meddling in their affairs. Plus a crossover from Division Five (foreign counterintelligence) to Division Six (criminal investigations) would lead to a new set of administrative hassles.

Months passed. I persisted. Finally, the folks in Philadelphia became so exasperated with the French, they offered John H. and me a hearing.

Mike and Ed, two tough special agents from the bureau's Fugitive Squad in Philadelphia, drove to Washington for a powwow in John H.'s room at the Marriott Wardman Park. Ed stood taller than six-foot-six and had a solid build. Though soft-spoken with gentle eyes, Ed was not a guy you'd want chasing you down. Mike, of shaven head, was smaller but sinewy. No slouch himself, he had wisecracked his way through the scummier parts of Philly.

They heard me out. I'd planned to insert myself into Einhorn's existence. Without going into details, John H. confirmed that I could do it. I told them I would strive to become Einhorn's confidant and friend. Then if Einhorn fled France, as we all expected of him at the penultimate juncture, I'd be one of the few people he'd tell, and we'd know where to find him. Mike wanted to know how I would pull this off.

"I've read Einhorn is writing a novel," I said. "So he must be looking for a publisher." I paused. "That's me."

"Einhorn is clever," said Mike. "People he meets get taken in by him, like he's hypnotized them into believing his story. And he'll probably see through you."

"Maybe," I said, "but I like a good challenge."

Mike and Ed exchanged glances. What did they have to lose? And, besides, Albuquerque would pay the tab—to start with, anyway. Finally Mike asked, "What do you need?"

"His e-mail address," I said. I had read that Einhorn's favorite pastime was surfing the Internet.

"That's it?"

I shrugged. "That's it."

"Easy."

So it began, on November 2, 1998, with an e-mail from me, posing as a literary agent, to user886114: "I am interested in your novel, have you found a publisher yet? I also have a few book ideas that might appeal to your sense of the cosmos (if not your sense of humor). I'd be happy to meet . . . chat about book publishing, writing, etc."

His curiosity piqued, Einhorn responded rapidly and invited me to phone him.

At ten the next morning, or mid-afternoon in France, I telephoned the number he gave me. Einhorn answered himself. He spoke in an easy-going, enthusiastic manner, punctuated with chuckles. As I'd expected, I found him to be full of himself and excited by the attention his case had aroused.

Einhorn told me he had written four novels. But publishers, he said, were only interested in his memoirs, which he wanted to hold back. He reasoned publishing a novel would be a litmus test and allow him to see if the Maddux family would try to freeze his earnings through pending wrongful death civil litigation. (Einhorn's reasoning was sound: Holly's siblings soon won a judgment against him for $907 million.)

I said, "Fine, we'll talk novels. The key to shielding your earnings is to be creative."

"Now you're talking!" replied Einhorn. "You've said the right word, *creative*. I only like to work with people who think creatively."

I'd said the right thing and gained the password to his thoughts. Einhorn welcomed me into his life. The only question he had was how soon could I visit. Einhorn went on to tell me he'd never planned to live in France but that he had "just dropped in like a Martian. I'm so happy here," he added, "I couldn't imagine living anywhere else."

"How about prison, buster?" I wondered. Thus, I reported to John H. and to Mike and Ed: "I have established an excellent rapport with our target. The next step, aside from communicating with him by e-mail, should be for me to travel to Champagne-Mouton to further earn his trust."

Einhorn and I zapped each other e-mails while Mike and Ed fought bureaucratic battles for a green light and funding. My time on this project was on Albuquerque's dime, but Philly would have to pay travel expenses.

I sent Einhorn a tape of his Connie Chung interview, which he had requested. And in early December I congratulated Einhorn for making the cover of a magazine published by the Fox TV program *America's Most Wanted*.

"Merry Christmas, Ira," I e-mailed Einhorn on December 25.

"And happy New Year to you," he zapped back five hours later.

We were practically old friends.

28

CANTOR DUST, OR "YOU BRING THE CROISSANTS"

On January 20, 1999, the thirty-five-seat prop plane—an EMB-80 Brasilia—lifted from Nice on the French Riviera into a flawless blue sky. As the noisy plane fought the clouds, I plugged my ears with my Walkman and listened to the High Llamas' *Cold and Bouncy*, which aptly described this flight. The plane circled the azure Mediterranean, gaining altitude to clear the snow-capped French Alps, then lurched northwest toward a region of France Ira Einhorn would soon describe to me as "the back end of nowhere." I fast determined that if the Charente region was indeed the rear end of France, the dismal village Champagne-Mouton, where Einhorn resided with his wife, was its butt hole.

Most of this plane's passengers disembarked at Clermont-Ferrand. Only a handful remained on board for the short hop to Limoges, famous for its porcelain.

A tall, skinny, bearded man greeted me at the small airport. "Mr. Eringer?" said Jean-Pierre Yot, a friend of Einhorn's who'd been tasked with fetching me from the airport. Einhorn never did a lot, and one thing he never did was drive. Yot was chatty during the hour-long ride to Champagne-Mouton. His questioning was gentle, his nonchalance pronounced. "A police informant?" I wondered. When he eventually got around to asking about my business with Einhorn, I responded with affable vagueness. About work, I never miss an opportunity to keep my mouth shut.

Yot told me he'd known Einhorn about three years. "I knew him when he was still 'Eugene Mallon' [Einhorn's alias]," said Yot. "Nothing much happens in the Charente, and people like it that way," he added. "People keep to themselves. If you live twenty miles away, you're considered foreign. It has become fashionable among the Dutch and English to settle here, for those who desire a simple, cheap existence in France."

We entered one end of Champagne-Mouton and exited out the other. A sign on the right side of the road said Moulin de Guitry. On the left side sat the Einhorn's old mill house. I climbed out of Yot's car and "found what I found"—Ira Einhorn, emerging from his front door.

"Welcome!" he called. Mercifully, the fifty-eight-year-old Einhorn was not naked; instead, he was dressed in a yellow button-down shirt, its tails hanging over his dirty blue jeans.

I crossed the street, shook Einhorn's hand, and looked deeply into his eyes. I expected to experience his alleged hypnotic powers. After all, wasn't this the highly intelligent Unicorn, the man who could supposedly brainwash people? But all I detected there was a possible thyroid condition. Einhorn's eyes, bloodshot either from age or the local wine, protruded from their sockets. He appeared sincere, yes, but truthful, no. I expected Einhorn to be more clever than the man with whom I locked eyes and with whom I expected to spend many hours in conversation. My ears would soon encounter an intense bluster and carefully articulated but flatulent psychobabble.

His wife, Annika, stood behind him and studied me with unsure eyes. She was tall and thin with a gaunt face. She and Ira led Yot and me into their residence, through a dark, cold foyer, and into a kitchen warmed by an old wood stove, the only source of heat in their abode.

Einhorn grabbed a bottle of wine. Announcing "A neighbor of ours made this," he poured four glasses. We all sipped. Silence ensued. Then Jean-Pierre Yot commented politely that perhaps it needed time.

I said, "Time won't help. It tastes like Welch's Grape Juice without sugar."

Einhorn laughed. "You're right. This neighbor of ours doesn't know what she's doing." He uncorked another bottle of barely drinkable plonk. It was immediately apparent that the Einhorns were in wretched financial shape, living on whatever pennies would buy.

Einhorn then dismissed Yot, reminding him to collect me the following morning from Hôtel Plaisance and to stop by for croissants and coffee. "You bring the croissants," he instructed.

While Annika prepared lunch, Einhorn gave me a tour. Adjacent to the kitchen was a multipurpose living and dining room and home office. At one end was a rustic dining table; at the other, Einhorn's computer station and Compaq equipment with a twenty-inch monitor. All these high-tech toys were gifts, Einhorn told me, from ABC News as a payoff for the Connie Chung interview. "She also gave me a color TV set, but I sold it for cash," said a gleeful Einhorn. "I think they broke every law possible by giving me this stuff."

The bathroom, basic, sparse, and unkissed by the wood stove, was very cold. Next, we visited the barn, which contained two large piles of chopped wood. Einhorn crowed about what a find this house had been and how he'd paid seventy-five thousand dollars for it, with Annika's money, of course.

We returned to the dining area, where Annika offered us lunch: potato and leek soup, country paté, hard cheese, a tossed salad, and baguettes. We ate and talked, and talked and talked, for hours. Meanwhile, Annika served us, cleaned up, hauled firewood from the barn to the kitchen, stoked the oven, and knitted, as Einhorn talked, occasionally listened, and bounced back and forth to his computer station to retrieve documents. Annika seemed in awe of her husband, though I discerned some tension between the two, perhaps because she did everything and he did nothing. While Annika waited on the ponophobic Einhorn, his role in this household was to read, study, pontificate, philosophize, and write, though Einhorn confided he'd been suffering writer's block ever since the French gendarmes had arrived at his door. "I was in the middle of my fifth novel," Einhorn sighed. "I could never get back into it after what happened."

Einhorn professed he was eager to know my whole background, although he constantly interrupted my spiel to eruct related tangents personal to him. Each time I allowed Einhorn to fully indulge his logomania. I had no doubt that, within twenty-four hours, he would regard me as his new best friend.

Einhorn then whined about having been deceived by Connie Chung and ABC News. They were not supposed to lead in their interview by describing him as "a fugitive who got away with murder." They had edited that introduction out of the videotape *they* had sent him.

Regarding Holly Maddux's murder and the ongoing U.S. extradition request, Einhorn said, "Maybe I did it and maybe I didn't. That has nothing to do with it [his case against extradition]." Then Einhorn tried to convince me that Holly was murdered to frame him and thus end his social activism.

I asked, "Who would do this?"

Einhorn jumped up, strode to his computer, printed out a document, and returned. "Ron Pandolphi," he said. "He's head of the 'Weird Desk' at the CIA."

"The 'Weird Desk'?"

"Yeah, uh-huh," said Einhorn. "That's the most interesting department. Covers mind control, Sidney Gottlieb. Pandolphi's also involved in the Chinese satellite stuff." He winked. "And Kit Green. He used to be chief of the CIA's Weird Desk. He investigated seven suspicious deaths. One was Holly. Another was William Franklin, a metallurgy professor at Kent State. Now Green is head of medical research at General Motors. You need a Q clearance to get into this stuff. But the main reason they framed me," Einhorn added, "was UFOs."

"UFOs?"

Einhorn nodded. "I know they exist. Monsanto and other companies have been developing technology retrieved from crashed alien spaceships—fiber optics, lasers. . . . They all derive from Roswell, New Mexico."

Einhorn zipped off somewhere. Annika, knitting at the table, leaned forward and said, "It's so good you are here. Ira has not been able to talk like this to anyone for eighteen years. The villagers don't understand him."

"Because of his English or his nonsense?" I wondered, but I did not ask.

Einhorn returned with new photocopies. "So what do you want to do with me, with my books?"

I didn't say what I was thinking: "To put you behind bars, asshole. Who gives a crap about the books?"

More to the point, Einhorn added, "How much money could I get?"

I asked, "Which of your novels excites you most?"

"*Cantor Dust,*" Einhorn replied without hesitation. "It's my fourth novel, my best."

"OK," I said. "That's the one I want to read."

"I haven't decided yet whether to give it to you," said Einhorn. "The important question is, how much could I get?"

"Obviously, I have to read it first."

"But let's suppose you read it and you like it. How much?"

"Maybe twenty or thirty thousand dollars."

"Good," replied Einhorn. "I really need twenty-five thousand dollars."

We finally adjourned at quarter of six. I gave Annika a box of soap, assorted fragrances from Provence, and for Einhorn, a biography of Nabokov he'd requested. I also gave him a copy of Edward Howard's book, *Safe House*, and mentioned that I had edited it.

"That must have been tough," said Einhorn.

"Just a rehearsal for you," I said, "and your book."

Later, as Annika drove me to the nearby Hôtel Plaisance, we exchanged small talk. I checked into room seventeen and had two hours to rest before dinner.

Champagne-Mouton is not Monte Carlo. And Hôtel Plaisance, one can be certain, will never make the *Michelin Guide*. It is family run and, like everything else in the pissant village, drab and bare.

Chambre seventeen was musty, dusty, and rusty. The size of a walk-in closet, it was illuminated by a naked light bulb that dangled from the ceiling. The room featured a worn, saggy mattress with a hard pillow roll and stained bedcover. Forget about a TV.

I dumped my bag and toured the damp and cold village, which lacked even an ounce of charm. The Café de la Paix—no relation to the famed establishment in Paris—beckoned me. I ordered a pastis and watched a group of men, who, in turn, watched me. One called, "Au revoir!" when I left.

At seven thirty, the Einhorns appeared outside Hôtel Plaisance to pick me up for dinner. Although it was cold, Einhorn did not wear a sweater or a jacket. "I've always been that way," he explained.

Annika drove, of course. I sat up front with her. She thanked me again for her gift. "It's my favorite soap," she said.

En route to Château de Nieuil's restaurant, which they'd booked for dinner, I asked Einhorn where he hoped his life would lead and what, ideally, he would do if he could do anything.

"My dream is to start a foundation," replied Einhorn, "the Unicorn Foundation."

"Where?"

"Right here in Champagne-Mouton."

"And its purpose?"

"To preserve the simple life we have in this region," said Einhorn. "There are people who want to change it, make it faster-paced. I want to stop them."

"Ira should lecture," said Annika. "He has so much to say, so much energy and ability to offer the world. It is not fair that he can't contribute."

I asked Einhorn about his willingness to travel for putting a foundation together, knowing that the French had ordered Einhorn not to leave the Charente for now.

"I suppose travel in France will be OK in a year or two. Then Europe."

The Château de Nieuil had one of the finest restaurants in the region. Our threesome enjoyed an elaborate four-course meal, starting with an aperitif called Pineau, a local specialty of cognac with grape juice. For full effect, I sprang for a fabulous bottle of red Bordeaux. The Einhorns oohed and ahhed over this liquid gold. They did not usually drink so well.

"Gee, if I lived in this area, I'd come here every week," I said.

"If I had the money to do that," Einhorn countered, "I'd fix my roof."

Money again. Einhorn said he needed $6,371 to repair the leaks in his roof. He needed money so badly, he asked if I could sell his story to a magazine or newspaper. "You have authority to speak on my behalf," said Einhorn, giddy from good Bordeaux.

Annika told me that her parents had not been aware of Einhorn's true identity until he'd been busted by the French police. "They were very upset," she said. Sweden was one country to which we thought Einhorn might flee, so learning that no warm and fuzzy family welcome awaited them was significant.

Annika got up to use the powder room. In her absence, Einhorn said, "She's a good woman, and I've had quite a few." He told me he'd commit suicide rather than be extradited, and he expressed his concern that Annika be taken care of financially. They'd been together eleven years, he said, adding that their relationship was strained sometimes because they were both always at home, in close quarters.

Annika returned and quizzed me, trying to assess a timeline regarding my interest in her husband.

I threw up my hands. "It's not the only thing I do," I laughed.

"But why are you so interested in Ira?" she pressed.

I leaned forward to draw her in. "I'm addicted to intrigue and lunacy," I said. "Can't help myself. Your husband qualifies."

Einhorn laughed while Annika studied me. Einhorn made fun of her seriousness. Then he blathered about how he'd never had a boss or worked

a day in his life at what most people think of as work. He said h,
would be to advise rich people on how to enjoy life. After dessert, t,
our enjoyment, I ordered a round of very smooth, very old cogna(

After dinner, on the drive back to my hotel, Einhorn asked wh
I'd been reading. It was a favorite question of his.

"Books about Cuba and Fidel Castro," I told him, "but one of n
ite writers is John Fante."

"Fante!" Einhorn whooped with delight. "His books are the bigge
in France right now."

We reached Hôtel Plaisance just past midnight. The Einhorns ;
and saw me inside.

Thus followed an eerie night in the discomfort of chambre sever
The little sleep I got was punctuated by dreams related to the mission. A
moment, I thought I felt the presence of Holly Maddox, urging me forv
"Right on, get this bastard."

I welcomed the sunrise and settled my tab of 201 French francs
about thirty-five bucks. Jean-Pierre Yot arrived, having dutifully picked
croissants first, and we carried on to Moulin de Guitry.

The Einhorns were up and about. Lying on the kitchen table was In
manuscript for *Cantor Dust*. Annika poured coffee. Einhorn handed me th
manuscript, as proud of me for being worthy to receive it as he was of him
self for having written what he considered a masterpiece. Then he descende(
into another bout of logorrhea, this time on digitalization and its catastrophi(
effect on mankind's future.

I told Einhorn he should pen a thirty-page monograph, *Blueprint for
the Future*.

He beamed. "Yeah, I can do that." Some called him a "guru" or a "mes-
siah," but Einhorn liked the label "futurist" best. "You can *really* communicate," he told me, meaning I said what he liked to hear.

My visit, less than twenty-four hours in town, was as short and as
sweet as I'd planned it. It was just short enough that Einhorn was sorry to see
me go.

29

FRAGMENTS OF ILLUSION

Within a few weeks of our meeting, Ira Einhorn pressed me for a critique of his novel *Cantor Dust*. I couldn't very well tell him what I really thought: it was the most incoherent crock I'd ever read. So I sent him an e-mail with this quick comment: "One of a kind. Astonishing in its depth."

Einhorn zapped me right back: "Remember, there are three more."

"Oh, joy," I said to myself.

My report to the FBI on this manuscript was somewhat different. I shared my honest opinion of what "Sam"—our code name for Einhorn, though we later changed it to "Fat Ass"—had written:

> *Cantor Dust* is a long, rambling essay disguised as a novel. Its most blatant flaw (and there are many) is this: a novelist is supposed to show, not tell. This manuscript tells, doesn't show. It is an amalgamation of great philosopher meets new age spiritualist, regurgitated in Sam's incoherent psychobabble.
>
> The protagonist—obviously Sam, himself—holds himself out to be the world's greatest genius and is a proponent of incest and sadomasochism.

When I next telephoned Einhorn, he focused again on money. All money talk should be communicated by fax, not e-mail, he decreed. "We have a secret bank account in Luxembourg," said Einhorn. "My book's gonna be big because I'm famous. And I've got some more writing I'm sending you. It's called *Fragments*, modeled after Nietzsche's style of writing."

Einhorn and I then sent e-mails to each other daily and talked by phone weekly. He gave me updates on his legal situation in France.

When I again met with John H., Mike, and Ed on March 16 at the Marriott Wardman Park, room 3035, the Philly boys were beside themselves. They marveled over how my relationship with Einhorn had flourished. Headquarters was so pleased with our progress, it pledged twenty grand for Albuquerque to support the mission.

For his birthday on May 15, I sent Einhorn a birthday card featuring an artsy montage of pens, bound journals, and handwriting. I telephoned him, too, and suggested, "Open a fine bottle of wine and blow out some candles. You know what to wish for."

"I sure do," Einhorn replied. "Thank you for calling. I really appreciate it."

Two and a half months later, a jury awarded the Maddux family a judgment against Ira Einhorn of $907 million. In his communications with me, Einhorn sounded overjoyed. First, he rationalized that the judgment made him _worth_ that much. ("With interest, I'm the one-billion dollar man!") Then he also believed "it elevates my case" toward getting a good advance for his novel. Einhorn sent me so many e-mails that wading through them was the most time-consuming part of writing _Ruse_.

In mid-August, I huddled with John H., Ed, and Mike at the Marriott Wardman Park again. It would be my last meeting with John H. before he retired from the FBI.

We agreed on two main issues regarding the Einhorn case. One, we would create a dummy book contract for Einhorn as we played for time—the drawn out extradition process. Two, I would push Einhorn to leave France so we could rendition him on the lam.

In September, Einhorn bubbled with excitement over the phone and told me _Esquire_ planned to do a story on him. He expected a photographer to visit his home any day. Einhorn said, "He's going to do a day in my life."

A month later the photographer had come and gone. And Einhorn reported, "They took photos of me getting out of the water naked. I hope they use them for the cover."

In mid-November, _Esquire_ hit the stands. The issue featured Einhorn's story by Russ Baker, whom Einhorn professed to have liked. I sent an e-mail to Einhorn stating, "I have Dec. *Esquire*. No cover. Opens with full page of frontal nudity. They appear to have cropped your dick to one inch. Will read presently."

Einhorn zapped back: "I was in forty-five-degree very cold water for a half hour, so shriveled rather than cropped, perhaps."

I sent him another e-mail two hours later: "I've read it. I don't think you're going to like Russ Baker anymore."

Einhorn's return e-mail said, "We never liked him. Use it, my friend, and laugh last."

"Precisely," I thought.

Come January 2000, Einhorn started to grow impatient. His roof was still leaking, and I hadn't gotten any closer to getting him any cash. I swore about shortsighted publishers no longer willing to take chances on experimental fiction, and I offered to buy his novel myself. For the sake of verisimilitude, I had sent a number of queries to likely publishers, but an Einhorn book was considered of such poor taste, nobody even responded.

Enter my operative Rick K., who evaluated *Cantor Dust* and offered another editorial opinion. Rick outdid himself. In the opening paragraph of his evaluation he wrote, "*Cantor Dust* is a powerful and provocative novel that provides a history lesson of twentieth-century culture and politics and stretches the intellectual boundaries of anyone who reads this book."

Rick K. recommended, in cahoots with me to buy more time, that Einhorn should revise the novel's ending "to enhance the book's literary impact." He also suggested that Einhorn rewrite the characters' dialogue because, basically, all his characters sounded the same.

Responded Einhorn: "Rick obviously got it, and his criticism is correct, especially as to the dialogue." Einhorn immediately went to work on his revising *Cantor Dust*, and I put Rick K. and Einhorn into contact with each other.

Then, in March, the FBI's Washington Field Office suffered a financial crunch and opted to scrap the operation. Mike and Ed drove down from Philadelphia. They wanted the operation to continue. They were pleased I had not frozen my contact with Einhorn the way Washington had frozen my funding. They promised to get their superiors back home to put pressure on my local field office.

In April, Einhorn told me he had Bryant Gumbel, *U.S. News & World Report*, Fox TV, and "that demon lady," Theresa Conroy, from the Philadelphia *Daily News* banging on his door. But it was me he wanted to see. By this time, *Cantor Dust* was in Rick K.'s hands for a total rewrite.

Come May 15, I sent another birthday card to Ira. He had turned sixty years old.

In July 2000, after several hearings on Einhorn's case, France approved extradition. Einhorn's lawyers appealed to Prime Minister Lionel Jospin, but they felt serious heat. If Einhorn had thoughts about running, this was a good time. The French, for their part, erected a twenty-four-hour observation post outside his house.

Also, come July, Rick K. was "about ten hours away from completing" Einhorn's rewrite. Einhorn, meanwhile, must have been pulling his hair out of his head with frustration as we bought time, pending new developments in his appeal to the French prime minister. And not a development went by without Einhorn reporting in detail what was happening, how he felt, and what he and his legal team were going to do about it. We knew what he was thinking, what he was doing, and what he was thinking of doing.

Einhorn, in an e-mail dated September 29, 2000, asked, "Any idea when the present phase of the book will be done AND when you will be here?" Rick had finished his revision, which Einhorn accepted and fully incorporated.

I replied, "I'm working on the galleys. Would like to bring them with me." Two months later, I had galleys, or typeset page proofs, in hand. I sent Einhorn this e-mail: "The galleys look great! I will dispatch them to you."

Einhorn answered, "Happy to hear that. You will feel my smile when I get them. . . . Now all we need is you." And on December 6, Einhorn wrote, "Arrived. What a good feeling! A lift! Thanks! Let us set a date [for your visit] as soon as possible, as we are in the middle of complicated legal actions." Einhorn set to work correcting the galleys.

It was amazing we'd been able to spin him for so long. Now the time was right for me to face the devil again.

30

OPERATION BEELZEBUB

The only way to fool Beelzebub is on his own terms, with a bottle of whiskey in one hand and a Cuban cigar in the other. With that determination I came head to head with Ira Einhorn on January 16, 2001.

We met at Le Claud Gourmand, a Restaurant-Hôtel de Charme, halfway between Saint-Claud and Champagne-Mouton. I extended my right hand, but Einhorn wanted to hug, ensuring that I caught a whiff of his putrid breath. Ira Einhorn had gained weight. It was almost exactly two years—and hundreds and hundreds of e-mails—since I had first met this fugitive killer. His face was now ravaged with stress, his cheeks swollen with malevolence, and his teeth and gums rotted.

On my tab, I checked Einhorn and his wife, Annika, into room two and myself into room three. This place wasn't the Ritz, but it sure beat Hôtel Plaisance in Einhorn's grim village. We settled in the parlor for tea and anchovy-filled croissants. We had the hotel and restaurant to ourselves. Indeed, we were its only guests.

Einhorn, ever the enthusiastic blabbermouth, desired an update on all my book activities since last we met. "Have you been to Cuba?" he asked. "How did that go?"

When I told him about my Cuban escapades—Vesco, Chesimard, Castro, a spy ring—Einhorn listened attentively. Then he said quietly, "That's where my lawyer has advised me to go, Cuba. He says he can make the introductions and arrangements. All my friends have been urging me to flee."

"So here it was," I thought. "This stinkard was planning an exit, stage left. Surprise, surprise." I asked him, "But aren't the French police watching you?"

Einhorn nodded. "I have three sets of surveillants," he boasted. "The local gendarmes, who take turns coming down from Lille; the antiterrorist squad in Paris; and the federal intelligence agency."

"So how can you flee to Cuba?"

"Very easy," Einhorn replied. "I'd only have to walk across my garden."

"But don't you have to check in with the cops every few days?"

"I'd have five days before they knew I was gone," Einhorn whispered. "Annika will stay and pretend all is well. She can't live underground again." He paused. "And in a worst-case scenario, I have a plan to kill myself. But let's not talk about that in front of Annika. It upsets her."

The last thing we wanted was for Einhorn to end up in Cuba. Scores of American fugitives freely roam there, courtesy of Fidel Castro, who routinely grants political asylum to American criminals. And Einhorn was within driving distance of Madrid, where he could catch a nonstop flight to Havana.

"Cuba sucks," I said. "I have another idea, and it sure beats dying."

"Yeah? What?"

"A plan that will generate massive publicity for your novel."

"Let's not talk about it here," Einhorn whispered. "Later."

Einhorn suggested a stroll through the hotel's grounds. He pointed out his watchers—one unmarked car with two policemen—and told me most of them had been friendly and sympathetic to his plight. Several had helped him stack firewood and had come into his home for New Year's drinks. He added, contemptuously, that one had even given Annika a kiss. Einhorn's smirk and body language implied that the liberty-loving French were helping him get away with murder.

"Annika and I are now separate," said Einhorn.

Annika stopped, upset. "Are you saying we're not married?" she asked him.

"Of course, we are," Einhorn said, patronizingly. "I mean we're separate financially. The house is in her name. I have nothing." Einhorn dug into his blue jeans pocket and held up a two hundred–franc note. "Except this," he chuckled.

We soon cut indoors from the cold for a round of Pineau. Einhorn seemed anxious to hear my publishing plan for *Cantor Dust*. I laid out this fantasy: we would print five hundred deluxe copies, bound exquisitely with slipcovers, and they would all be numbered. The first hundred would bear his signature. Signed books would sell for $250; unsigned for a hundred dollars. We would also print 250 bound galleys for reviewers.

Einhorn grew excited. "I need fifty bound galleys," he said. "I need to demonstrate to the French that I am a man of letters. This will help my case."

"Through our special deluxe edition," I continued, "we would hope to attract a large publisher to publish a mass-market, paperback version. Interest would depend on the amount of publicity you could generate."

Einhorn nodded. It all made such sense to him. "I need an advance," said Einhorn. "We're broke. The roof still has not been repaired and is leaking like a sieve. I almost mentioned it to you before you came, so maybe you would bring some money." Einhorn shrugged sheepishly. "Is twenty thousand dollars possible?"

"Maybe," I said. "I'd have to calculate the total cost of publishing, and see what I can afford. Maybe I should have your bank details?"

"Give it to him, Annika," Einhorn instructed.

Annika dipped into her handbag and produced a handwritten note:

Annika's Bank Account, Annika Flodin, Moulin de Guitry, 16350 Champagne-Mouton, France; ████████████████ Banque Generale de Luxembourg, Agence B6L "Royal Monterey" 27, Avenue Monterey, L - 2163 Luxembourg SWIFT B6LL LU LL.███████████████
████████████

Annika's concern was timing. "How soon could you publish the novel?"

"How fast can you correct and return the galleys?" I asked.

"You can have them tomorrow morning," said Einhorn. "We appear to be the only dinner guests this evening, so whenever we want to eat, they'll serve us."

I suggested we get on with it. Dining room lights switched on, and we took our seats at a round table in the corner. Proprietor-chef Jean Marc Rougier appeared before us and suggested a five-course truffle dinner. Who could say no? Chef Rougier scooted to the kitchen and then reappeared with a big grin and a jar of fresh truffles. I asked him to recommend a fine red wine to accompany our meal.

"How about," he suggested, "a selection of wine to compliment each course?"

"You kidding? Do it."

Chef Rougier descended to his wine cellar and returned with three half bottles of red wine. He uncorked and poured the first, a Domaine Saint Vincent Saumur-Champigny 1999. Then he served the first course, warm sliced truffle over a piece of garlic toast atop a bed of mixed greens. It was heavenly.

"What are you reading?" Einhorn asked me his favorite question. He considers himself the world's most voracious reader.

"*On Writing* by Stephen King," I replied. "I don't read books about writing any more, but I flipped it open at a bookstore, and it looked good. I learned a few important things."

"Like what?" asked Einhorn.

"The road to hell is paved with adverbs." Needless to say, I considered Einhorn's novel well paved.

Our second course was even better: Sliced warm truffle with pan-sautéed foie gras in a rich butter sauce and accompanied by Ampelidae 1998. With the French doors closed, Einhorn proclaimed it safe to speak as we got into our third course of truffle potpie with a Clos les Côtes Pécharmant 1997.

"Poland," I whispered. "I've kept up a relationship with the former underground activists from Solidarity. Using a network of old safe houses, these guys could hide you, settle you in a city like Krakow. It's full of intellectuals like yourself."

Einhorn absorbed everything. He liked the plan, saying it was the best he'd heard. "And very doable," he declared.

"Traveling by car, you could cross the border into Germany without identification, then drive across Germany to the Polish border. That's where you would need papers," I said. "My Polish friends would be able to organize that."

Einhorn said it would mean separating from Annika. "She can't live underground again," he repeated.

Annika confirmed that an underground existence could no longer work for her. She'd be happier with the stress of litigation than living on the lam. However, she added, for Ira life in Poland would be better than his plan to commit suicide.

"If the court goes against me," said Einhorn, "I will kill myself in a very public demonstration."

"How?" I asked.

"Self-immolation," replied Einhorn. "I plan to set myself on fire in a public place." (When Agent Mike from Philly heard about Einhorn's plan later, he quipped, "Can I bring the marshmallows?")

As much as Einhorn liked my escape-to-Poland plan, he was in no hurry to leave France and separate from Annika. He believed he had many, many months, perhaps years, before his pro bono lawyers would exhaust their appeals. Ultimately, they hoped to get to the Court of Human Rights in Strasbourg.

Then we dug into course four, a sliced truffle with a fried egg. And finally we had dessert, which was a truffle inside warm peaches, with a scoop of vanilla ice cream, topped with cocoa powder, and a chilled bottle of Sauternes. This area of France being cognac territory, Chef Rougier then poured snifters of the best of the best: Paul Beau Cognac Hors d'Age Vieille Grande Champagne.

Afterward, I suggested a Cuban cigar. Einhorn concurred. I returned to my room and retrieved two Montecristos. We lit, drew, puffed, and drank fine Armagnac as we conspired into the night.

The next morning, Einhorn joined me for breakfast and produced his corrected galleys. Einhorn told me he and Annika had labored intensely. Finally he was satisfied with the novel's ending: "She once again glanced at him with the eyes of the nineteen-year-old and calmly walked to the hook on the wall that held the strap they had used to beat each other and shyly smiled at him as she reached for it. Daddy's little girl was home again."

Again, we agreed to fax all our sensitive communications. I devised a code for the escape plan. We would refer to it as a "documentary." So if I could get him a false Polish ID, I would fax the following: "The documentary producer has offered a contract."

As I settled the hotel and restaurant tab, a tough-looking character with a shaved head, black leather jacket, and commando boots strode by to get a fix on things. I went outside and then returned to the lobby. Baldy and another cop were chatting with Chef Rougier.

My departure plan had called for Annika to drive me to the airport, but when we got in her Fiat, it wouldn't start. The battery was dead. By sheer luck, a taxi rounded into the forecourt to take Einhorn home.

"I'll take the taxi," I said, not planning to miss my flight and not wishing to stick around with Baldy. The French Napoleonic code allows the French police to hold anyone they want for weeks just for the hell of it. And who knew what they thought of my presence.

"I must check with Ira," said Annika, who wouldn't as much as belch without Einhorn's permission.

"To hell with Ira," I thought, as I stowed my bag in the taxi's trunk and got in the backseat.

Annika returned. "Ira says it's OK."

"As if it really mattered," I thought to myself.

Many hours later, during a long hot shower, I endeavored to scrub away every last trace of Beelzebub's breath and persona.

31

THE INSECT GETS SPRAYED

We now believed that if Ira Einhorn chose to flee, he would do it my way and go to Poland. Of course, I would be along for the ride. And the Philly Fugitive Squad, Mike and Ed, would be just inside the Polish border to greet Einhorn and take him to the States.

Now we needed to wait, watch, and monitor Einhorn's appeal process and his state of mind. In a stall for time, we gave him as little progress as possible on his novel's publication. We knew he was desperate for money and that, in his mind, I was his only hope for making any. We would play his situation to our advantage.

To commence the stall, I sent Einhorn an e-mail saying I had consulted a lawyer—at his suggestion—regarding the structure of a foreign entity that could pay Einhorn an advance and escape the scrutiny of those enforcing the civil judgment against him. The (imaginary) lawyer, I wrote, had been *negative* on the whole project.

"On what basis?" Einhorn shot back by e-mail. "Has the First Amendment disappeared?"

I pretended to seek a second opinion. Then I "decided" to use a British lawyer, but obtaining one would have to wait until I next visited London "in the very near future."

Einhorn's anxious e-mails to me soon became caustic and frustrated. I was winding him up and enjoying the process. But by mid-February, Einhorn outright demanded that I produce bound galleys for him, and on the twentieth, he snapped. He zapped me a menacing e-mail: "I have shared what you are proposing [the escape plan] with two close advisers, one in the media, who are aghast at what you are proposing. I am preparing to go on the

Internet with the story and will do so if I have not heard from you by tomorrow night."

I groaned. "Fat Ass was trying to blackmail me into publishing his wretched novel!" I phoned Einhorn. "Hey, chill out," I said. "What's the problem?" I listened a full five minutes while Einhorn vented his spleen, acid reflux rising to a gorge. "But the galleys are almost ready," I said. "Do you want them or not?"

Einhorn finally calmed down. "Would it be OK," he asked, "if I provide my own colophon?"

"Sure," I said.

"A calligrapher friend of mine in Philadelphia has drawn a unicorn."

"Get it to me," I said. And one week later, a unicorn colophon arrived by post from Einhorn's friend, Roy David.

I wrote a follow-up memo for Mike and Ed in Philly:

Short of new pressure from France, Einhorn remains content to sit where he is and wait out the next round of his appeal. It could be a year or longer before he decides his liberty is in danger. Only then will he consider my Poland option—or implement his lawyer's advice to seek refuge in Cuba.

The only way for me to remain on good terms with Einhorn would be for me to provide him with bound galleys of his novel. I am loath to do this as Einhorn will use these galleys to attempt to improve his standing in the French media by depicting himself as a man of letters.

Perhaps we should inform the French police of the contempt Einhorn has shown for them in his private conversations with me and of Einhorn's scheme to flee France for Cuba. The French would be greatly embarrassed if Einhorn was able to escape.

The Philly boys concurred. But in the interest of buying more time and remaining in sync with Einhorn, they requested that I bind some galleys and keep him moderately happy. Thus, in mid-March, I sent Einhorn a small batch of bound galleys.

In mid-April Einhorn wanted more bound galleys. I told him I'd send a box of ten but did not. Then I expressed surprise when the box did not arrive.

"What copies?" Einhorn e-mailed back, his blood pressure rising.

> Our mail is very well handled here, so that can't be a problem. If it would get to here, WE WOULD GET IT. All packages should be marked *gift* and listed as being of no value [he got that right] AND WELL WRAPPED. This could be the only answer IF you sent a package. THE POST IS NOT GENTEEL!! I have been buying books from the USA for over three years, about 100 individual packages—NOTHING HAS FAILED TO ARRIVE. Please confirm, as I don't want to turn this into S. J. Perleman [*sic*] writing to his Chinese laundry man.

In keeping with his wishes, I replied with one word: "OK." It touched off a round of e-mails.

Einhorn: "Has your package gone missing? Your very cryptic reply didn't confirm that."

Me: "Apparently so."

Einhorn: "Nothing we can do about that. Please send me 10 copies and confirm that you have done so."

Me: "All right."

When I dragged my feet about sending galleys to a number of addresses Einhorn had supplied, he turned to menace again. "Call me today," he vented in an e-mail on June 3, 2001, "or deal with the press and the police as I have consulted a number of people about what you have done, and none of them is against my doing what I am about to do. You agreed to do something which you have miserably failed to do."

I telephoned Einhorn and attempted humor. The niddering buffoon launched into me, as I gather he launched into Holly Maddux, though she had the misfortune of standing with her back to him the last time. In my case, the only weapons Einhorn had at his disposal were words, which he lashed with risible venom. "You have to get over here within a week and talk to me, or I'm exposing you!"

"That's impossible," I said.

"Then it's all over," Einhorn spewed in a murderous, high-pitched voice. "I'm going to ruin your life!"

"But you seem bent on this path whatever happens," I said calmly.

"Don't you understand what you've done to me?" hollered Einhorn.

"Not only did I understand, I hadn't finished," I thought. "Done to you?" I said. "I've paid money to print and bind galleys and mail them to you. Instead of gratitude, all I get are threats."

"You don't grasp what I'm saying!" yelped Einhorn. "You have held me up two and a half years!" Blah, blah, blah. The onslaught continued another ten minutes. "I don't know what's going on in your mind!" he concluded with a guttural rasp.

"If he only knew," I chuckled to myself.

Once Einhorn had spent his rage, we carried on as before, as if nothing had happened to upset him. I told him that I would dispatch galleys to persons on his list. Einhorn then changed the subject to insects, or rather the absence of insects from the Charente this season after all the spraying. "I feel very close to insects," mused Einhorn.

Holly Maddux's siblings—two sisters and a brother—no doubt had similar feelings about the orthopterous Ira Einhorn. And when they met in early June with Attorney General John Ashcroft, they shared their feelings. Before their scheduled appointment, Ashcroft had naturally asked his minions for a briefing on the Einhorn case. When he learned Einhorn was plotting an escape to Cuba, he presumably telephoned his French counterpart and demanded action.

Because on July 10, months ahead of schedule, a French judge announced that Einhorn's appeal would commence the following day, with a decision expected the day after. Not only that, forty police officers then surrounded Einhorn's house.

Einhorn sent me this e-mail:

Some judge freaked. No one knows why. It should have been September or October or later. The [French] government is pushing. There are now 8 cars parked outside and they have set up a customs post outside our house so that when Annika leaves without me, the car is searched for alcohol and tobacco, as I might be hiding in the 18" by

18" box in the back of our very small car. They also have posted men in the field around my house [thus cutting off the backyard route Einhorn intended to take when it came time to flee]."

I sent an e-mail back: "This sounds serious. What the hell is going on?" Einhorn replied, "House now surrounded by a small army. The entire area is blockaded, and no one is allowed in without questioning."

The court's decision went against Einhorn. To protest his imminent extradition, Einhorn invited a French TV crew into his house and, while they filmed, pierced his own neck with a kitchen knife. If Einhorn meant to kill himself—and I am certain he did not—he failed miserably. All he bought himself was one week before the French authorities declared him fit enough to travel.

Tension reigned supreme on the Fugitive Squad in Philadelphia. They still worried Einhorn would make a run for it. On July 18, Einhorn planned a party at his home, part celebration of Annika's fiftieth birthday and part bon voyage bash for himself. Philly was concerned Einhorn might use the party to mask an escape.

But at eight o'clock the next morning, Einhorn confirmed his presence at Moulin de Guitry in an e-mail to me: "The media are gathering outside. . . . A SWAT squad has joined the seven other police services in town. *C'est fou* [It's crazy]."

This e-mail message wasn't good enough for the guys in Philly. "Call him," said Mike. "Make sure he's there."

I phoned, spoke with Annika, and heard Einhorn yakking in the background. Then I phoned Philly. "He's there."

At two o'clock French police officers took Einhorn into custody and drove him to Charles de Gaulle Airport outside Paris, where a U.S. government–chartered plane awaited his arrival. At about 1:10 a.m. Paris time, I received a call from Ed, who'd just cuffed Einhorn and buckled him into a seat. "We got him!" Ed sounded ecstatic. "We're just about to take off."

Ed and Mike phoned me the following day from Philadelphia. "Sorry we didn't get to do it in Poland," said Mike.

"You kidding?" I said. "The evil scumbag is behind bars. Mission accomplished."

"Get this," said Ed. "On the plane, Fat Ass told me he had a publisher for his novel. When I asked him who was publishing his book, he wouldn't give you up. He thinks his future as a famous author depends on it."

Einhorn, who considered himself the smartest man in the world, still didn't get that he had been outsmarted.

On October 24, Einhorn wrote me from state prison in Houtzdale, Pennsylvania: "According to Annika, you have just disappeared. When we last talked, you said you would work to get *Cantor Dust* published. . . ." Blah, blah, blah. Fat Ass still did not realize he'd been stung!

32

DÉJÀ VU ALL OVER AGAIN

In June 2001, I moved from Washington, D.C., to Santa Barbara, California. As a result, a bureau fracas ensued over which FBI field office would work with me and prioritize (the upside) and administrate (the downside) my sting operations. Would I remain with the Washington Field Office? Or with the Einhorn ruse under way, should Philly take over? Should Ventura, the nearest FBI office to Santa Barbara, or Los Angeles oversee my work? Or should I revert to Albuquerque, where I'd started, not least because I was still "passively active" on the Edward Lee Howard case? My diverse cases perplexed protocol.

In the midst of this wrangling, headquarters had its own idea about how to proceed with the Howard case. I learned of its bold new initiative just one week before I left Washington, when at a Starbucks I met with Special Agent James O., a Russia specialist. He was one of the two guys with whom I'd spent an engaging evening in London, along with John H., on my first rebound from Moscow six years earlier.

Headquarters' new thinking was I might have been burned by Robert Hanssen, who, before his arrest in February, was believed to have gained access to casework on Edward Lee Howard. Hanssen had evidently uploaded computer files on Howard. Big-time counterintelligence, dubbed by one comic in the business as "smoke and urinals," had cut in. The bureau told me, "Don't visit Russia or Cuba any time soon, for any reason."

Taking this new situation into account, a plan was presented to me. On the assumption that I'd been burned by Hanssen, I would organize a rendezvous with Edward Howard in Switzerland. I could tell him that I had been working for U.S. intelligence but that I was fed up with those bastards and open to offers from his friends in Moscow. Howard would most certainly convey my overture to his KGB friends, and it would undoubtedly reach a specific senior FSB officer who handled all the important American agents but who rarely left Russia. I would lure this officer to Switzerland, and the FBI would have a crack at recruiting him.

If it sounded a tad cheesy, well, at least somebody at long last was thinking creatively. When I offered to reach out to Howard and set it up, however, they declined. The Russia specialist needed more time to outline the plan to his superiors, attend meetings, obtain approvals, and so on. (With hindsight and a dash of paranoia, the bureau—given its widespread disconnection within its system—might have lost me in a wilderness of mirrors and misconstrued an approach to the Russians as the real thing!)

By the time the Cheese Family signed on to James O.'s proposal, in mid-July, it no longer mattered anyway, because someone at another bureaucratic level determined that my operations would revert to FBI Albuquerque. What's more, John H. had been asked to step out of retirement and consult on the Howard case, which was great news indeed. It suggested that the bureau had finally resolved the "related conflict" that had stymied Howard's rendition for six years.

Next, I had a phone call from Jackie J., the special agent who had taken over from John H.'s successor and had been assigned to Howard's case in Albuquerque. Pregnant and unable to fly, she invited me to visit her and John H. in New Mexico.

A few weeks later, in early September, I flew to Albuquerque. Over Tex-Mex cuisine with my old partner John H. and Special Agent Jackie J., I recounted the odyssey I had undertaken with the Washington Field Office: visiting Prelin and Sokolov in London, sparing with the Cubans in Washington, and getting Michael S.'s instruction to "stop billing as of today" despite the multiple stand-downs that would result. They listened raptly, for all of it was news to them. What's more, they had not even heard about James O.'s three-month-old plan to lure a specific senior FSB officer out of Russia. But since it was headquarters' scheme and not FBI Albuquerque's concern, that was the end of that.

Then I asked, "Did you know Howard was prepared to travel to New Mexico?"

John H. and Jackie J. expressed their astonishment. John H. could not have known, having retired and been out of the loop, but I was surprised news of Howard's proposed visit to his old haunts in the southwestern United States had never reached Jackie J. or her predecessor, who'd handled the case after John H. left. Neither the Washington Field Office nor headquarters had bothered to notify FBI Albuquerque about the potential opportunity to snare Howard in its own backyard!

"But we still have a warrant for Howard in New Mexico," said Jackie J.

"I know," I sighed. "The main thing is, you're finally ready."

John H. and Jackie J. exchanged glances. "Well, not quite," said Jackie J. "We can't do anything yet." She paused. "But we're getting real close to a green light. We'd like you to hang in there and remain in contact with Howard till we're ready." The old "related conflict" apparently was *still* unresolved. To quote Yogi Berra, "It was déjà vu all over again."

In the meantime, unknown to me until he sent me an e-mail a few weeks later, Edward Howard had visited Thailand to investigate a job offer with a residential development company called AIH (Thailand), Ltd. The company promised to move him from grim Moscow to Phuket, a tropical paradise island. On his return to Russia, Howard's e-mails reflected his elation about the prospect of living in a beach house, driving a Jeep, and shepherding prospective buyers to new condo developments.

33

MAKE SOME ARRESTS

FBI Special Agent Jackie J. had her baby, took maternity leave, and then left the bureau permanently for personal reasons. At our last meeting, when I dropped her at Santa Barbara Municipal Airport, she told me, "Never, ever go to Moscow—even if they [the bureau] say it's safe."

A pretty, young special agent, Christine H., stepped into Jackie J.'s shoes and telephoned me soon after her predecessor's departure with an update on the Howard case: "We're still in a holding pattern, but we'd like you to stand by."

I considered this stall. "It's been over eight years since I started work on Howard," I finally said. "I've been standing by for seven of them. I need a sense that you folks aren't just pulling my chain. How about a letter from your director saying that your shop is serious about this operation?"

"That's doable," said the gung ho new special agent.

Two weeks later I received a presentation binder with a generic certificate thanking me for my "cooperation and assistance in an investigation of great importance" that was signed by FBI director Robert S. Mueller III. Not only was this document *not* what I had requested, but based on what I'd been doing (and continued to do) for the bureau going on nine years, it was an absurd, if typical, way for headquarters to respond to a field request.

Three months later, Albuquerque stirred. Christine H. wanted to discuss Howard and asked if we could meet in Washington. Of course, I agreed.

She and a female colleague from Albuquerque flew into Washington. We sat down for dinner at Clyde's in Chevy Chase, where we were joined by another gal from headquarters. I looked around me at the three pretty female agents. "Are you women taking over the shop?" I asked.

They giggled. "Yeah, we are."

"Eight years ago," I said, "I would've been sitting at this same table talking about Ed Howard with a bunch of big ugly guys. So what's up?"

They wanted to know if I could still rendition Edward Howard.

I shrugged. "Sure. When do you want him?"

"Well, not yet."

"No, of course not."

"But it looks very promising," said Christine H. from Albuquerque.

"Sure it does." I chuckled.

"This is the first time," said Christine H., "that the initiative to rendition Howard has come from headquarters."

I turned to the gal from headquarters. "Yeah?"

She nodded earnestly. "That's right."

What had apparently transpired was in the wake of congressional and media criticism over the FBI's pre–9/11 disconnections, the bureau decided it needed a public relations fix. Hence, FBI director Mueller issued this directive: make some arrests.

The gal from headquarters continued, "I need to present a plan to my superiors. How would you rendition Howard?"

"Easy," I said. "I'd tell Howard we finally have a publisher for *Spy's Guide*, but we need to update it. I could get him to visit any number of European capitals."

The G-women exchanged glances. One asked, "*Spy's Guide*? What's that?"

I should have cashed in my chips on the spot. Instead, I actually responded, "It's a long story, documented in your case file, which you should probably read. The upshot is this: I can lure Howard to just about anywhere in Europe. You need to tell me where you want him." I'd already been through this drill so I knew what they needed to do better than they. "You need to find a country that will let you nail him in the international corridor of an airport."

As the gal from headquarters scribbled notes, I continued, "If I got burned by Hanssen, Russian intelligence hasn't told Howard. I would have noticed something in his commo [communications] with me. I don't think they trust him anymore."

"No, why not?"

"Because if you read your files, you'll find that for years he's been selling out everything he learns from his KGB buddies to me." I had become the FBI's institutional memory on Edward Lee Howard.

"OK, don't do anything yet," said the gal from headquarters. "We need to run this up the ladder."

"Of course."

They were still running it up the ladder when, seventeen days later, Edward Lee Howard met a freakish death in Moscow under circumstances that remain murky.

34

NO RISK, NO GAIN

When Harold Macmillan was prime minister of Great Britain, he took a good hard look at the intelligence services at his disposal. He declared, "Anyone who spends more than ten years in espionage will go mad. Or they were bonkers to start with."

For nine years, I lived a clandestine life of intrigue and lunacy and engaged in the world's second-oldest profession for FBI foreign counterintelligence. At the risk of going mad—or maybe I was bonkers to start with—I would have stuck around another ten years to finish what I'd started with Edward Lee Howard. I felt it was an important case. The international apprehension of a fugitive traitor—one who had given up important secrets and had caused the execution of at least one Russian CIA asset—would have been a precedent worth setting, regardless of any so-called related conflict. But Howard died, and with his death came the unexpected resolution to the main case on my docket.

I was able to serve my country in a way I felt best suited to serve. Even better, I did it on my terms, as a maverick freelancer, with a license to think *and* operate outside the box. I learned a few things, taught others a few things, and had one hell of a ride working with good people and dealing it to bad people.

Along the way, I witnessed firsthand just how cumbersome a bureaucracy the FBI had become. And this was ultimately exemplified by its inability to foil Osama bin Laden's 9/11 terror attacks on New York City and the Pentagon. The bureau supposedly did not have enough clues to prevent what the intelligence service had been created to prevent. As everyone now knows, the FBI had *plenty* of clues about what al Qaida was planning to do. Lest anyone interpret my comment as conspiracy theory, the awful truth is less palatable: the FBI was simply too slow and inefficient to piece the clues together. Headquarters hampered or scuttled whatever leads flowed in from the field.

Congress, the media, and, more important, the bureau itself recognize the FBI's problem of widespread disconnection. The FBI knows it has become a muddled bureaucracy fraught with petty turf rivalries and an aversion to risk taking and timely decision making. One can only hope its leaders will do more than pretend to overcome the bureau's serious deficiencies.

Most of the FBI special agents I operated with in the field are well meaning and hard working; however, they are let down horribly by middle management, whose unofficial job description is to pile paper, hide behind it, and, above all else, avoid taking risks. Intelligence, by its very nature, is a risky business. When practiced correctly, it is based on balancing risk versus gain. Avoiding risk for fear of embarrassment or demotion defeats the bureau's purpose and puts the American public in harm's way. The FBI's cumbrous machinery thus needs a major overhaul if it is ever to regain its integrity and effectively protect Americans from those who wish us harm.

"Nobody's going to get into trouble for not doing anything on this," I was told with regard to the Edward Lee Howard case. "But somebody might if he does something and it goes wrong." This bureau-cratic mantra led to, among other things, 9/11.

I urge everyone in the FBI who subscribes to this dysfunctional dictum to resign and do something else. They must make room for those individuals who truly want to make a difference and fight the good fight, efficiently, creatively, and without fear of reprimand for making an honest mistake.

Capturing Edward Lee Howard would have sent shivers up the spines of any traitors still in place. And it would have sent this signal to any would-be traitors: once uncovered, the world becomes a small and dangerous place. You can run and you can hide, but you'll forever be looking over your shoulder, never able to trust anyone anywhere for fear of getting rused, renditioned, thrown in the clink, tried in court, and potentially sentenced to death.

The FBI could have captured Ed Howard—and didn't.

EPILOGUE:
"BLACKMAIL, VODKA, AND
THREAT TO KILL"

Soon after Vladimir Putin assumed the presidency of Russia, he surrounded himself at the Kremlin with his former KGB colleagues, just as former KGB colonel Igor Prelin had forecast. In fact, Prelin was one of those Putin installed in a Kremlin job, along with their old chief, Vladimir Kryuchkov. The pair became "security consultants," and their placement did not bode well for what Russia would soon become.

My distinct impression from Edward Lee Howard and his KGB friends, as far back as 1998, was that the old crowd was out to settle scores. And now they are the *in* crowd.

When Putin assumed office, he had three priorities:

- put the oligarchs out of business, consolidate the energy sector as an instrument of Russian foreign policy, and then use it to blackmail foes into submission, especially the former Soviet republics
- siphon billions of dollars for himself through several trusted bankers and money launderers from the St. Petersburg Tambov criminal organization, which has created a complex network of oil-trading and distribution companies throughout Europe to this end
- strike back at those who were perceived to have betrayed the Motherland

Regarding the final point, he has given top priority to those who compromised Aldrich Ames and Robert Hanssen. Although Boris Yeltsin had refused to exfiltrate Ames from harm's way when he had the chance, the former president was untouchable after a secret immunity deal that was orchestrated to replace him with Putin.

When my association with the CIA's Former Spymaster surfaced on the Internet in September 2001, it would have been standard procedure for the Russian FSB to conduct a damage-control assessment of my regular dealings with Ed Howard and, by extension, Prelin, Kryuchkov, Batamirov, Sokolov, and others. One hypothesis the FSB would naturally develop is that Howard knew all along I was working for U.S. intelligence and that he was a witting participant in fulfilling requests to introduce me to others and in keeping me updated on Russian intelligence gossip. The Russians knew he grew desperately unhappy in their country and that he would have done anything to be able to return to the United States without threat of imprisonment, including sell them out.

So we ask the question: how could Howard have been privy to information the Russians would consider sensitive to their national security? The answer is, often in the intelligence business, the "need to know" devolves into corridor chitchat or after-work boozy boasting. (As the late former CIA official Miles Copeland used to joke, "You can trust me with any secret that doesn't have entertainment value.") Howard's information, among many other things, established that after Ames's arrest another mole existed at a senior level within the U.S. intelligence community.

If the Russians concluded that Howard was *not* a witting participant in my work, they would have seen his involvement with me as a screwup that embarrassed and compromised them, including the much-revered chairman of their service. Either way, it meant trouble for Howard. In mid-July 2002 he was quite likely among the first casualties of Putin's campaign to get even with those he perceived as having hurt the Motherland.

Others felt Putin's wrath. The oligarch Boris Berezovsky fled to exile in the United Kingdom. Another prominent, if less fortunate oligarch, Mikhail Khodorkovsky, was arrested, tried, convicted, and sent to prison in Siberia. Both men had stood in the way of Putin's energy interests.

What came next in Putin's campaign was truly brazen: the systematic assassination of Russian investigative reporters who were slowly piecing together evidence of Putin's corruption and laundering of state money for his own personal coffers and eventual safety net. The man who had once pledged to crack down on oligarchs who exploited privatization in Russia has himself become the number one oligarch. The best known of these felled journalists was Anna Politkovskaya, who was shot to death in her apartment building's elevator on Putin's birthday, October 7, 2006. A reporter named Yuri Shchekochikhin was poisoned with thallium and died on July 3, 2003—one year after Edward Lee Howard's death—following the publication of his book *Slaves of the KGB.*

Arytom Borovin, another high-powered investigative reporter, died in the mysterious crash of a small private plane on March 9, 2000.

Putin's purge has not been limited to oligarchs and journalists, however. Russian politicians who dared to speak out about Putin's massive corruption have been threatened, harassed, physically attacked, beaten into submission, and murdered. On August 21, 2002, the Liberal Russia Party's cochairman, Vladimir Golovlyov, was shot and killed on a Moscow street. On April 17, 2003, within hours of officially registering the Liberal Russia Party to participate in parliamentary elections, Sergei Yushenkov, a democratic politician, was shot dead near his home.

Then on February 2, 2004, Ivan Rybkin, formerly speaker of the Duma and the Liberal Russia Party's presidential candidate, published a full-page ad in *Kommersant* that accused Putin of shady financial dealings and also identified by name a mysterious ex-KGB officer from St. Petersburg as Putin's personal banker and money launderer. Three days later, in what has all the hallmarks of an intelligence operation, Rybkin was lured to Kiev under false pretenses and given tea laced with drugs. He awakened four days later in another location and was shown a compromising, perverse video of himself. Soon after, Rybkin abandoned his candidacy. Moreover, he never again mentioned Putin's plunder nor his partner-in-pillaging.

Even American reporters are not immune from Putin's purge. Paul Klebnikov, the Moscow-based editor of *Forbes Russia* magazine, was shot dead in the Russian capital on July 9, 2004. At the time of his death, Klebnikov was in hot pursuit of a story about Putin's mystery banker, the same man Ivan Rybkin revealed as Putin's shady business partner before he was drugged and compromised five months earlier. It seems that anyone and everyone who delves into Putin's get-rich relationship with Geneva-based moneyman Gennady Nikolayevich Timchenko puts himself or herself at enormous personal risk.

And if all the above were not quite enough, this Putin-inspired campaign to murder and terrorize was followed by a Russian state-sponsored assassination of Alexander Litvinenko, a nationalized British citizen on UK territory, resulting also in radioactive contamination on UK soil. Quite aside from breaking international law, this FSB operation broke the unspoken rules to which professional intelligence services normally adhere with one another. For all the theories and political spin, clearly the FSB as an institution, not some rogue element, executed Litvinenko, a former KGB officer himself who had quit and sought asylum in Britain.

FSB chairman Nikolai Patrushev would have had to personally approve the operation, and his boss, President Putin, would have had to sanction it. Contrary to movie culture, professional intelligence services do not make policy; instead, they *implement* the executive's policies, even if it is part of their brief to provide their leader with plausible deniability. The FSB bungled the Litvinenko operation, using ten times the lethal dose of polonium-210 and thereby leaving an unplanned trail of publicity, furor, and the radiation poisoning of, among others, their own agents or assassins.

When Igor Prelin told me over dinner in London that he and the KGB-in-exile crowd would like to kill Oleg Kalugin, I took it as no idle threat. Had Kalugin chosen to exile himself in Western Europe instead of the United States, he quite likely would no longer be alive.

So far as re-creating the Soviet Union goes, Putin and his cronies now understand that they do not need to achieve this politically or militarily. That's what Gazprom—Russia's largest corporation—is for. The Ukraine, Belarus, and the other former republics are learning that if they want to fuel their cars and heat their homes, they'd better cooperate with Moscow.

And multinational oil companies are discovering that their ironclad contracts to build multibillion-dollar refineries in places like Sakhalin Island are not so ironclad after all. When one such oil company's top brass threatened to take legal action after their refinery was arbitrarily confiscated and turned over to Gazprom, Putin's regime told them, "If you sue us, we'll charge you with criminal offenses for violating our environmental laws, and, when you come to Moscow, you'll be arrested and thrown into jail."

In Vladimir Putin's own words: "The only way to influence people is blackmail, vodka, and threat to kill."

Not unlike 9/11, the bold, brutal regime of Putin was foreseeable—but only to those who cared enough to pay attention and assemble the clues. The Cold War was over, so the U.S. intelligence community paid scant attention to Russia in the years leading up to 9/11. The agencies preferred to appease and make allowances for the Russian leadership and overlooked signals that all was not well, to our detriment. And we've paid too little attention to Russia's intelligence offensives since 9/11 because we devote most of our resources to the wars in Afghanistan and Iraq and on terrorism only as it applies to Islamic fanatics. We have ignored, and continue to ignore, state-sponsored terrorism emanating from Russia, hoping that this big bully will get tired and leave us alone. Bullies do not tire from acquiescence, however; they grow stronger and more monstrous.

As I've said, Edward Lee Howard was likely one of the first to feel Putin's wrath. Alexander Litvinenko will not be the last.

ABOUT THE AUTHOR

Robert Eringer has enjoyed a wide-ranging career in the information business as a journalist, novelist, private intelligence consultant, undercover operative, and, most recently, director of an intelligence service.

Eringer began his writing career as a London-based correspondent for the *Toronto Star* and the *Blade* (Toledo, Ohio), filing feature stories and high-profile interviews from around Europe. As an investigative reporter for British large-circulation Sunday newspapers, Eringer raked the gutter, exposing sleazeballs and scumbags. His specialty was infiltrating extremist groups, including violent anarchists, neo-Nazis, and the Ku Klux Klan. He still possesses a red robe and hood the KKK tailored for him.

Eringer evolved from journalism to private intelligence before embarking on a ten-year career operating undercover for FBI counterintelligence. Using his intelligence experience as grist, Eringer merged both his writing and spying skills to author a cluster of humorous espionage novels that combine intrigue with lunacy. As a novelist, Eringer inhabits a world of master spies, billionaires, royalty, and delusional lunatics. In reality, he keeps the same company.

Two decades ago, a petition to the U.S. Supreme Court in the *Liberty Lobby v. Jack Anderson* case called Eringer "mysterious" and questioned his actual existence. Eringer questions his own existence, usually over a glass of pinot noir, while dividing his time among London, Monte Carlo, Washington, D.C., and Santa Barbara.